AP

Praise for

MAKE It a WINNING Life: Success Strategies for Life, Love and Business

"Wolf Rinke has the unique ability to tell you what successful people have known, in a manner that we can not only understand but employ in our daily lives. His book came at a critical time in my life and helped me immeasurably."
> **Lou Holtz, Head Football Coach, University of Notre Dame**

"Wolf Rinke ignites a fire in your belly and shows you how to keep it burning while you achieve your dreams. His book is a milestone in the field of personal development, and reading it can be a milestone in your life."
> **Scott DeGarmo, Editor-in-Chief/Publisher, *Success* Magazine**

"*Success* is a slippery word and has many meanings. Wolf has defined it interestingly, and I think it may help you transform your life."
> **Art Linkletter, author, lecturer, and television star**

"This is a wonderful book on individual success and personal empowerment. Anyone can use these six 'PEP' principles to go far beyond anything they have ever done before. You learn how to achieve things you may never have thought possible!"
> **Brian Tracy, President, Brian Tracy Learning Systems, and author of *Psychology of Achievement***

"Many authors write about winning and success, but few ever live their words. Wolf Rinke 'walks his own talk' and has lived every chapter of his book. His philosophy has worked for him, and it can work for you in all that you do!"
> **Denis Waitley, author of *The Psychology of Winning***

"Wolf has the formula to help you take charge of your life. Use his principles and enjoy your ride to the top!"
> **Dianna Booher, author and business communications expert**

"It's the one book to buy if you want to get motivated and energized and learn how to maximize your potential. It's humorous, entertaining, and wise."
> **Congressman Robert L. Livingston, U.S. House of Representatives**

"Why not go first class on life's journey? Wolf Rinke's book buys you that ticket."
> **Danielle Kennedy, author of *Selling—The Danielle Kennedy Way***

"I love this book! It's full of witty and upbeat advice that will help bring to you all the good things in life!"
> **Roger Dawson, author of *Secrets of Power Negotiating***

"This is not just another positive thinking book. This is a positive *action* book. Congratulations Wolf, it's a winner and so are you!"
> **Kristi Krafft, USA world championship gymnastic coach**

"As a minister for the past 35 years, I must say Wolf Rinke's book should be required reading in every Sunday school and church."
> **Dr. Donald N. Sills, President, Family Entertainment Network, Inc.**

"From a teacher who helps children discover and define their essence—I keep envisioning a classroom of students using your book as a course curriculum... for life. It needs to be a mandatory program for teachers and everyone else who will impact the lives of children!"
> **Ann Rousseau, Founder, Your Center for Health Esteem**

"After missing the big tackle on John Riggins in the 1983 Super Bowl, I felt I had failed my team, but after reading Wolf Rinke's book, I now know I stand in great company. Some of the best failed at first, but succeeded in the end."
> **Don McNeal, former Miami Dolphins cornerback**

"Wolf Rinke can make a major change in your life. It will be well worth your time and money to read his book."
> **Dr. Peter B. Petersen, professor of management, Johns Hopkins University**

"Give this book to every one of your employees and watch the incredible improvements in productivity, effectiveness, and customer service."
> **Anita Owen, R.D., President, The American Dietetic Association (1985–1986)**

"This is one of those rare books that crosses the boundaries of home and professional life and is equally as effective in both environments."
> **Ed Foreman, President, Executive Development Systems, Inc.**

"What an inspiration! But, more importantly, what a powerful call to action. Don't read this book unless you sincerely want to be happier, more in control of your life and more successful."
> **Al Walker, President, National Speakers Association (1992-1993)**

"A solid work on a timely topic. Sure help for any success-minded person. Easy to read; much to learn. Highly recommended."
Nido R. Qubein, Chairman, Creative Seminars, Inc.

"Buy this book! But don't quit there, READ it! It will help you to shape your future today."
Daniel Burrus, Burrus Research Associates, Inc.

"This book is an action plan for success. An absolute must-read for anyone who wants to make it to the top."
Patricia Fripp, author of *Get What You Want*

"Wisdom, humor, innovation, suspense, joy, all rolled into one book!"
Stew Leonard, Chairman, Stew Leonard's World's Largest Dairy Store

"This book is a winner! As I began to read it, it made me want to read more. It is fun, participative, and powerful. If you follow its advice it will make you a winner too!"
Anthony J. Alessandra, Ph.D., author of *The Art of Managing People* and *Non-Manipulative Selling*

"Wolf's book made me think, smile, laugh, and feel energized!"
Elizabeth Pan, CEO, PSI International

"If you desire large doses of life, light, love, and laughter, read this book again and again!"
Joe Batten, author of *Tough Minded Management*

"Haven't you often wished you had a guru—or at least a book—that would tell you how to accomplish all your goals in life and do it in such a way that even your rivals would admire you for it? Stop wishing right now. You've just found both. Wolf Rinke is the guru. The book is in your hands."
John McCaleb, author of *Amerikajingo* (best selling Japanese book series)

"Wolf Rinke helps us believe in ourselves by offering six practical techniques for becoming the best we can be."
Jerold W. Apps, professor of adult/continuing education, University of Wisconsin, and author of *Mastering the Teaching of Adults*

"This is one of those rare, valuable books that's actually *fun* to read. Every page offers a change of pace, unique twist, or hearty laugh. And it's loaded with Power Talking!"
George R. Walther, CPAE, author of *Phone Power* and *Power Talking*

"I'm from Missouri and have to be shown. Some books are entertaining, some are informative, some books are inspiring, and some are empowering. Wolf Rinke has shown me that *MAKE It a WINNING Life* does all four extremely well."

Congressman Richard H. Ichord,
U.S. House of Representatives

"For top performers, people who really make a difference, survival is not enough. Wolf Rinke shows us how to go *beyond survival* to emerge from our challenges or adversities smarter and tougher than we would have otherwise been."

Gerald L. Coffee, Captain U.S. Navy (Ret.),
speaker, author of *Beyond Survival*

"If you are interested in improving quality, delivering excellent service, and building a winning team, provide a copy of this book to every one of your team members. But do it quickly, before the competition beats you to it."

Colonel Donald A. Johnson, M.H.A.,
M.A.C.H.E., Chief of Staff, Walter Reed Army
Medical Center

"Wolf Rinke is a winner, and *MAKE It a WINNING Life* can help make you one too."

W Mitchell

"You are what you eat, right? Read Wolf Rinke's book and you will find out that you are what you *think* you are. *MAKE It a WINNING Life* is a powerhouse, a classic. It will put you, your family, and your employees on the fast track to success."

Susan Finn, Ph.D., R.D., Director, Nutrition,
Ross Laboratories

"If you want to help your organization succeed, grab a copy of *MAKE It a WINNING Life*. It's a winner!"

Mark J. Tager, M.D., President,
Great Performance, Inc.

"By combining his own ideas and anecdotes with the insights and contributions of others, Wolf Rinke has created an easy-to-follow, enjoyable approach to personal success.

Robert W. Reasoner, Executive Director
Center for Self-Esteem

"If you don't like losing and want to know how *you* can do something about it, read this book!! Wolf Rinke's formula—the double PEP Principles—will give you the tools to take charge and plot a clear course to a winning life!"

Robert C. Karch, Ed.D., Executive Director,
National Center for Health/Fitness, The American
University

MAKE It a WINNING Life™

Success Strategies for
Life, Love and Business

WOLF J. RINKE, Ph.D.

Foreword By Anthony Robbins

ACHIEVEMENT PUBLISHERS
Rockville, Maryland

MAKE IT A WINNING LIFE:
SUCCESS STRATEGIES FOR LIFE, LOVE AND BUSINESS

Published by:

Achievement Publishers
P.O. Box 5640
Rockville, MD 20855-5640
USA

Copyright © 1992 by Wolf J. Rinke
Printed in the United States of America
1 2 3 4 5 6 7 8 9 10

Publisher's Cataloging in Publication
Rinke, Wolf J.
Make it a winning life: success strategies for life, love and business / Wolf J. Rinke.
p. cm.
Includes bibliographical references and index.
ISBN 0-9627913-8-5
1. Success—United States. 2. Success in business I. Title.
BF637.S8   646.7   91-075609
QB191-1445

Generous bulk discounts for *MAKE it a WINNING Life: Success Strategies for Life,
Love and Business* are available for sales promotions, premiums, fund raising,
educational use or other programs.

For details regarding quantity purchases, contact:

Achievement Publishers
P.O. Box 1289
Olney, MD 20830-1289
USA
(800) 828-9653

Dedicated to Marcela,
my wife, best friend, and superwoman,
who has helped me to MAKE *it a* WINNING *life,*
and to my daughters, Jeselle and Nicole,
the future winners.

Table of Contents

Foreword

Why on earth would anyone want to read another success book?

People often ask me why I've attended so many personal development seminars, read so many books, and listened to so many tapes (some more than once). My answer is always, "No matter how well I *think* I know the material, every time I hear it in a new way I make new distinctions and new connections between what I'm learning and what is happening in my life." You see, every time is different—*you're different*. Perhaps this will be the time that really clicks for you, that allows you to put it all together and compels you to take action.

Beyond presenting a simple prescription for success, Dr. Wolf Rinke engages both your heart and your head. He provides powerful scientific evidence that will convince you once and for all that positive thinking and success are a choice, not a coincidence. At the same time, he shares revealing personal experiences that have transformed him from an "eternal pessimist" to an "unabashed optimist."

Because he writes from experience, Wolf can help you translate theory into practice. After beginning to work full-time at age 14, with only an eighth-grade education, Wolf propelled himself to the top by relentlessly practicing the principles contained in this book.

MAKE It a WINNING Life contains delightful insights and humor, including interviews with some of the people I respect most. You'll learn about inspiring survivor, W Mitchell, a paraplegic who still flies his own plane, goes skydiving and river rafting, and consistently pursues his dreams. You'll meet Captain Gerald Coffee, eloquent speaker and author who not only lived through but learned from his captivity in the infamous Vietnamese Hoa Lo prison. You'll be introduced to the father of Tae Kwon Do in the United States, Grandmaster Jhoon Rhee, my own personal coach and coach to many famous individuals, including over 100 members of Congress. You'll also have the privilege of meeting Dr. Ruth Bennett, an international traveler and marathon racer who shares her beliefs about what it takes to remain vibrant and alert at age 94. You'll have the opportunity to find out how a young black man, Benjamin S. Carson, was able to overcome seemingly insurmountable obstacles to become an incredibly successful physician. Dr. Carson attained national prominence when he headed the 70-member surgical team at Johns Hopkins Hospital that successfully separated the Binder Siamese twins. You will also learn from Danielle Kennedy what it took to sell enough real estate (while pregnant with her fifth child) to earn the title of "Six-Million Dollar Woman."

Their inspiring stories and strategies for success are not to be overlooked. These are true winners who have transformed their lives by practicing six principles that Wolf calls PEP², Positive self-esteem, Purpose, Energy, Education, Positive attitude, and Perseverance.

It is these amazing success stories and the author's warm commentary that make this truly enjoyable and inspirational reading. Wolf Rinke's passion and optimistic celebration of *your* limitless potential will help energize, motivate, and empower you to *MAKE it a WINNING life!*

Anthony Robbins
Author of national bestsellers
Unlimited Power and *Awaken the Giant Within*

Acknowledgments

So many people have helped me *MAKE it a WINNING life*—and have contributed to this book—that it is hard to pick out just a few. Here then is my attempt to say thanks and to express my appreciation, incomplete and inadequate as it may be:

First and foremost, my wife, Marcela, who, more than anyone else, has been and continues to be my best friend, partner, and guide on *our* journey to success. She is always there to help me maintain my PEP², and to provide me with guidance, reflection, sound advice, encouragement, and inspiration. She is truly my superwoman.

My daughters, Jeselle and Nicole, for keeping me on my toes, putting things in perspective, and making me proud while they are struggling to *MAKE it a WINNING life.*

My parents, for providing me with a solid work ethic and sound value system.

Anthony Robbins, author of the bestsellers *Unlimited Power* and *Awaken the Giant Within,* acclaimed master of personal achievement systems, and supersuccessful businessman, for his outstanding foreword and for helping me dream big dreams.

Denis Waitley, author of *The Psychology of Winning,* for helping me change my life and contributing to many of the principles in this book.

Brian Tracy, author, speaker, and entrepreneur par excellence, for inspiring me to always reach for the top.

Nido Qubein, speaker, leader, and unexcelled businessman, for getting me excited about joining the National Speakers Association, the largest group of winners ever assembled in one organization.

Zig Ziglar, master motivator, public speaker, author, and entrepreneur, for convincing me that I can get anything in life I want, if I just help enough other people get what they want.

Dr. Susan Calvert Finn, of Ross Laboratories, and president of the American Dietetic Association, for being a friend and mentor.

Anita Owen for teaching me that there is more to life than "contemplating your navel."

Richard J. Harty, originator of *Creative Conditioning,* lobbyist, and entrepreneur, for putting me together with other winners and teaching me the fine art of networking.

Dr. Peter B. Petersen, professor of management at the Johns Hopkins University, for his early review of the manuscript.

Richard Frishman, my agent from Planned Television Arts, for helping me make this book a bestseller.

Katherine V. Givens, my editor, for her invaluable suggestions and patience in helping me sculpt this book.

Jackie Egan, my administrative assistant, for her dedicated loyalty and for keeping me "straight."

My numerous audiences, workshop participants, and students at the Johns Hopkins University, for keeping me on the cutting edge and revitalizing my PEP^2 on an ongoing basis.

The many unsung winners behind the scenes, including Robert Howard, Gordon Shifflet and Elise Mahaffie for the outstanding artwork on the cover and throughout the book, and the folks at The Composing Room, Nighthawk Design, and Book Press, Inc., for typesetting, indexing, and printing a first class "masterpiece."

And last, but certainly not least, Jhoon G. Rhee, Captain Gerald L. Coffee, Dr. Eunice R. H. Bennett, Dr. Benjamin S. Carson, Danielle Kennedy, and W Mitchell for sharing so freely how they maintain their PEP^2 and *MAKE it a WINNING life.*

The End

The END? You have got to be kidding!

Well, yes and no.

Yes, because it is the end to
   Zapping
   Stinking thinking
   Doom
   Low self-esteem
   Hatred
   Pessimism
   Vindictiveness
   Defeat
   Indifference
   Misery
   Animosity
   Resentment
   Gloom
   Negativism
   Ignorance
   Wariness
   Cynicism
   Losing
   Anguish
   Bitterness
   Anxiety
   Whining
   Aimlessness
   Worrying
   Listlessness
   Malice
   Depression
   Fear
   Hostility
   Anger
   Failure

No, because it is the beginning of your journey to success in life, love, and business—a journey that will empower, energize, and motivate you to levels that you have never imagined possible—a journey that will help you *MAKE it a WINNING life.*

1

Road Map for Your Journey to Success

Success is a journey, not a destination.

—Ben Sweetland

As you are about to embark on a journey, it will help you to have a road map—a road map that will show you not only where to go, but more important, how to get there. That is why I begin this book—and each chapter—with a brief overview, which I call "Preview of Coming Attractions."

PREVIEW OF COMING ATTRACTIONS

This chapter will provide you with a sense of direction; it is a road map illustrating how you can *MAKE it a WINNING life.* First I will give you an idea of why I wrote this book and what it will do for you. Then I will make some commitments to you and—you guessed it—ask you to make some commitments to me (to yourself, actually). I will also tell you why habits are more important than knowledge and suggest how you can get the most out of this book by thinking holistically and by having fun. So, let's start with a very important question.

WHY THIS BOOK?

You and I live in a very tough and unsettling era. At the same time, however, we also live in a very exciting time. It is the beginning of a new decade, and not just a new decade, but a new millennium. And if that is

1

not exciting, I don't know what is. After all, it comes around only once every 1,000 years. It will not happen again in our lifetime. Some authors consider this the decade of "megatrends"; others refer to it as a "powershift," an era that will literally transform our perception of power and influence as we know it. I see it as a rapidly changing world, a period in our history when things are indeed changing all around us at hyper-speed. Such rapid changes can leave you and me feeling stressed, anguished, depressed, and defeated. Alternately, we can feel that we "possess a front-row seat to the most challenging yet most exciting decade in the history of civilization."[1]

According to John Naisbitt and Patricia Aburdene, ten new major social, economic, political, and technological changes are unfolding as we move into the new millennium. The tenth major trend, according to Naisbitt and Aburdene, is that at the conclusion of the 20th century individuals are more powerful than ever before. They go so far as to suggest that "the most exciting breakthroughs of the 21st century will occur not because of technology but because of an expanding concept of what it means to be human."[2] Power will shift from that of institutions to individuals and the "primacy of the consumer."[3] As a result, the triumph of the individual will become the great unifying theme.[4]

Similarly, Alvin Toffler predicts in his new theory of social power that wealth creation will no longer be driven by mass production and money as in the industrial age, nor by military might and violence. Real social power in a future "super-symbolic" economy will "increasingly be dependent on the exchange of data, information, and knowledge."[5] Force and wealth, according to Toffler, "are the property of the strong and the rich."[6] Knowledge, on the other hand, has a truly revolutionary characteristic; it can be grasped by the weak and the poor, and therefore will become "the most democratic source of power."[7] Toffler further maintains that "the new hero is no longer a blue-collar worker, a financier, or a manager, but the innovator (whether inside or outside a large corporation) who combines imaginative knowledge with action."[8]

To take advantage of the innumerable exciting challenges and opportunities that are unfolding before us, to get that "front-row seat," you and I must master powerful strategies that will enable us to deal effectively and productively with the dizzying changes that are being thrust upon us. But we must go beyond that. We must put ourselves in the driver's seat of our lives. We must put ourselves in charge of our personal destinies. We must empower ourselves so that we not only survive, but thrive, in this rapidly changing world. In short, we must learn how to *MAKE it a WINNING life*. That is the very purpose of this book. It will provide you with powerful principles (the PEP^2 principles—the double PEP) that you will need to succeed.

Now that you know what this book will do for you, let me outline some of the premises that I have attempted to adhere to throughout the book to ensure that you and I have a productive and enjoyable journey.

Insight Break

Success is simply a matter of luck. Ask any failure.

—Earl Wilson

THE *KISS* PRINCIPLE

Keep it simple, stupid (KISS) is an axiom whose time has come. In fact, perhaps we should make it the 27th amendment to our Constitution. (Just kidding, although don't you wish our politicians would live by it?) Keeping things simple seems to have gone out of fashion. It almost seems that in order to be successful at something you have to make it complex. What I have found from personal experience, however, is that the opposite is true. For example, as a professional speaker I used to cram my presentations full of information. My assumption was that I wanted to give people a lot of value for their money. As I became more relaxed, however, I began to notice that people's eyes glazed over and they began to get a distant look, as if they were somewhere else (Hawaii, for instance). Although no one ever fell asleep on me (I create too much excitement and make too much noise), I began to doubt my effectiveness. My doubts were reinforced time and time again by participants' letters and feedback from attendees, especially those who had heard me speak more than once. Invariably, what had made a real impact on listeners were the simple but memorable concepts. These were the principles that people could relate to, and because they could relate to them, they were able to use the concepts to change their lives. In other words, it was the uncommonly simple strategies that people remembered and internalized.

The importance of keeping it simple is supported by many things that you and I encounter every day. For example, think of the products that you love to use. I would like to submit that they are simple to operate, or in the current marketing vernacular, that they are user friendly. Consider the first videocassette recorder (VCR) I owned, for example. It had six buttons. I knew what each button did, and I could get it to do what I wanted it to. I can't say that about my current "entertainment system." It consists of four pieces of equipment—television, radio (wait, I think that's called a tuner now), compact disc (CD) player (that's what we now "have to have" to get the best music—or is it so the record companies can sell us the same thing more than once?), and VCR—all "controlled" from one central processing unit. (I think it was the comedienne Carol Burnett who said that she would buy a CD player only if it came with a guarantee that there will be no other new stereo equipment inventions.) I put the word *controlled* in quotes because it is a misnomer. The entertainment system really controls me, because it forces me to get an engineering and electronics degree and/or take the time to read several volumes of instructional manuals in order to operate it.

There are many other examples as well. There are only three primary colors, but just think of what Michelangelo and van Gogh were able to do with only those three primary colors ($82.5 million for *Portrait of Dr. Gachet* is not too shabby for one painting). Similarly, there are only seven musical notes. Think of what Mozart did with only those seven notes (and what Elvis Presley did with only two!). (If you are not chuckling, you are not with me. Perhaps you should do a couple of stretching exercises or get yourself a cup of coffee or tea before going on.)

In short, I have done everything possible to make this a user-friendly book, one that is uncommonly simple yet provides you with powerful success strategies while keeping you entertained, energized, and motivated.

Humor Break

Think you're having a tough day? You haven't seen anything until . . .
—You call Suicide Prevention and they put you on hold.
—Your twin brother forgets your birthday.
—You wake up and your braces are locked together.

KNOWLEDGE IS NICE BUT . . .

In my workshops and seminars I like to ask the audience this deceptively obvious question: How many of you agree that knowledge is power? Even after I warn them that it is a trick question most participants agree with the statement. (I guess we have been influenced (or is it brainwashed?) by such authors as Alvin Toffler.) How about you? Let's take a look at it.

Researchers generally agree that you and I store everything we have ever learned in our brain, that 3½ pounds of pinkish-grey matter located right between our ears, the most powerful biocomputer ever built. In fact, even with today's advances in artificial intelligence, microchips, and related technology, no computer, regardless of size, can do something as simple as generate an original thought. Even more startling, according to Roger Penrose, controversial Oxford mathematician, physicist, and author of *The Emperor's New Mind,*[9] computers will never be able to think, reach insights, or think creatively. Why? Because, according to Penrose, the laws of nature do not allow it. Of course, you, as well as all other *Homo sapiens,* do all of these things "at the drop of a hat." More than that, we take it for granted, never even giving it a second thought. If you want to test this, you can have yourself admitted to a specialized clinical center. A specialist can run an electrode into a specific part of your brain, causing you to relive a certain event. Depending on where the electrode is placed, you may reexperience your 5th birthday party, recall a fact you learned in 7th grade, or visualize the first drawing you ever drew. Each of these experiences will feel as if it is happening at that very moment, in living color, accompanied by all of the sights, sounds, and smells you experienced at the time. It will be as if you are being transported in your own time machine. In short, I am suggesting that "it's all in there." All you have ever learned is captured inside of that fabulous biocomputer of yours, the brain.

Now, you are probably saying, Wolf, if it's all in there, how come I'm having so much trouble? Well, there are several reasons. For one, the program that allows you to access the stored knowledge does not necessarily work the way you want it to work. But the biggest reason is that most adults do not think very much any more. Adults are creatures of habit. We operate on autopilot. You don't believe it? Let's test it. Think about the way you go to work. (This assumes that you are commuting most days to the same place.) Let's say that a friend tells you that a new highway has been built that would allow you to cut your travel time by about ten minutes. Your friend tells you that if you want to take advantage of it, you must make a right turn at the third intersection instead of your customary left turn. (For this discussion I am assuming that you have made a left turn for at least the last 21 days.) You thank your friend for the tip and plan to take advantage of this shortcut the next day. Tomorrow, when you get to the intersection, which way will you turn? If you said *left* (the old way), you are probably correct! Why? Because it is a habit, and to change that habit you will have to consciously and consistently remind yourself—literally *force yourself*—to make a right turn (the new way). At times, you may even have to turn back after you have made the habitual left. You will have to do this for about 21 days, or 3 weeks, whichever comes earlier![10] (Are you chuckling?) After about 3 weeks, you will have developed a new habit and will make that right turn automatically.

Mental Stretch Mini-Break

Is there any federal law against a man marrying his widow's sister? (See end of chapter for answer.)

HABITS: THE GOOD, THE BAD, AND THE UGLY

One more thing about habits. As you probably learned from your mother, there are at least two types of habits: good habits and bad habits. An unfortunate thing about habits is that bad habits are easily acquired, but they are very, very tough to give up. (Think of habits such as overeating, smoking, alcoholism, and drug abuse.) Good habits, on the other hand, are extremely tough to develop, but they are relatively easy to give up. (Think of such wonderful habits as flossing your teeth, exercising regularly, and eating breakfast.) What this means is that you have to minimize your exposure to bad habits and be very tenacious when you want to acquire good habits. In fact, the better the habit, meaning the greater its potential to make the biggest positive difference in your life, the longer it will take to acquire. So be liberal with the 21-day rule, and be prepared to extend that time frame when necessary to acquire truly important positive habits.

What is the moral of all this? The moral is: Knowledge is important (that's why I dedicate an entire chapter to it), but habits, the right kind of habits, the ones that are the toughest to acquire, are even more important because they will make the biggest difference in your life.

Because you are serious about success (you are reading this book, aren't you?), be sure to go beyond just reading the simple but powerful principles that I am sharing with you. Commit to them, at least to those that you think will help you on your journey to success, and translate them into empowering new habits that will set you free and allow you to make the most of your life.

Insight Break

He who does not go forward goes backward.
—Johann Wolfgang von Goethe

HOW TO THINK WITH A FULL DECK

Research appears to support the notion that human beings have a bifunctional brain. (I hedged my bets here because the most recent research talks about the front and back brain instead of the left and right brain.)[11] In any case, the left/right brain model maintains that the left cerebral hemisphere, in the 95 percent of us who are right-handed, is responsible for our analytical, sequential, and linear problem-solving capabilities. This is the part of the brain that helps us with the three Rs—reading, writing, and arithmetic. (To remember this, I suggest the mnemonic device *left = linear* or *logical.*) It is, so to speak, our rational—linear mind. The right cerebral hemisphere, in contrast, is responsible for our intuitive, holistic, spatial, and artistic abilities. It is this part of the brain that lets us see the whole or, to use a fancy German term with which to impress your friends, the gestalt. To clarify the differences, it is the left side of the brain that helps you recall a person's name and the right side that helps you remember a person's face.

In accordance with this model, you have the left side of your brain engaged while processing the information you are reading right now. That is not good enough for me, though, because I want you to maximize your learning utility. So that you get the most out of this book I want you to have both the left and right sides of your brain engaged.

Another motive for wanting to help you keep the right side engaged is that I want to enhance your creative potential. I want to help you reawaken your innate creative ability. In working with adults in my creativity workshops I have found that all adults have the ability to think creatively. Unfortunately, most of us have compromised that skill because we live in a world that rewards conformance rather than performance. This situation is in fact an oxymoron (a contradiction in kind), because we live in a world that is changing at hyper-speed. Management guru Tom Peters has gone so far as to suggest that we need to learn to thrive on chaos.[12] Similarly, Les Brown, a well-known motivational speaker, has referred to this era of rapid change as the era of the three Cs: accelerated *change,* overwhelming *complexity,* and relentless *competition.*[13] This rapidly changing global environment in which we live requires us to think more creatively, more innovatively, or, if you will, more holistically. (Don't let the word *creative* intimidate you. Creative thinking is nothing more than looking at the same thing as everyone else but thinking something different.)

To facilitate your thinking creatively, I have scattered weird mental stretch breaks throughout the book. To find out what I mean, solve Exhibit 1-1. Solve each one as it appears and you will reawaken your slumbering creative potential, reengage the right side of your brain, learn to think holistically, and keep your mind fit. (Just think, you will get all that at absolutely no extra charge. What a bargain!)

Mental Stretch Break

Exhibit 1-1 contains 8 drawings. Your task is to translate each of them into a meaningful and easily recognizable word or short phrase. For example, the first one stands for *mental blocks*. The rest work just like it, so put on your creative thinking cap, go for it, and enjoy! (See end of chapter for answers.)

Exhibit 1-1 Brain Teasers

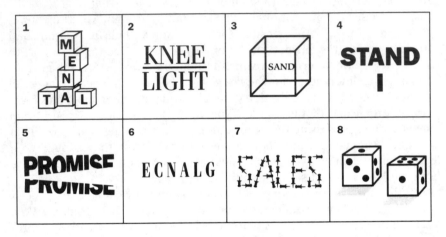

ARE YOU HAVING FUN YET?

Having fun, learning, working, and, for some people, even living just don't seem to go together. Regarding learning, it was Mrs. Jones, the silver-haired English teacher, who did it to you. Remember when she told you in front of the whole class that you were here to learn, not to have fun? At work, it was Mr. Brown, your first supervisor, who told you that you were here to work, not to mess around. In your personal life, it was your Uncle George (I'm keeping my fingers crossed that it was not your spouse) who thought that having fun was a sin against humanity. In fact, Uncle George had what well-known master motivator Zig Ziglar calls "stinking thinking." Uncle George was so grumpy that when he left a party, the party began. If he was like my Uncle George, he "died" at about age 45 and waited the rest of his life to be buried.

Nothing is more debilitating than losing one's sense of humor or taking one's self too seriously. I am not sure how I came to be so vehement about this. Perhaps it was the 679th deadly college lecture that I endured, the 950th boring textbook that I read, or the 1,000th numbing "professional presentation" that I attended that led me to promise myself that if I ever became the "doer" instead of the "doce" I would make sure that every book I wrote or presentation I made would consist of about two-thirds education and one-third entertainment.

Insight Break

If it's fun—
it gets done.

—Wolf J. Rinke

Within this book, I would like to live by the adage expressed by Robert Townsend, of *Up the Organization* fame, who said, "If you are not in business for fun or profit, what the hell are you doing here?"[14] Having fun is a critical success strategy by itself, but it is much more, especially if you can go beyond having fun and make yourself laugh.

Experts tell us that during a laugh the throat goes into spasms that cause you to expel blasts of air at 50 miles per hour with gusts of up to 80 miles per hour. The body goes into overdrive and begins to pump adrenaline. Your heart gets excited and beats at an accelerated rate. And your brain, not wanting to be left out, begins to secrete endorphins, the body's natural painkillers. Getting your engine revved up like this requires more oxygen, so your lungs begin to work double time, taking in more oxygen and getting rid of greater volumes of carbon dioxide. If you do this really well, your eyes get into the act too, cleaning themselves with streams of tears. And, if you keep at it long enough, you can get your face washed at the same time. Most importantly, your muscles lose their tenseness and become very relaxed, leading some experts to claim that laughter is one of the best natural stress reducers. Incredible as it may sound, it may even be more than that. For example, Norman Cousins reported in his classic *Anatomy of an Illness* that he belly-laughed himself to health from an incurable illness by watching Marx Brothers films.[15]

No matter what, having fun and laughter are good for you! So, what are you waiting for? Just laugh! I can see that you want me to make you laugh. To help you with that and to make sure that you keep things in perspective and have fun on this journey, I have inserted "humor breaks" throughout the book. But you have to give me a hand. Just as with everything else we will talk about, I will provide the stimulus but you have to respond. After all, Shakespeare was absolutely correct when he said, "Nothing comes from doing nothing."

Humor Break

Notices written in English and posted in foreign countries:

Magazine cover in Moscow hotel: If this is your first visit to the USSR, you're welcome to it.

Swedish bar: Ladies are requested not to have babies in the bar.

Polish zoo: Please do not feed the monkeys. If you have the right food give it to the zookeeper.

Chinese hotel: You are invited to take advantage of the maid.

I have told you what I am committed to. Unfortunately, what I do will do nothing for you unless you are willing to do your part. (I guess that is a major insight: No one can do success for you; you have to do it for yourself.) Listed below are several commitments that I would like you to make to yourself and to me. (If you are not sure of what I mean by commitment, think of a high-cholesterol breakfast of eggs and bacon. The chicken is *involved;* the pig is *committed.*)

THINGS TO DO

- *Read actively.* This means that you stay tuned instead of running off to imaginary islands while reading. This happens to all of us because the mind processes information four to ten times faster than we read. Here are several ways to help you read actively:
  —Underline things that are particularly meaningful.
  —Read the beginning of each chapter first, specifically the "Preview of Coming Attractions." This will provide you with an overview of the chapter. Then skim the headings and read the summary. (I call this section "A Trip Back to the Future.") This will prime your mind and give you a general idea of what the chapter is about. Then go back to the beginning and read the chapter, from beginning to end

in one sitting if possible. Note that this is how you should do all of your readings, because this method increases your reading speed and retention.

- *Take notes.* The best way to take notes is to extract one critical concept gained from each part of the book. This could be a strategy you want to incorporate into your behavior or something you want to change. To make this happen, state the strategy in the active present tense and write it on two index cards. For example, from your reading so far you may want to generate the following: "I am in charge of my success." Put one of these cards next to your mirror, where you will see it at least twice each day. Put the other one on your desk or in some other place where you will see it several times a day. (More about this technique in Chapter 4.) These cards will have to remain in place for at least how many days? (This is a review for you. If you don't know the answer, or worse, don't even know what I am talking about, you left me during an earlier part of this chapter. You will need to go back to find the answer. In fact do not pass GO or collect $200.)

- *Search and apply.* While reading, stop and search for ways that you can apply a principle, idea, or concept to your personal or professional life. The principles in this book are like the concepts in a diet book. You can't just read about them and expect results. You have to *take action,* so go ahead and do it.

- *Keep an open mind.* Avoid idea-killers such as "This will never work for me" or "This is all fine in theory, but. . . ." (There is very little theory in this book. These principles have worked for me and for many others I have studied.) As a general rule, forget about your "but" (get it?). The reason? Every time you say "but," you have opened an escape hatch to failure. Remember the last time your boss paid you a compliment that was followed by "but"? For example, "I appreciate you finishing this project on time, but. . . ." That's right, you forgot the compliment and heard only what came after the "but." (That's your boss's escape hatch; what came after "but" is really what she meant to tell you. The rest was just filler to soften the blow. This is also referred to as sandwiching criticism.)

- *Practice NOW!* Practice your new skills consistently for at least 21 days. (You already know why.) But, whatever you do, do it while it is still fresh in your mind. Consider your employees, your boss, your family members, and anyone else you interact with on a regular basis as your "laboratory." Try out new behaviors to see what results you get. Although it may not be a major revelation, keep the IYDWYAD-

YWGWYAG principle in mind. (Don't know what that means? It means *If you do what you always do, you will get what you always got.*)

- *Practice what you know.* This is directly related to practicing now instead of putting it off. Avoid saying to yourself "I know this already" or "I have heard this before." You probably have, but *are you practicing it?!?!* When it comes to human behavior, there is very little that is new. What makes it new is when you translate knowledge into a change in behavior. In study after study researchers have verified that what people know is generally *not* reflected in their actual behavior. For example, after conducting a 15-year in-depth study of management consultants, Chris Argyris stated that people's "espoused theory of action [that's what people say they do] has very little to do with how they actually behave."[16] As I said, "knowledge is nice, but. . . ." To help you translate theory into practice I recommend that you refer to and apply the "Success Action Steps" listed at the end of each chapter. These are the critical concepts that will help you translate knowledge into action and assist you on your journey to success.

Insight Break

The one serious conviction that a man should have is that nothing is to be taken too seriously.

—Samuel Butler

OTHER IMPORTANT THINGS TO DO

- *Avoid wasting your mental energy.* Don't bother attempting to prove to yourself or to me that I do not have all the answers. I don't! (I won't know that you are doing it, so why bother?)
- *Share the information.* Pass the critical principles in this book on to your spouse, your employees, your boss, your children, and anyone else who will listen. When you share things or teach someone else you make what you have learned part of you, and you will develop those powerful new habits much more quickly.
- *Read the information in the order it is presented.* I have written this book so that each concept builds on the preceding one. That means for your first reading you will get more out of it if you read it in the order I have presented it.

- *Reread the book, and refer to it often.* This time you do not need to read it in order. Instead, focus on your highlighted outlines and the 3 x 5 cards you have generated from the book. The more often you refer to this book and your cards, the more likely you are to translate what you know into a change of behavior and habits, which is exactly what we both want. (You do want to succeed, don't you? Great, because that is what we are going to talk about in Chapter 2.)

SUMMARY: A TRIP BACK TO THE FUTURE

- Success is a journey, not a destination.
- The individual will become the great unifying theme of the 21st century.
- We get more out of things that are simple and fun.
- Our brain is the most powerful biocomputer ever built.
- Adults are creatures of habit.
- Developing a new habit takes at least 21 days of constant and conscious repetition.
- "Good" habits take longer to develop than "bad" habits.
- Learning is enhanced by engaging both the left and right sides of the brain.
- All people have the ability to think creatively.
- Having fun and laughing are very therapeutic.
- To get the most out of this book and maximize your journey be sure to:
  —Read actively.
  —Take notes.
  —Search and apply.
  —Keep an open mind.
  —Practice NOW.
  —Practice what you know.

SUCCESS ACTION STEPS

- ❏ Neatly copy the axiom at the beginning of this chapter: "Success is a journey, not a destination." Place it on your desk or on your refrigerator to remind yourself that *you* are in charge of your destiny.
- ❏ Think of a change you want to make. Write the new desired behavior on two 3 x 5 cards. Place one card near your mirror, the other where

you will see it several times each day (for example, on your desk). Remind yourself and practice this new behavior for at least 21 days or until it becomes a new habit.

❑ Evaluate what type of climate you have in your organization or family. If it is a negative and boring climate, get together with your team members or family members to figure out what collective actions you can take to make it a positive and fun climate.

❑ Catch yourself when you come up with an innovative idea, make a mental note of it, and put your right hand on your left shoulder and give yourself a sincere and hearty pat on the back.

❑ Copy the headings from *Things to Do* on an index card and use it as a bookmark. Review the list prior to the start of each reading adventure.

❑ Smile. Or better yet, *make* yourself laugh as you read this book! Once you get the hang of this, you will have learned the basics of what it takes to *MAKE it a WINNING life.*

NOTES

1. J. Naisbitt and P. Aburdene, *Megatrends 2000: Ten New Directions for the 1990's* (New York: Avon Books, 1990), p. 338.

2. Ibid., p. xxii.

3. Ibid., p. 333.

4. Ibid., p. 322.

5. A. Toffler, *Powershift: Knowledge, Wealth, and Violence at the Edge of the 21st Century* (New York: Bantam Books, 1990), p. 238.

6. Ibid., p. 20.

7. Ibid., p. 20.

8. Ibid., p. 239.

9. R. Penrose, *The Emperor's New Mind: Concerning Computers, Minds, and the Law of Physics,* 6th ed. (New York: Oxford University Press, 1989).

10. M. Maltz, *Psycho-Cybernetics: A New Way to Get More Living out of Life* (New York: Simon & Schuster, 1975).

11. N. McAleer, "On Creativity," *Omni* 11 (April 1989): 42–44, 98–102.

12. T. Peters, *Thriving on Chaos: A Handbook for a Management Revolution* (New York: Knopf, 1987).

13. L. Brown, "Personal and Professional Mastery," *Insight* 87 (1990): 26–42. Audiotape program with accompanying written materials. Nightingale-Conant Corp., 7300 North Lehigh Avenue, Chicago, IL 60648.

14. R. Townsend, *Up the Organization* (New York: Knopf, 1970), p. 58.

15. N. Cousins, *Anatomy of an Illness As Perceived by the Patient* (New York: Norton, 1979).

16. C. Argyris, "Teaching Smart People How to Learn" *Harvard Business Review* 69 (May–June 1991): 103.

Notes about the book:

   I have built on the works of many in this book and have made every effort to give credit to my sources. The axioms are attributed to what I believe were the original sources. That is easier said than done, because often multiple authors claim credit. When that occurred I attempted to determine who the original author was and provided credit accordingly. To make these determinations I relied on *Peter's Quotations: Ideas for Our Time,* by Laurence J. Peter. The brain teasers are from my personal collection, which I have accumulated from a variety of sources, handouts, and exercises. Also, to deal with the gender issue, I elected to randomize male and female roles throughout the book instead of resorting to the cumbersome he/she, him/her designations.

ANSWER TO MENTAL STRETCHING EXERCISE
Page 6

   There is no law against it, but it would be tough to do. To have a widow, the man would have to be dead.

ANSWERS TO BRAIN TEASERS
Page 8

1. Mental blocks
2. Neon light
3. Sandbox
4. I understand
5. Broken promise
6. Backward glance
7. Sales tax
8. Paradise

2

Success: A Model
for Action

*If one advances confidently in the direction of his dreams,
and endeavors to live the life which he has imagined,
he will meet with a success unexpected in common hours.*
                                        —Henry David Thoreau

Success. Everyone wants it, but few attain it. Why? I suppose there are many reasons, but an important one that comes to mind is that a lot of people have no idea of what success means to them.

PREVIEW OF COMING ATTRACTIONS

In this chapter, we will analyze what success means to you. After all, if you don't know what you are looking for how will you know that you have found it? While we are at it, I will also dispel a few myths. After taking away some of your crutches, I will share with you the most functional definition of success that I have found. Then I will provide you with insight into how your beliefs can get in the way of maximizing your potential. And last, but not least, I will provide you with a success model—your very own PEP² rocket. You will want to learn to fly this rocket, because once you know how, it will take you to the top. If you commit to operating it according to the principles I will outline for you, your PEP² rocket will take you as high as you are willing to go. But, let's not get ahead of ourselves. Let's begin by figuring out what success means to you.

SUCCESS: NOW YOU SEE IT, NOW YOU DON'T

This book is about *MAKING it a WINNING life* and succeeding in life, love, and business. But first, what is success to you?

When I ask that question of audiences, the most common response is "I want to be happy." The next most popular response is "I want money, lots of it!" Is that what you said to yourself when I asked what success is to you? Is that what you really want?

If that is what you want, then let me help you get it. In fact, happiness is fairly easy to obtain. (I bet you didn't expect that you could get that from reading a book.) To help you get happiness, I am going to teach you how to use a modified neuro-linguistic programming (NLP) technique. NLP, which deals with the effects of verbal and nonverbal language on the nervous system, is a technique developed by Richard Bandler, a German psychotherapist, and John Grinder, a professor of linguistics at the University of California.[1] This technique was popularized by Tony Robbins in his best-selling book and audiotape program, *Unlimited Power.*[2] You can use this technique to put yourself into any state, including happiness. The steps are as follow:

1. Sit in a comfortable chair (a recliner would be ideal) in which you can really relax.
2. Loosen any tight clothing and put yourself in as relaxed a state as possible. The room should be very quiet, without any outside distractions.
3. Close your eyes and think of the last time you were really happy. It makes no difference what the occasion was. It could have been during a birthday party, during a vacation, when you received a promotion, or at your wedding. It can be whatever caused you to be happy, by *your* definition.
4. Form a clear image in your mind of what each of your senses experienced while you were happy. What did you feel, see, smell, taste, and hear?
5. Zero in on each of your senses, and isolate what you experienced. For example, what did you feel?
6. Now that you have isolated that sensation, enlarge it by making it bigger, stronger, brighter, more colorful, and more powerful so that all of your thoughts are occupied by what you were feeling when you were happy. Push all other feelings out of your mind. All that should be in your conscious thoughts are the feelings that you experienced while you were happy.

7. Once you have accomplished that, concentrate on what you saw while you were happy.
8. Repeat the process for what you smelled, what you tasted, and what you heard. For each sense, be sure to enlarge the sensation by making it bigger, more vibrant, more colorful, and more powerful. If I were with you and you were doing this correctly, I would see a happy, relaxed person in front of me.
9. Before returning to the here and now, make a mental note of what it felt like to be happy.
10. Slowly bring yourself back to the present by opening your eyes.
11. Remain seated until you are fully present.

You now know how to be successful. If your definition of success is to be happy, then you have reached that goal. All you have to do to be successful is to recall what you just experienced. Or, if you can't recall it, simply repeat the exercise above and you will be happy.

Insight Break

Happiness is a perception, which you can create at any time.
—Wolf J. Rinke

But, you may say, I don't just want to be happy. Success is having lots of money. Would doubling your money make you successful? If you said yes, I can help you accomplish that right now, without any risks on your part. What a deal! Take out all the money you have in your wallet. Fold it over once and put it back into your wallet. You have just doubled your money. (Are you chuckling? If you are not, you are taking this money thing too seriously.)

Humor aside, let's find out just how important money is to you. Let's assume that I am in the business of buying body parts and organs (don't wince, this is only make-believe). I act as a middleman; I sell the body parts that I acquire to hospitals, medical centers, and other organizations that have a legitimate need for them. These institutions buy the parts that I sell to help less fortunate people, people who have been in accidents, or people who have lost the use of body parts or organs because of disease. Suppose I ring your doorbell one afternoon. You open the door, I introduce myself, and you invite me in. I tell you what I do and offer you $1 million for your eyes. I explain to you that there is someone who desperately needs your eyes (in fact, it is my father, who has lost his eyesight to glaucoma). Would you sell your eyes for $1 million? I bet your answer is not just *no*, it's *HELL, NO!* What about your legs? Same answer? Your arms? How about just one arm? I bet the answer is still no.

What if I were running an adoption agency and were looking to buy children? Would you be willing to sell one of your children (assuming of course that you have children) for $1 million? (No, I am not interested in slightly used mothers-in-law.) I bet your answer is again hell, no. (Unless, of course, I caught you right after your two-year-old just finished throwing a terrible temper tantrum, when you might offer me that much just to take him off your hands.)

All this talk of money reminds me of an exercise. Let's take a brief mental stretch break.

Mental Stretch Break

I have in my hand two U.S. coins that total 55 cents in value. One is *not* a nickel. Please bear that in mind. What are the two coins? (See end of chapter for answer.)

I have another proposition for you. What if I were a magic genie and I offered you anything you wanted. The price, however, is that you have to give up 14 hours per day, every day, for the rest of your life. In addition, you must give up 1 additional hour per day for each wish granted to you. (Nice try, but you can't wish for time back.) Would you go for it? I bet you wouldn't! (This is exactly what happens to some people who lose track of what money is—a means to an end, not the end itself.)

Now, if you answered no to these wonderful propositions, we would have to assume that money is not nearly as important to you as you thought. It certainly is not *the* most important thing in your life.

Insight Break

Money often costs too much.

—Ralph Waldo Emerson

SUCCESS: A DEFINITION

If it is not money, what then is success? To find an answer to that question I conducted a brief survey. I discovered that to some people success is fame; to others it is serenity. To some people success is making

$30,000 per year; to others it is making $3 million. Some people want to live in a big house; others don't want the headache and would rather live in an apartment or condominium. Some want to be parents of successful children; others want no children. Some want a successful marriage; others want to change their marriage partner as often as they change their shirt. (As Johnny Carson said to one of his wives, "I won't keep you very long.") Some want to live exciting lives; others want to live low-stress lives. Some want to work all their lives; others can't wait till they retire. In other words, success, perhaps more than anything else, means different things to different people. This can be better expressed as "Different strokes for different folks."

Somehow, that seemed like a cop out. So I continued my search for an all-encompassing definition of success. The old axiom that those who seek shall find proved to be true. I finally found a definition of success that seems to be "right on the money." This definition is from the late Earl Nightingale, the dean of self-development, who defined success as "the progressive realization of a worthy goal."[3]

SUCCESS: THE JOURNEY

Of all the definitions of success I have come across, I like Nightingale's the most. It incorporates several important elements. The words *progressive realization* tell me that success is something that one continuously pursues. This definition makes it clear that the greatest joy comes from traveling the journey, from being fully engaged in something that we enjoy and value doing, something that stretches us and demands excellence and even sacrifices from us, something that tests our commitment and resolve. Those are the accomplishments that give us joy and satisfaction, not the things that are given to us on the proverbial silver platter, not the things that we receive free, especially when we know we do not deserve them. (In the military this is referred to as "backing up to the pay table.")

You can test this for yourself. Think back to when holidays such as Christmas or Hanukkah were a super-positive occasion in your life. (For most of us who have not yet reached grandparent status, that means back to when we were children.) What was the most exciting time for you? Was it the time before the holidays, when you were anticipating and waiting for all the wonderful presents? Or was it the time after the holidays, when you had opened your presents and were playing with them? I bet your answer is the time *before* the holidays. In fact, after you had opened the presents you probably felt let down.

This definition also acknowledges that goal attainment is not a static, one-time achievement, but is rather an ongoing, fluid process. It is a process in which we, on reaching one major goal, set other goals so that our entire life is a continuous journey of goal setting, striving, and achieving.

The importance of having continuous lifetime goals has been proven to me more than once. For example, there is my Uncle John, who, as a German merchant seaman, jumped ship in New York City because he could find no legal way to enter the United States. Toiling all his life, he progressed from literally possessing nothing other than the shirt on his back to becoming a successful small restaurant owner in Philadelphia. And, yes, he also became an American citizen. To him, however, running his own business and being financially independent was an intermediate goal. His major lifetime goal was to be able to retire and do nothing. After 62 years of working 6 or 7 days a week, 10 to 12 hours a day, he finally made it. He retired and began to enjoy *doing nothing*. Without any other major goals, though, without the goals that had driven him and given him a sense of purpose, his life lost meaning and direction. As a result, Uncle John's life of leisure did not last long. Only about one month after his retirement (in fact, just after he received his first Social Security check) Uncle John died peacefully in his sleep.

Insight Break

Death is not the greatest loss in life.
The greatest loss is what dies inside of us while we live.
                                                —Norman Cousins

---

Another example directly related to the importance of goal setting is my parents' story. Although I love my parents dearly, I have had difficulty understanding and relating to them all my life. By the way, my feelings toward them changed only after I accepted them the way they are instead of the way I think they should be. That change was the result of my taking complete responsibility for my life by living in accordance with the axiom "If it is to be it is up to me." (But back to my parents.) As a result of my upbringing and my early life experiences, I have been endowed with many positive attributes: a burning desire to be number one and a drive to pursue success and "the good life," balanced by a conservative approach to risk taking. (My father defined it as follows: You know you are successful when you perspire while eating and are cool while working.) My parents attained this ideal by working feverishly, 40 to 60 hours every week, and saving every penny, allowing themselves virtually no luxuries, vacations, or anything that would detract from their goal of independence. Success to my parents meant being able to buy a comfortable house with a piece of property large enough so that they could feed themselves and become self-sufficient. Success also meant retiring early so that no one could tell them what to do or when to do anything, so that they could "enjoy life." They accomplished half of that goal in 1965 when they bought a 34-acre farm with a comfortable house, a large barn, several farm buildings, and all the farm equipment to go along with it. They continued working very hard; in fact, they worked harder than before, because now they also had a farm to take care of. They worked that way for another eight years, until 1973 when they "retired" at the early ages of 49 and 51. For many people, this would be a dream come true. Who at age 49 or 51 would not like to own his own farm, raise virtually all his own food, and be almost totally self-sufficient?

But is it really success? If you asked my parents, the answer would be yes. If you asked me, I would say no. Why? First, there's the obvious reason: Different strokes for different folks. But there is more. Once my parents achieved this lifetime goal, they lost their drive, their passion, their focus. Whereas before they had traveled to many parts of the world, they were now prisoners of their own creation, the farm, which could not be left because someone needed to be there to take care of the animals. (No one else could be trusted to do that.) Whereas before they had had a zest for adventure and travel, they began to stay at home, because, after all, the farm had everything they could possibly want (nothing else was good enough). They even found it virtually impossible to visit my wife and me, or even their grandchildren, even though we lived only a three-hour drive away. Whereas before they had been frugal, saving their hard-earned money so that they could attain their goal, they now had become cheap. Saving money had turned into an obsession that was continued even after their primary goal had been reached. Instead of spending it on themselves to make their lives more enjoyable and rewarding, money was to be saved at any price, even if it meant forgoing essential medical care. Money had become the end, the end that was needed to ensure that they would never have to go to work for anyone else again. Whereas before they tended to be positive, flexible, upbeat, and highly motivated, they became negative, inflexible, skeptical, and morose because they had isolated themselves in their "prison," rarely venturing out to expose themselves to other people and other ideas, sights, sounds, tastes, and smells. Instead, they formed their opinions about the outside world from the news media, the prime purveyors of stinking thinking. (If you are detecting sadness, you are right. But keep in mind that I am the one who is sad. My parents say that they are "happy." I think that is a rationalization, because happiness is a relative emotion. If things, even great things, are always the same, how can they make you happy? Think of your own bed. Don't you appreciate it the most when you return from a trip and have *not* slept in it for several days? In other words, true happiness is hard to come by unless you have change, challenges, and even deprivation.)

Humor Break

I don't have time to die, I'm booked.

—George Burns, age 95

To continue to enjoy the benefits of traveling the journey and to avoid that let-down feeling, you must be sure to always set new goals. Now, that does not mean that you should become a workaholic. It simply means that you should always be striving toward something that turns you on. Once you have reached a goal, you should reward yourself by celebrating with those who have helped you accomplish the goal and those who have had to sacrifice to ensure your success. But then, after the celebration has worn off, it is time to begin another journey. It is time to get on the road again, pursuing yet another worthy goal.

Nightingale's definition of success also tells me that people who are traveling the journey are by definition successful, provided of course that they are pursuing goals that they and society consider to be worthy. Conversely, this definition also acknowledges that success is not possible unless we have positive goals, goals that give us positive feelings and enrich or benefit ourselves and others. (Goals that are at the expense of others, such as becoming the most successful drug lord in the city, do not fit this definition because they would not be deemed worthy according to society's standards.)

All kinds of other people, however, are successful in accordance with this definition. They include the individual who is striving for a promotion in her company, the homemaker who has the goal of being a first-rate parent and spouse, the student who is working on an advanced degree, the runner who is striving to extend his distance, the husband who is allocating a specific amount of time to spend with his wife each week to ensure that he has the most successful marriage possible, the nurse who is going to night school to make herself more marketable, the person who expects to earn $80,000 per year at age 30, and the select other few, the minority, the approximately 3 percent of the population who, in our abundant society, have clearly defined goals that they have written down and that they are currently pursuing.

Mental Stretch Break

Before I call you to action (you did know that this was going to get serious, didn't you?), take a brief mental stretch break to reengage the right side of your brain. Your task, just as before, is to translate each of the figures in Exhibit 2-1 into a meaningful word or short phrase. (See end of chapter for answers.)

Exhibit 2-1 Brain Teasers

1	2	3	4
dump dump dump dump dump dump dump ↓	oven oven oven oven oven oven	b (lo⌀use)	WO (HILL) ODS
5	**6**	**7**	**8**
ONCE / 4:45	CHAIR	OHOLENE	AGES

SUCCESS: ARE YOU READY FOR THE JOURNEY?

Now for the important question: What about YOU? Do you consider yourself successful? Are you getting what you want from life? Do you have the tools that will allow you to maximize your personal potential and propel you to success? Regardless of how you answered that question, this book is for you. If you said no, this book will provide you with the tools to enable you to reach the top. Even if you answered yes, this book will be equally meaningful to you. You see, my study of successful people has confirmed that the people who are full of PEP[2] are the ones who recognize, more than anyone else, that success is a journey. They also know that traveling the journey is enhanced by lifelong learning. These are the people who are full of PEP[2], the ones who have internalized the idea that real learning occurs after you think you know it all.

Insight Break

The proper function of man is to live—not to exist.

—Jack London

Yes, I'm Ready for the Journey, But . . .

There are three other groups of folks. (They are the toughest; that is why I have left them for last.) These are the folks who think they have arrived. They erroneously believe either that they know it all or that they do it all, or they feel that they are so successful that they become conceited and close themselves off to new information. I don't believe that you are one of these folks, however, because few of them read books like this one. But let me say a few words about each group just in case.

I Know It All

The first group, the ones who know it all, are those who have fallen into what has been referred to as the intelligence trap.[4] Because of this, they are virtually unteachable, and generally only a major failure such as losing a job or going bankrupt can shake them up sufficiently to unclog their "categories." They are the zappers who are afflicted with a killer self-development disease, "opinionitis," which, according to Karl Albrecht, author of *Brain Power,*[5] afflicts more people than all other diseases combined. These people are easy to recognize; they have what anthropologist Ashley Montagu calls "psychosclerosis," or hardening of the categories.[6]

I Do It All

The second group comprises those folks who engage in what Harvard professor Chris Argyris refers to as "single-loop" learning.[7] They know how to solve problems in single-loop fashion, but they are unable to be introspective and self-critical, that is, to practice "double-loop" learning. They are often highly educated and extremely successful professionals who not only believe that they know it all, but also firmly believe that they do it all. They often do so well that they do not know what to do with failure when it comes, as it ultimately does. Instead of being able to accurately reflect about their own behavior, they externalize any failure that they may experience (i.e., it's so-and-so's fault). These "water walkers" are unable to be introspective and self-critical because their "espoused" theory of action is entirely different from their "theory-in-use." In other words, these single-loop learners have the correct knowledge, but their knowledge has very little to do with how they actually behave. These very successful, highly educated professionals shut down their learning when they need it the most. As a result, Argyris maintains, "the smartest people find it the hardest to learn."[8] (You may want to reread this paragraph if you are a highly educated, successful professional who thought that this obviously does not apply to you. If you thought that, this paragraph probably applies *primarily to you!*)

I Have Arrived

People in the third group have "successitis." In the early stages of this disease, people feel that they have arrived (see my parents' story above). In fact, you may have a touch of it, particularly if you have had major successes in the past, have had considerable experience, and perceive yourself to be quite successful (for example, you are an executive secretary for a *Fortune* 500 company, make $100,000 per year, have an MBA degree, are a regional manager, or are the president of your own company). Although I would agree that you are very well accomplished, you are not successful by our earlier definition. The reason? Success is a journey, not a destination. Why do I say that? Because success is measured not by what you have accomplished or even by what you have accomplished relative to others. Success is measured by what you are *capable of accomplishing*. Most of us can accomplish much more than we give ourselves credit for. After all, we use only 0.1 percent to 10 percent of our brain's potential.[9] (Peter Russell, author of *The Brain Book,* contends that most of us use less than one-tenth of 1 percent.[10]) I contend that we, more than any external factor, are the primary obstacle to our own success.

People with advanced successitis, which is better known as conceit, are of course much more readily recognizable. These people are the zappers who perceive themselves to be so successful that all others should worship them. If you have associated with any of these folks I encourage you to stay away from them. They are the losers in life who delight in zapping you at every opportunity. On the other hand, if you are infected with this disease it is time to get yourself inoculated so that you are protected for life. You can make that happen by internalizing and applying the principles in this book.

Insight Break

Conceit is a weird disease that makes everyone sick except the person who's got it.

—Zig Ziglar

SUCCESS: READY, FIRE, AIM

Ready or not, let's get going. (No, the section heading does not have a typo in it, but I am glad that you are being attentive.) To facilitate your journey to success, I will provide you with a vehicle (theorists would call this a model) that will expedite your travels. This vehicle, which we will build throughout the pages of this book, is a rocket that will help you to *MAKE it a WINNING life* and propel you to success (you do want to get there fast, don't you?).

This rocket has six major parts. Part 1, the assembly building and launch site, represents your **P**ositive self-esteem. It consists of the assembly building, where your rocket will be constructed and assembled, and the service structures, where support personnel will check the rocket before it is launched. Of all the rocket components, your positive self-esteem represents the foundation for your success. If your rocket is not assembled properly, that is, if you have poorly developed or low self-esteem, no matter how well all the other components work, your journey will be doomed from the beginning. In fact, soon after liftoff, if you make it off the launching pad, your rocket will begin to self-destruct. Part 2, the control center, your **P**urpose, will control and direct the launch and the flight of your rocket. It will ensure that you remain focused on your target. Your purpose will provide for constant course corrections and ultimately, with all the other components of your rocket functioning at optimum performance, ensure that you reach your destination. Part 3, the fuel, the **E**nergy in your rocket, will lift you into space and keep you constantly moving toward the attainment of your goals. Part 4, the on-board computer, your **E**ducation, will collect data and intelligence about the performance of your rocket's vital systems and about your actual course of travel. Because this information makes your rocket "smart," it is analogous to your education. Part 5, the oxidizer, your **P**ositive attitude, is a fuel additive that will supply oxygen to the fuel to ensure that your rocket will be propelled to the highest levels. Part 6, the engines, your **P**erseverance, will work their guts out to get you to where you want to go. For an illustration of your PEP^2 rocket, see Exhibit 2-2.

Exhibit 2-2 Your Complete PEP² Rocket, with Assembly Building and Launch Site

CONTROL CENTER

ON-BOARD
COMPUTER

OXIDIZER

FUEL

ENGINES

ASSEMBLY AREA I

To help you on your journey, you will complete a self-assessment before each new stage, just as astronauts check out their rocket prior to liftoff. These self-assessments will help you to determine where you are and what you have to work with before you begin. Knowing your strengths and weaknesses will help you to identify your learning needs and will allow you to establish a more effective action plan. All of this will help you get your success rocket to the zenith in the shortest possible time.

At the end of each chapter, I will introduce you to someone who has mastered the art of *MAKING it a WINNING life* by excelling in one of the six PEP² principles. I will summarize each chapter in a section I call "A Trip Back to the Future." After that, I will outline "Success Action Steps," which are intended to help you to translate theory into action and knowledge into practice. Practice (which I know you will repeat consistently for at least 21 days) will result in new habits—habits that will change your behavior and help you to *MAKE it a WINNING life*. I will keep you awake and entertained with my famous (or is it infamous?) brain teasers and the insight and humor breaks sprinkled liberally throughout every chapter. (I won't leave you stranded; the answers to the brain teasers and mental stretching exercises are at the end of each chapter.)

Mental Stretch Break: How Well Do You Follow Directions?

But now, before we get into the thick of it, let's pause for a moment to have you briefly assess how well you follow directions. After all, this book is full of it—directions, that is. Turn to Exhibit 2-3 and do the following:

Block 1: Put a dot on the letter *j*.
Block 2: Write the six letters which make up the PEP^2 formula in the blank spaces.
Block 3: Block 3 represents a barn. In the barn are a baby bull, a papa bull, and a mama bull. Circle the one that does not belong.
Block 4: Circle one word that does not fit with the others.

(See end of chapter for answers.)

Exhibit 2-3 Worksheet: How Well Do You Follow Directions?

1	2
J	— — — — — —
3 BB PB MB	4 Drum Child Dog Sex

Source: Adapted from *Games Trainers Play* by J. W. Newstrom and E. E. Scannel, p. 207, with permission of McGraw-Hill Book Company, © 1980.

SUMMARY: A TRIP BACK TO THE FUTURE

- Success means different things to different people.
- Happiness is a perception, not a goal.
- Money is important, but it is not nearly as important as you think it is.
- Success is the progressive realization of a worthy goal.
- Happiness is derived from traveling the journey, not from arriving at a destination.
- You are successful as long as you are striving to reach a worthwhile goal.
- Succeeding requires that you
  —believe that success is a journey, not a destination; and
  —recognize that success, like learning, is a lifelong process.
- Success is measured by what you are capable of accomplishing.
- Success requires that you maximize your PEP[2]:
  —Positive self-esteem
  —Purpose
  —Energy
  —Education
  —Positive attitude
  —Perseverance

SUCCESS ACTION STEPS

❏ On your next day off from work, get up one hour before everyone else in the house. Make yourself your favorite brew, sit down with paper and pencil, and list all of the things that you would have to accomplish in order to consider yourself successful. Check off those that you are currently working on. For each of the remaining items on your list, ask yourself if you are willing to pay the price necessary. Hold on to this list; you will use it frequently.

❏ Take the list that you completed in the first action step. Make yourself very comfortable and relax. Pick the most important goal from this list and visualize what you are doing when you reach this goal. Make what you imagine as realistic as you can. Experience what you see, feel, touch, hear, and smell when you reach this goal. Enlarge it so that it fills all of your conscious thoughts. Make it brighter, more colorful, more vivid, and more realistic. Put yourself in the middle of it all. Make it feel as if it has already happened to you. Anchor this perception in your mind so that you can call it up any time you feel discouraged, disillusioned, or defeated. Remind yourself that your brainpower plus the tools contained in this book will help you reach this destination, provided you are willing to pay the price.

❑ Write the PEP² principles on the back of your business card. List what each letter stands for. Put the card in your wallet. When you encounter an obstacle on your journey to success, pull out the card, and review which principle you have to reengage to keep yourself on target.

❑ Identify how you see yourself. Are you a traveler on a journey, a person who knows all that he or she needs to know, or a person who has arrived? If you characterize yourself as one of the last two, reread this chapter, and/or visit your local library or bookstore to check out any of the other success books noted at the end of this book. Also, talk to successful people to find out how they see themselves. Continue this search until you have convinced yourself that success is a journey, not a destination.

NOTES

1. R.B. Dilts, J. Grinder, R. Bandler, J. DeLozier, and L. Cameron-Bandler, *Neuro-Linguistic Programming I* (Cupertino, CA: Meta, 1979).
2. A. Robbins, *Unlimited Power* (New York: Simon & Schuster, 1986).
3. E. Nightingale, "The New Lead the Field," (Chicago: Nightingale-Conant, 1986). Audiotape program.
4. B. Tracy, "Seven Secrets of Self-Made Millionaires," *Insight* (Chicago: Nightingale-Conant, 1987). Audiotape program with accompanying written materials. Nightingale-Conant Corp., 7300 North Lehigh Avenue, Chicago, IL 60648.
5. K. Albrecht, *Brain Power: Learn to Improve Your Thinking Skills* (Englewood Cliffs, NJ: Prentice-Hall, 1980).
6. Ibid., p. 102.
7. C. Argyris, "Teaching Smart People How to Learn," *Harvard Business Review* 69 (May–June 1991): 99–109.
8. Ibid., p. 99.
9. P. Russell, *The Brain Book* (New York: Hawthorn Books, 1979).
10. Ibid., p. 7.

ANSWERS TO MENTAL STRETCHING EXERCISES
Page 20

The two coins are a 50-cent piece and a nickel. (I said *one* was not a nickel—pretty tricky. I stoop to anything just to keep you turned on and tuned in.)

Page 30

How well were you able to follow directions?

- In block 1, did you place a dot *on* the letter *j?*
- In block 2, did you place the letters PEP[2] *on the lines,* or in the blank spaces as instructed?
- Which one did you circle in block 3? If you circled *MB* you are right! Why? Because there is no such thing as a mama bull!
- Which one did you circle in block 4? The object here is to come up with one that does not belong with any of the others. Many different answers and rationales can be generated. One of my workshop participants came up with the following answer: "I circled sex, because you can beat a drum, you can beat a dog, you can even beat a child, but you just can't beat sex!" (See Exhibit 2-4.)

Exhibit 2-4 Solutions: How Well Do You Follow Directions?

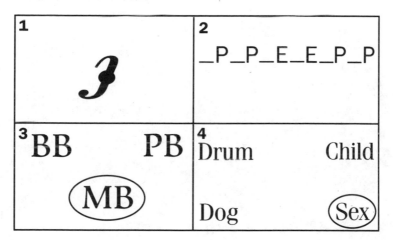

ANSWERS TO BRAIN TEASERS
Page 25

1. Down in the dumps
2. Microwave oven
3. See-through blouse

4. Over the hill and through the woods
5. Once upon a time
6. Highchair
7. Hole in one
8. Dark Ages

3

Positive Self-Esteem

To be what we are,
and to become what we are capable of becoming,
is the only end of life.

—*Robert Louis Stevenson*

What, you ask, does positive self-esteem have to do with success? Everything and nothing. Everything, because your positive self-esteem provides the foundation for success. No positive self-esteem, no success. Nothing, because if you have a high level of positive self-esteem but experience no success, your positive self-esteem will soon begin to diminish, and you will end up demoralized and beaten. (It's kind of like the riddle of the chicken and the egg, which came first?)

Because we have to start somewhere, let's begin by getting into the assembly building so that we can assemble the best PEP[2] rocket money can buy (see Exhibit 3-1). This is truly the foundation of your success; to have success you must have a high level of positive self-esteem that is internalized and integrated into all of your behavior.

PREVIEW OF COMING ATTRACTIONS

Let's begin by finding out how well you do in the self-esteem department by completing the Self-Esteem Assessment Scale (SEAS). Then we will consider the following question: What is self-esteem, anyway? After that, I will provide you with two quick self-assessment strategies that you can use at any time to find out how well your rocket has been built. Next, I will share with you some data about your marvelous body that will immediately make you feel a lot better about yourself. Following that, we will roll up our sleeves and learn some specific strategies that you can use to maximize

35

Exhibit 3-1 Your PEP^2 Rocket—Part 1: The Assembly Building and Launch Site (Positive Self-Esteem)

your self-esteem. To help you, I will reveal the secret to success; discuss the importance of accepting 100 percent responsibility for your life; teach you how you can use positive affirmations; and finally, conclude by sharing seven specific steps that will help you *act* like a winner.

POSITIVE SELF-ESTEEM: A SELF-DIAGNOSIS

To assess your self-esteem before you learn powerful enhancement strategies, complete the Self-Esteem Assessment Scale (SEAS) shown in Exhibit 3-2.

POSITIVE SELF-ESTEEM: A DEFINITION

Positive self-esteem has been defined by Denis Waitley, author of *The Psychology of Winning,* as the deep-down, inner feeling of your own self-worth.[1] Checking my trusty *Webster's New Collegiate Dictionary,* I find that *esteem* refers to "estimating worth, value . . . regard highly and prize accordingly." How do you regard yourself? What do you think you are worth? To find out, let's play a little game. Let's pretend that you are going to "check out" of life. Just like a business that goes bankrupt, you will need to do an inventory before you can go out of business. Let's begin our inventory with your eyes. In Chapter 1 I offered you $1 million for them. You turned down $500,000 for each of your arms. Your legs should each be good for at least $500,000 as well. What about your brain? I recently read about a young woman who had sustained permanent brain damage in an automobile accident who was awarded $12 million for damages in a suit against the automobile manufacturer. What about the other important parts of your body, such as your lungs, your heart (assuming that was not stolen on a previous occasion), your kidneys, your liver, and so on? I have lost count, but I think you would agree that we are up to several million dollars.

Insight Break

The longer I live the more beautiful life becomes.

—Frank Lloyd Wright

You are an incredibly sophisticated creation. Just look at some of the things that you have going for you:

- a body that has the capability to repair itself continually at the rate of 2 billion cells per day. (Don't you wish your car could do that?) As a result of this marvelous system, you replace 98 percent of all of the

Exhibit 3-2 Self-Esteem Assessment Scale (SEAS)

Instructions

Using the scale below, circle the number that most closely indicates the frequency with which each statement applies to you. (People have different preferences and opinions; therefore, there are no right or wrong answers.)

1	2	3	4	5
Never	Almost Never	Infrequently	Almost Always	Always

1. I feel that I am in charge of my life.   1 2 3 4 5 _____

2. I catch myself wishing that I could be more like someone else.   1 2 3 4 5 _____

3. I hesitate to take on new projects because I fear that I might fail.   1 2 3 4 5 _____

4. Upon making an error, I tell myself, "That's not like me," and get on with it.   1 2 3 4 5 _____

5. When meeting new people, I introduce myself by stating my full name.   1 2 3 4 5 _____

6. I feel that I can do just about anything.   1 2 3 4 5 _____

7. I think that getting ahead in life is primarily a function of luck and being in the right place at the right time.   1 2 3 4 5 _____

8. When asked to volunteer for a new project, I tend to focus mostly on why it might *not* work out.   1 2 3 4 5 _____

9. When I kid or tease others, I focus on their negative attributes.   1 2 3 4 5 _____

10. When paid a compliment, I answer with "thank you."   1 2 3 4 5 _____

11. I am constantly improving.   1 2 3 4 5 _____

12. When I make a mistake, I get on my "case," telling myself such things as "You are a dummy," "You will never learn," or "I knew you couldn't do it."   1 2 3 4 5 _____

13. When interacting with others, I focus most of my mental energies trying to recognize their positive attributes.   1 2 3 4 5 _____

14. When things work out well for me, I attribute it to circumstances.   1 2 3 4 5 _____

15. I believe that my self-image controls my life.   1 2 3 4 5 _____

16. I respect other people's opinions, even if they are very different from mine.   1 2 3 4 5 _____

Exhibit 3-2 continued

17. I find criticism very hard to take.   1   2   3   4   5 ____

18. I tend to be envious of successful people.   1   2   3   4   5 ____

19. I look for ways to help others even if there is   1   2   3   4   5 ____
    absolutely nothing in it for me.

20. When my boss is talking to me, I tend to think   1   2   3   4   5 ____
    about what I will say next, so that I come across
    positively.

Total Score   ____

Scoring Instructions

Score items 1, 4, 5, 6, 10, 11, 13, 15, 16, and 19 in accordance with the number that you circled. For example, if you circled a 2 for question 1, you earned 2 points, which you should write on the line next to question 1.

Reverse-score items 2, 3, 7, 8, 9, 12, 14, 17, 18, and 20. This means that you have to turn the scale around to score these items, so that 1 = 5, 2 = 4, 3 = 3, 4 = 2, and 5 = 1.

Examples:

1. I feel that I am in charge 1   2   3   4   ⑤   = 5

2. I catch myself wishing that 1   2   3   ④   5   = 2

3. I hesitate to take on new 1   ②   3   4   5   – 4

Total your points.

Interpretation of Your Score

91–100   *Excellent.* You have the ability to walk on water. You might consider skipping this chapter. On the other hand, people who score this high tend to be winners, and winners always want to learn new strategies that will help them to maximize their potential.

81–90   *Very Good.* Your self-esteem is in good shape. Tune in, and you will learn lots of new strategies that will enable you to get even better.

71–80   *Good.* You are on the road to optimizing your self-esteem. You will do better if you make a commitment and plan to apply the strategies delineated in this chapter.

61–70   *Average.* You have an opportunity to learn lots of valuable strategies. Be sure to study this chapter carefully and plan how to maximize your self-esteem.

<60   It is time to put that drink aside and pay attention to the principles presented in this chapter.

atoms in your body in less than one year. More specifically, you change
—your skin about every 20 days,
—your stomach about once a month,
—your liver about every 6 weeks,
—your skeleton once every 3 months, and
—all of your brain cells every year.
   This means that if you did not like yourself yesterday, don't fret.
   You are changing all the time. You simply need to decide to change
   for the better, which is what this book will teach you.

- a brain that has about 8 billion cells and a virtually limitless capacity to store and process information
- a brain that contains 100 billion neurons, with each neuron capable of transmitting an impulse 80 times per second
- a brain that thinks at the rate of about 800 words per minute
- a circulatory system consisting of 60,000 miles of blood vessels and a heart that beats about 100,000 times per day and that will have pumped at least 46 million gallons of blood by the time you are 70 years of age
- a nervous system consisting of about 7 miles of nerve fibers with the capability to send messages at the rate of 100 yards per second
- a set of kidneys, each containing about 1 million filters (nephrons), that will have removed 1 million gallons of waste products from your blood by the time you are 70 years of age
- about 600 muscles
- about 200 bones
- about 20 square feet of skin
- eyes containing about 100 million receptors
- ears containing about 26,000 fibers[2]

Of course, we could get a bit more precise and calculate the worth of your body from a scientific perspective. According to a DuPont engineer, if we utilized the electronic energy in the hydrogen atoms of your body to estimate your worth, you, assuming that you are close to being an average person, are worth about $85 billion, give or take a couple billion dollars.[3]

But I think we are still underestimating your worth. In fact, I would like to suggest that you are priceless (I know you have heard that from your sweetheart before). Here is my rationale. Vincent van Gogh's *Portrait of Dr. Gachet* was sold for $82.5 million. Startled by such an incredible price (would you know what $82.5 million looked like?), I began to reflect on what could possibly make any painting worth that much money. Is it the paint, the canvas, the frame? All could be purchased at your local art supply store for under $200. So, what could account for the enormous difference? It has to be because it is unique, because there is only one original *Dr. Gachet* painted by van Gogh to be found on the earth.

Mental Stretch Mini-Break

Since today is my birthday, here is a riddle for you. Quickly, how many birthdays does the average man have? What about the average woman? (See end of chapter for answer.)

BUT NOW FOR THE BILLION-DOLLAR QUESTION: WHAT ABOUT YOU?

Of the 5.5 billion people who currently inhabit the earth, of all the billions of people who have ever lived, there never has been, nor will there ever be, another *you*. You are even more unique than all of van Gogh's paintings combined because you are the rarest, most precious commodity *you* will ever own! Keep that in mind the next time you get out the proverbial whip and flagellate yourself for a mistake that you have made, the next time someone attempts to "build you down" below their level, the next time someone zaps you, or the next time you criticize yourself. Think about how you feel when someone makes a derogatory comment about what you wear, your new car, or an important project you just completed. You get quite upset about it, don't you? Why are you letting others get away with making derogatory comments about you? Or worse, how dare you say anything but positive things about something as precious as you?

Feeling better? Better about yourself? Better about your perceived worth or value? Good. You are beginning to learn how to enhance your self-esteem. You are beginning the process of building a high-quality PEP[2] rocket.

Insight Break

It is one of the most beautiful compensations of this life that no man can sincerely try to help another without helping himself.

—Ralph Waldo Emerson

SELF-ESTEEM: A QUICK CHECKUP FROM
THE NECK UP

Before we continue with this building process, let me share two quick methods to check your self-esteem so you can monitor your progress at any time. First, pay close attention to how you respond internally to mistakes. Are you an expert at self-flagellation? If you mess up, do you give yourself a good "beating" by saying to yourself, "You dummy, you will never . . . ," "You can never do anything right," "I knew you couldn't do it," etc.? If you respond to your own mistakes in this fashion your self-esteem is in bad shape. Second, take notice of how you kid others, especially the people who are the most important in your life, such as your spouse, your children, and your employees. When you jest or interact with them, do you habitually look for their strengths, highlighting those by complimenting, stroking, and catching them doing things *right* and letting them know about that? (I call these PEPers.) Or do you continually "build them down" by focusing your mental energies on catching them messing up or by zeroing in on their weaknesses and teasing them about those? (I call these zappers.) If you prefer to operate as a zapper, then your self-esteem is on the skids, and you might just need what Zig Ziglar calls "a checkup from the neck up."

If you read the previous paragraph carefully, or if you majored in English, I probably made you shudder with the way I mangled the English language with the term *building down*. I used that term on purpose, because I have found that people tend to remember oxymorons. Oops, I think I may have just violated the KISS principle, so let me explain. An oxymoron, according to our friend Webster, is "a combination of contradictory or incongruous words," such as *cruel kindness* or *jumbo shrimp*. Some of my favorites are *Postal Service* and *Internal Revenue Service*. Service? Who are they kidding? Another one I particularly like after 20 years in the military is *military intelligence*. How about *pretty ugly?* Does that make you think of Madonna? What about *political ethics?* Does that remind you of anyone we know? Do you ever ask anyone for an *original copy?* Or are you getting on in years and consider *happy birthday* to be an oxymoron? You can tell I think that these are *awfully good* fun. So let me shut up (I mean sum up) before I really get carried away. But wait, as we are talking about the English language, let me share a quick funny one that all the English teachers of the world will love.

Humor Break

Hearing a knock on the pearly gates, St. Peter asked, "Who is there?" The answer, delivered in a sweet, melodious voice, was "It is I." St. Peter turned to one of the angels in waiting and exclaimed, "Oh no, not another English teacher!"

SELF-ESTEEM: HOW TO MAKE THE MOST OF WHAT YOU'VE GOT

Now that you have a sense of what you are worth and know how to assess your self-esteem on an ongoing basis, you are ready to learn specific strategies that will help you increase your self-esteem to incredible new heights. To help you, I want to share with you the secret to success; discuss the importance of accepting 100 percent responsibility for your life; teach you how to use positive affirmations; and finally, conclude by outlining seven specific steps that will help you act like a winner.

Take Advantage of the Secret to Success

Many people spend a great deal of time looking for the secret to success. The irony is that there is such a thing, that it has been around since the beginning of time (I believe Aristotle first identified it), that it is totally free, and that it is relatively easy to learn. That secret, which Nightingale[4] popularized about a decade ago as the "strangest secret," is this: Your thoughts govern your behavior, and all you have to do to change your behavior is change the way you think! Dietitians and nutritionists misguide people by telling them that you are what you eat. The more correct statement is that *you are what you think you are,* most of the time, *because your self-image controls your life.*

You can check the validity of this axiom for yourself by asking whether you would have volunteered to sail around the earth during the time of Columbus. Or would you instead have been more conservative because you knew that you would have fallen off when you got to the end? There is another way to look at this. What did you just do? Perhaps you picked up a glass and had a sip to drink. Or maybe you underlined the previous sentence. I think that you would agree that these are all voluntary actions. Before you can execute such an action, what must you do? I bet your answer was: "Think about it." (Great, now I know that you are paying attention.) Now we know that *thoughts lead to actions.* What if you repeat an action over and over again for about 21 days or 3 weeks, whichever comes earlier? What will you have then? (This is review.) If you said "a habit," you are doing great! If you said something else, reread Chapter 1, and pay attention! Next question: What do you have when you put together all of your habits into a human body? If you said "behavior," you win the first prize, because you are really with it! (See Exhibit 3-3.)

Exhibit 3-3 The Thoughts–Behavior Connection

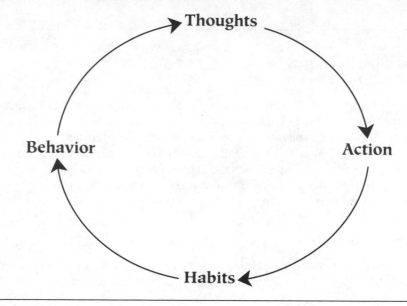

Here it is, one more time, because it is critically important that you internalize this concept. *If you want to change your behavior, all you have to do is change what you put into your mind.* What I am saying is that *psycho,* your mind, controls *soma,* your body. But you knew that already. Think of the last time you worked hard at getting something right. Maybe it was making a difficult shot while golfing. After missing it, you exclaimed, "I knew I was going to miss that shot!" And that indeed is what you did, because the body simply executes what the mind tells it. Another example, although a bit sadder, is a young man who had been jailed for committing a burglary. He admitted, "I didn't let my Dad down. I did exactly as he expected. He always said to me, 'Young man, someday you'll end up in jail.'" You will come across this concept many more times in this book. It is, after all, the secret to success.

Insight Break

Your actions are driven by your thoughts. Past thoughts represent your current performance. Current thoughts represent your future performance.

—Denis Waitley

Accept 100 Percent Responsibility for Your Life

To build your self-esteem you must begin by taking 100 percent responsibility for your life. You must recognize that you are in command, that you are the captain of your own ship, that life is somewhat like a game in which you are on the playing field every minute of the day. You are the player, the coach, and the umpire all in one. In this game you have control of the here and the now, no control of the past, and just a little control of the future. You also must recognize that just as in a game, you don't *have* to play, but you *want* to play because it is so much fun. In fact, I would like you to recognize that you really have to do only one thing in life, and that is to die. Everything else is your choice!

At this point you might be saying that that is not true. You might say that you have to go to work, that you have to pay taxes, and so on. Do you? No, you don't! You *want or choose* to do those things because you do not like the alternatives. You want to go to work because you are rewarded with money that can be readily exchanged for the things that you need to survive, such as food, shelter, and medical care, and the things that bring you joy, such as a new automobile or a vacation. You choose to pay your taxes because you don't want to pay the price of not doing so.

This is not just an issue of semantics, but rather a question of whether you conduct your life as an "external" or an "internal." Psychologists tell us that externals blame everything on something or someone else. They attribute their failure to poor parents, little education, bad luck, or anyone or anything else they can point a finger at. *Time* magazine referred to these folks as "busybodies and crybabies."[5] Internals, on the other hand, recognize that they are in charge and that it is not luck, karma, or their astrological signs that will determine whether they succeed in life. Instead, internals live by the belief that *if it is to be, it is up to me.*

Come to think of it, this would make one hell of a political slogan for the next presidential election. It is a belief that all of America could benefit from. Collectively we are suffering from what *U.S. News & World Report* called "it's-not-my-fault syndrome," also referred to as "victimology."[6] Just about all of our bad habits and deviant behaviors have been turned into "diseases." It started with drinking too much, "alcoholism," and smoking excessively, "nicotine addiction," and abusing drugs, "drug addiction." All of these I can accept intuitively, although I must tell you that I have never put anything into my mouth or body *accidentally.* But it has gotten out of hand. The *Diagnostic and Statistical Manual of Mental Disorders* has an excuse for any deviant behavior you can think of. There is the Pete Rose disorder (pathological gambling), Marion Barry's disease (alcoholism), dependence on cola or coffee (caffeinism), and inhalant dependence (reliance on aromatic hydrocarbons). But that seems to be just the beginning. A number of disciplines, including law, neurology, biology, nutrition, psychiatry, and psychology, have joined forces to usher in this new age of "it's-not-my-fault."[7] Combine law and psychiatry and you get the anabolic steroid defense. A bodybuilder robbed six Maryland homes and set fire to three. A judge determined that he was not criminally responsible because the excessive use of anabolic steroids caused him to be "suffering from organic personality syndrome." Although he was found guilty, he received no jail time.[8] Law and nutrition produced the convenient "Twinkie defense" (sugar made me do it). Law plus pop psychology plus technology gives us "computer addiction." Computer hacker Kevin Mitnick, who broke into various corporate computers, was "sentenced" to a year of "treatment" for his "new and growing" impulse disorder.[9] If all else fails, one can always be a sex addict. If you enjoy it too much and chase every person of the opposite sex who comes your way, don't worry, it's not your fault. Just get help. Search for the "right" psychologist and he will help you by giving it a fancy name, or join a support group such as Sexaholics Anonymous (come to think of it, that may be an interesting group to join). Things have gotten so bad that Roger Conner, executive director of Washington's liberal American Alliance for Rights and Responsibilities lamented that "the R word in our language is responsibility, and it has dropped from the policy dialogue in America."[10] Conner continued on to say, "A society can't operate if everyone has rights and no one has responsibilities."[11] Clearly, it is time to stop this nonsense and take charge of our lives by reaffirming that each one of us, and no one else, is the only person occupying our driver's seat. Make that happen now, by living your life in accordance with the axiom *If it is to be, it is up to me!*

I have been challenged on this point in my success workshops. Participants have said that that is easy for me to say. After all, they think, I have a Ph.D., am the president of my own company, have lots of experience, and am successful. If you are thinking along the same lines, I would like to quickly take away that crutch before you rely too heavily on it. Although I do not want to take up too much space by sharing my entire career with you, let me just tell you that I started my formal career after I completed an 8th grade education in Germany. I began working full time at age 14 as an apprentice steward in the German merchant marine, working 10 to 14 hours per day, 7 days a week on a ship that returned to home port after four months. No, I did not have wealthy parents either. In fact, they lost virtually everything in World War II. This meant that I had to pay for my education myself by working two or three part-time jobs. Given that English is my second language, I have no reservation that you can do as well as I have. Indeed, you can do better! It simply is a question of whether you are willing to pay the price.

Mental Stretch Break

Before we talk about how you can program your mind, take a minute to reengage the right side of your brain by doing a brief mental stretching exercise. Again, your task is to translate each figure in Exhibit 3-4 into a word or short phrase. (See end of chapter for answers.)

Exhibit 3-4 Brain Teasers

1 **FISHING** C	2 YOUR NONO RIGHT	3 C O M I C
4 $$\frac{0}{\begin{array}{cc} PhD & MD \\ MS & LLB \end{array}}$$	5 *house* *prairie*	6 T M A U H S W T
7 **jink jink jink**	8 **8** OF SPEECH	9 ƎƆAꟻ

Use Positive Affirmations

The mind, or more precisely, the subconscious, is analogous to the soil of a garden. Do nothing with your garden and before you know it, weeds will have taken over. These weeds, like thistles and poison ivy, will prick and sting you, causing much aggravation and pain. Conversely, if you tend your garden; plant things that you want to harvest; and nurture, cultivate, and water it as needed, in time you will be able to harvest nutritious and healthy vegetables or admire beautiful flowers. Can't relate to an agricultural model? Well, let's get into the information age and compare your mind to a computer. You may be familiar with the acronym "GIGO," which stands for "garbage in, garbage out." Just like a computer reading its programs, your subconscious mind reads the instructions you provide it to control your behavior and your life.

Insight Break

If you think you can or can't, you're always right.

—Henry Ford I

To translate this metaphor into a practical illustration, let's pretend that you are uncomfortable with computers. You would rather stand in a long line inside your bank instead of using the automatic teller machine at the drive-up window. In fact, you wish that computers had never been invented. But here it is, the 20th century. It is Monday morning, and there on your desk is a brand-new computer. Your boss pops in, unaware of your computer angst (Oops, violated the KISS principle again. Well, it is a nice German word you might try on your friends. It means fear.), to advise you that henceforth you will be using that computer on a daily basis because the firm has implemented an automated inventory control system. She further tells you that each computer is supplied with a complete set of manuals, but you really won't need them because these computers are "extremely user-friendly." She departs saying, "These computers are so easy to operate a baby can use them."

Here you are, with sweaty palms and lumpy throat, having a computer phobia attack. Your subconscious is solidly programmed with the knowledge that "I'll never be able to operate a computer." However, you are not about to give up. After all, you like this job, you need the money (you have already spent this week's paycheck), and you have no intention of demonstrating to anyone that you are less intelligent than a baby. You muster all of your energy and turn on the computer. To your surprise, there is no magic, only a blinking blip (you later find out that's called a cursor). Where is the user-friendliness your boss mentioned? It didn't even say "good morning." But you don't give up that easily. You move on to plan 2 and start studying the manuals. You are diligent and really give it a try, but you can't even get past "square one." After struggling for about two hours, you call a friend who is a computer whiz. (That's what you call anyone who has a computer at home.) You explain your problem. She points out that you have omitted one minor, but very crucial, step. After being confronted with the obvious, you hit yourself on the head and say, "That proves it. I just don't know how to operate computers." That negative affirmation is recorded by your subconscious and is added to the information that you have previously stored, further strengthening the shackles of the self-fulfilling prophecy. That initial affirmation started as a weak notion that hinted to your subconscious that you were incapable of operating a computer. That flimsy notion gained in strength with each negative affirmation until it became a self-fulfilling "reality." This is also referred to as the Pygmalion effect (see Chapter 5).

Insight Break

Success belongs to those who believe in their abilities.

—Wolf J. Rinke

Social scientists have clearly demonstrated that the subconscious records everything we ever experience and tell ourselves. But the subconscious is not able to distinguish among images, perceptions, and actual experiences. This means that *your perception is your reality.*

To check the validity of this important statement, look at Exhibit 3-5 and identify where the dot is in relation to the pyramid. You have four choices:

(1) toward the top   (2) in the center
(3) toward the left   (4) toward the right

Exhibit 3-5 Dot Exercise

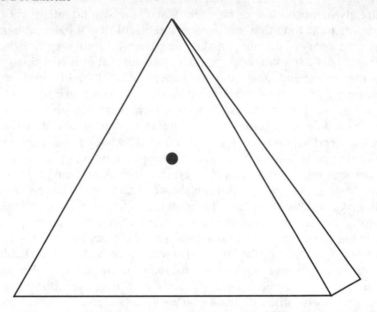

My guess is that you said (1) toward the top. Now get out a ruler and measure it. You will find that the dot is exactly in the center. Because of a perceptual distortion created by the pyramid your mind tells you that the dot is toward the top. Unless this is pointed out to you, and you are willing to amend your opinion, the off-center dot is your perception, and thus your reality.

Because your subconscious accepts everything you feed it as reality, *you become what you think about most of the time.* If you assume that you are unable to do something, such as operate a computer, then you will likely be unable to do it, no matter how hard you try.

The way to resolve this dilemma is to program your subconscious with positive messages or affirmations such as "I can operate computers," "I can run two miles in under 20 minutes," and "I will weigh my ideal body weight by the end of the year." If you are presented with a disconfirmation of a positive message (i.e., you mess up or don't succeed at something), then you must learn to treat that incidence as an *exception*. This can be accomplished by telling yourself, "This is not like me," or "I made a mistake this time, but I know that I will succeed next time." The secret to programming your internal computer is to recognize that your subconscious is equally as "stupid" as a computer. It cannot distinguish right from wrong; it simply records everything you feed it. So it behooves you to "feed" your subconscious positive affirmations. I recommend that you do that, even if initially you have to "fool" yourself. (No, you are not fibbing. You are just telling the truth in advance!) Those positive affirmations, right or wrong, will in the long run become your reality and will ultimately govern your behavior. (See Exhibit 3-6.)

Exhibit 3-6 My Robot

I have a little robot
That goes around with me.
I tell it what I'm thinking.
I tell it what I see.

I tell my little robot
All my hopes and fears.
It listens and remembers
All my joys and tears.

At first my little robot
Followed my command
But after years of training
It's gotten out of hand!

It doesn't care what's right or wrong
Or what is false or true.
No matter what I try now,
It tells ME what to do!

Source: Reprinted from *The Psychology of Winning Workbook* by D. Waitley, with permission of Denis Waitley, Inc., ©1983.

Act Like You Are a Winner

Another technique for building your self-esteem is to act like you are a winner. This was stated succinctly by the late actor Cary Grant, who was once asked how he transformed himself from his humble beginnings to an elegant, worldly, and debonair gentleman. He answered, "I started to act like the person I wanted to be, and eventually I became that person."

To clear up any misunderstandings, let me define what I mean by winning. To me, winning means reaching the goals you desire, but not at someone else's expense. Exhibit 3-7 provides an overview of winning and losing behaviors and attitudes, which you can readily use to diagnose your own behavior as well as that of others.

Exhibit 3-7 Characteristics of Winners and Losers

A winner says, "If it is to be, it is up to me."
A loser says, "I can't help it."

A winner translates dreams into reality.
A loser translates reality into dreams.

A winner empowers.
A loser controls.

A winner says, "Let's find out."
A loser says, "Nobody knows."

A winner is part of the solution.
A loser is part of the problem.

A winner is not afraid of losing.
A loser is afraid of winning.

A winner works harder than a loser.
A loser is always "too busy."

A winner says, "I was wrong."
A loser says, "It wasn't my fault."

A winner "wants to."
A loser "has to."

A winner *makes* time.
A loser wastes time.

A winner makes commitments.
A loser makes promises.

A winner says, "I'll plan to do that."
A loser says, "I'll try to do that."

A winner says, "I'm good, but not as good as I can be."
A loser says, "I'm not as bad as a lot of other people."

A winner listens.
A loser just waits until it is his or her turn to talk.

A winner catches people doing things *right*.
A loser catches people doing things *wrong*.

A winner learns from others.
A loser resents others.

A winner sees opportunities.
A loser sees problems.

A winner does it.
A loser talks about it.

A winner feels responsible for more than his or her job.
A loser says, "I only work here."

A winner says, "There ought to be a better way."
A loser says, "That's the way it has always been done."

Exhibit 3-7 continued

A winner celebrates others.
A loser complains about others.

A winner is willing to pay the price.
A loser expects it on a silver platter.

A winner expects success.
A loser expects failure.

To supplement these behaviors and attitudes, consistently apply the following seven strategies, and you will convince yourself and others that you are a winner.

Practice the Double Win

Practicing the double win technique, which maintains that ultimately if you win, I win, has an especially positive potential. Most people see life as a fixed pie or zero-sum notion (as I did until I taught myself otherwise). They assume that for them to get something, someone has to give up something. They focus on one or two obvious solutions when most of the time there are literally hundreds of options. To find those options, however, requires us to change the way we think and behave. It requires us to develop a new habit of working together to defeat the problem instead of the person or persons. It requires us to shift from win–lose thinking to problem solving, as shown in Exhibit 3-8.

Exhibit 3-8 Problem Solving versus Power

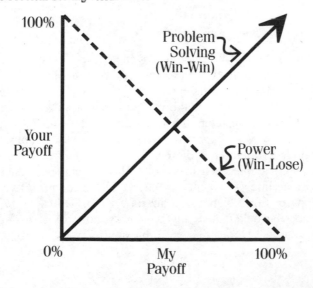

There are many examples of this paradigm shift and the positive results it will have for you. A husband and wife have had a particularly busy week and want to reward themselves with a special treat. She says, "I want to go to the theater—it has been ages since we have been." He says, "I just want to have a leisurely dinner and relax." Two obvious solutions, perceived as a fixed pie. "If we go to dinner I have to give in, and he always gets his way," thinks the wife. "If we go to the theater I have to give in, and she is already so bossy," thinks the husband. Both are using their abundant mental energies to defeat the other person. Instead, they could be operating under a win–win premise, wherein each is committed to finding out what the other person *really* wants and then using their mental energies to mutually generate as many options as possible that meet *both* of their needs. In a win–win mode, they would express themselves using "I" language. The wife would say, "I want to be entertained." The husband would say, "I want to relax." If they put their heads together to generate ideas that meet both of their needs, they would probably come up with many options, including dinner theater, a real win–win outcome. Of course, other possibilities would arise as well, such as dinner first, then a comedy club, or a catered dinner at home and a trip to the movies.

Insight Break

You can get anything in life you want if you will just help enough other people get what they want.

—Zig Ziglar

Give Yourself Away

David Dunn, author of *Try Giving Yourself Away,*[12] says that too many of us are still operating in the "me" generation, contributing to the win–lose behaviors of jealousy, selfishness, and greed. Selflessly giving yourself away, even in small ways, will make you feel good about yourself and will help you build your self-esteem. There are many "treasures" that you can give away, including your expertise; we all have a skill, competence, or ability that will help others. But there are many intangibles that can make a big difference in people's lives as well. These include kindness, active listening, genuine interest, loyalty, courtesy, tolerance, a positive attitude, love, and appreciation. Dispensing liberal doses of all of these will not, contrary to popular belief, take anything away, nor will it hurt you in any way. Having doubts? Here are several inexpensive ways that you can try this to see if it will work for you. At the next opportunity, hold the door open for someone else, and not just if they are of the opposite sex and good looking; let someone into the lane in front of you while driving (if you feel compelled to use sign language while driving, make it positive sign language—wave at the other driver instead of giving him the digit); pick up something that someone has lost and return it before looking at it to see how valuable it is; distract a small child that is giving his parent a hard time at the supermarket checkout counter; smile at others as they pass by you; express empathy to a person who is serving you; make peace with your enemies; and compliment someone you envy. All of these actions will build confidence in yourself because nothing builds your self-esteem more effectively than building the self-esteem of others. Actions like these will also restore your positive perception of human nature. As you now well know, life is just like a mirror: You will get back, in the long run, what you give. In fact, you will get back more than you give because giving yourself away is just like money in the bank (a solvent bank, that is). It will pay you interest and dividends.

Abide by the following rules to give yourself away effectively:

- Speak from the heart, not the head.
- Never fib or make up something.
- Mean what you say or don't say it.
- Walk your talk.
- Do it NOW.
- Do it first (don't wait for the other person to start).
- Do it without expecting anything in return.

The reason you must abide by these rules is that people, regardless of their level of education, are extremely street-smart. If you do not mean what you say, they will, no matter how convincing your words are, know that you are not sincere. Another reason is that people pay a lot more attention to your behavior than to your words, so always mean what you say and practice what you teach.

Insight Break

You can help others maximize their potential by catching them doing things *right*.

—Ken Blanchard

Catch Others Doing Things Right

As a manager, I used to concentrate on people's weaknesses, generally assuming that people were lazy and wanted to get away with doing as little as possible. (For those of you familiar with management theory, McGregor called this Theory X.[13]) Because people were basically "no good," I had to supervise them closely, making sure that they did things the way I wanted them done. And, if they did not comply, I was quick to point out what they had done wrong. Because people see themselves the way others see them (psychologists refer to this as the looking-glass theory), and because it is not possible for others to consistently do things exactly the way I would do them, I set people up for failure before they ever started. Failing makes people feel demoralized, depressed, and devalued and lowers their self-esteem. Their performance of course continued to further diminish, and before I knew it, they had fulfilled both my self-fulfilling prophecy and their own. And so, I was "right" again. Just as I suspected, they were indeed "no good."

Once I learned to focus my abundant mental energies on catching others doing things *right,* I began to reverse this destructive cycle. What I found, contrary to my earlier beliefs, was that most people want to do a good job and are trustworthy and dedicated, provided that is what is expected of them and they are treated and rewarded accordingly. This change came about not because of other people, but because I took ownership of *my* actions, recognizing that most people deliver in the long run what I expect from them. This reinforces our earlier lesson: If it is to be, it is up to me. Now I make it a practice to treat all human beings as if they are winners, team members, and adults. (Hold it, wait with rolling your eyes until you read the next sentence.) I continue to operate under that belief *until they prove me wrong.* (I don't want to get further off the track, but if you are a manager and this stuff gets you excited, I can recommend a highly praised management book [written by yours truly] that will provide you with many more specific tools for empowering your employees.[14] Don't let the title mislead you. It is a management book with universal appeal and application.)

Whatever you do, however, do not limit yourself to catching only your employees doing things right. Apply this strategy generously whenever you can find an opportunity. Why? Because one of the best ways to raise your self-esteem is to raise someone else's self-esteem! Make that important positive call to one of your friends, say the important positive words to your co-workers, and find something to praise your children about. Tonight, when you kiss your children good night, tell each of them how happy you are to be the proud parent of such a "dynomite" child. Don't forget to catch your spouse doing something, anything, right, and then tell him or her how fortunate you are to be married to such an exceptional human being. Whatever you do, remember to do it *now,* because a positive thought kept to yourself is not worth anything.

Insight Break

There are two ways of exerting one's strength:
one is pushing down,
the other is pulling up.

—Booker T. Washington

Set Your Own Internal Standards

Set your standards always just a bit out of reach, but not so far away that you perceive them to be unattainable. And most importantly, use yourself as your own "gold standard," against which you compare your accomplishments. The trick here is not to try to be *the best,* but rather to be *YOUR best.* Why? Because when you attempt to be the best you will likely set yourself up for failure, stress, indigestion, and maybe even ulcers. (Ulcers come not from what you eat, but from what is eating you.) Even though all human beings are endowed with the seeds for greatness, we are not all endowed with the same seeds. Some of us have far more natural abilities than others. For example, even though I think I am pretty smart, I am rather dumb at the same time. Let me explain. I am rather smart (whatever that means) if you compare me to me. But if you compare me with Albert Einstein I'm pretty stupid. Fortunately for me, though, that is an illogical comparison. After all, I'm not Albert Einstein (lucky for me, as he is dead), I am me. I can only build on my own innate abilities. The more important question to ask is What have I done to take advantage of and maximize *my* abilities? What have I done to help me be all I can be? What I am trying to say is don't waste your mental energies by comparing yourself with others. No matter what you do, *you will never be like anyone else.* (My daughters, Jeselle, who is 19 going on 22, and Nicole, who is 15 going on 19, could benefit from this advice. (They get it, but they are not ready to hear it.) They have not yet internalized this concept, and so they spend extraordinary amounts of effort and money (most of it mine) to look like someone else. (Don't you think it is strange that many people who have straight hair spend a lot of money to get their hair permed, while those who have curly hair have it straightened?)

It is not only the young who struggle with this. Recently, a rather attractive woman came up to me after one of my motivational presentations to ask several questions and compliment me. She exclaimed, "Wow, what a presentation. It was a tour de force. I really admire the way you speak. In fact, I would give ten years of my life to be able to speak like you." I thanked her, chuckled, and answered, "Your estimate is right on. That's about how much of my life I have dedicated to public speaking." You see, we admire others for how well they do things *now,* but we forget how long it has taken them to get to where they are. Most of us want to be just as good, but we don't want to pay the price!

Instead of wishing you were like someone else, the trick to life is to build on your own strengths. In fact, I consider this to be another key to success. Every human being is a composite of strengths and weaknesses. (Do you know what yours are? More about this in Chapter 4.) Luckily for all of us, there are no perfect people. Can you imagine how boring that would be? Learn from professional athletes who gain satisfaction from being just a little better this time than the last time, who persevere, and who, sooner or later, by continually beating their *own* record, beat their opponent. No matter how hard you try, you will never be like anyone else. So quit wasting your abundant mental energies. Instead, accept that you are the most valuable asset you will ever own. You are the only asset that belongs to you that has the potential to truly appreciate. Most everything else you own depreciates—your money, your car, your spouse (just kidding). So be sure to take the time to invest in yourself.

Insight Break

Don't explain. Don't complain. Just do it!

—Wolf J. Rinke

Accept Value Paid

Denis Waitley[15] says that the best way to spot a winner is to see how they respond to value paid. You should always accept compliments with an unequivocal and courteous "thank you." Don't be like the young lady who upon being paid a compliment about her beautiful dress replied, "This?" pointing to her dress. "Oh, I was going to give this to Goodwill." Or like a friend who had made an excellent presentation who answered when complimented, "You are just trying to make me feel good." Only losers have difficulty accepting value paid. Their level of self-esteem prevents them from recognizing that they are in control of their lives and that success is primarily a function of hard work and preparedness, not good luck. I believe it was Napoleon Hill, author of the success classic *Think and Grow Rich*,[16] who defined good luck as "preparedness meets opportunity." (Someone recently said to me, "You are so lucky." I answered, "Yea, I have noticed that the harder I work, the luckier I get.") Never say "Shucks, that was nothing," because very few things in life are the result of good luck or karma. Instead, accept value paid with a sincere and courteous "thank you."

Humor Break

A city-bound priest was riding through the countryside and was struck by the absolute beauty of a dairy farm. The meadow was well kempt, lusciously green, and surrounded on all sides by a beautiful white picket fence. The cows all looked as if they had been scrubbed from head to toe (or nose to tail?). It was truly a sight to behold. As he rode down the country road the priest noticed the farmer repairing the picket fence, so he took the opportunity and stopped to chat. To get the conversation started the priest said, "My son, God has blessed you with a beautiful farm." The farmer answered, "Yes sir, I'm grateful, but you should have seen this place when He had it all to himself."

Act and Look Your Best at All Times

"None of us will get a second chance to make a first impression." This is no idle old wives' tale. Various research studies have supported this. For example, I recall reading about a study in which a man went into various offices dressed rather casually. He later visited a second set of offices that were similar to the first set. This time, however, he was "dressed for success" in a traditional high-quality business suit with all the trimmings. In each case his goal was to get the secretary to provide him with certain confidential information. To control the independent variables, the same man made all of the visits, and the type of offices and the language and approach used were standardized. Although I cannot recall the specifics, I do remember that the results clearly demonstrated that when he was well dressed the gentleman was able to obtain the confidential information much more frequently than when he was casually dressed. This finding is further amplified by the fact that it takes roughly seven repetitions to reverse an initial impression. This means that if I perceive you as being negative when you and I meet for the first time, you would have to be on your best positive behavior for the next seven encounters before I would revise my initial impression. This is compounded further by the fact that most people tend to form a relatively stable impression in about five seconds. I am sure some of you are saying that that's not fair. I agree with you, but unfortunately, that's how they (you and I and whole bunch of other human beings) play the game. Instead of bemoaning that the world is an imperfect place, I suggest that you take advantage of this phenomenon and act and look your best at all times.

Mental Stretch Break

To keep you on your toes, here is a different type of exercise for you.

Quickly add the numbers in Exhibit 3-9. Add them in your head from the top to the bottom. (No calculators, please.) (See end of chapter for answer.)

Exhibit 3-9 Addition Exercise

1000
10
1020
10
1030
10
1010
10

Let Your Body Say Positive Things About You

One way that you can be sure to act and look your best at all times is to let your body convey positive messages. Walk briskly, erect, and, most importantly, with a smile on your face. In a recent success seminar I was challenged on this point by one of the attendees. Jane said, "How can I behave like this when I'm depressed?" I asked Jane to come up front to demonstrate how she walks when she is depressed. She walked to the front of the room slowly, taking small shuffling steps, with her head slightly bowed, and with an ever-so-subtle frown on her face. I asked her to next demonstrate how she talks when she is depressed. She answered that she talks in a nasal, bitchy voice. I complimented Jane on her excellent demonstration. Then I asked her to repeat this walk, but this time I asked her to walk erect, with her chin up, her shoulders back, and her chest out; to take purposeful steps with long strides; and to put a big smile on her face. She did this very well. At this point I said, "Jane, tell us how you feel now." She answered sheepishly that she felt much better. Your body, your posture, and especially your face say a lot about you. If you make the decision that you want to be depressed, your body will reaffirm that. Conversely, if you "pretend" repeatedly and convincingly that you feel good, your body will reflect that. (Doubt it? Try jumping up out of your chair, à la Toyota commercial style, shouting: "I'm depressed!" I bet you can't do it. Because if you do it, you won't be depressed.)

This is especially true if you learn to adopt one of the most powerful success strategies of all times: SMILE. Smiling improves your "face value" and communicates to all other human beings, regardless of their language or nationality, that you and they are OK. The other benefit is that smiling is contagious. (There is that life is like a mirror bit again.) Try it on the grumpiest person you know to see if sooner or later you don't get a smile back. Smiling also influences your posture. Check it out for yourself by standing, putting your chin *on* your chest, and trying to smile. (I do this exercise with my workshop audiences, and you should see how funny they look when they are grimacing like this. Don't gloat, though—get a mirror and see for yourself that you are not doing much better.) Now put your chin up, stand up straight, and smile. (Check the mirror now. What is your face telling the world now?) I think you will agree that this is much better. Your body is a living, moving, multidimensional billboard. Your "billboard" can advertise doom, gloom, and defeat or hope, courage, energy, and success. It is *your choice!*

Humor Break

That reminds me of something that happened recently. I met a good friend who was apparently in a grumpy mood. I asked him the customary "How are you doing?" He answered automatically, "F-i-n-e." Given that he was a good friend, I said, "Why don't you tell your face!"

Now before I introduce you to someone who has mastered the PEP[2] principles, you may find it useful to make a promise to yourself (Exhibit 3-10).

Exhibit 3-10 Promise Yourself

Promise Yourself—

—To be so strong that nothing can disturb your peace of mind.
—To talk health, happiness, and prosperity to every person you meet.
—To make all your friends feel that there is something in them.
—To look at the sunny side of everything and make your optimism come true.
—To think only of the best, to work only for the best, and to expect only the best.
—To be just as enthusiastic about the success of others as you are about your own.
—To forget the mistakes of the past and press on to the greater achievements of the future.
—To wear a cheerful countenance at all times and give every living creature you meet a smile.
—To give so much time to the improvement of yourself that you have no time to criticize others.
—To be too large for worry, too noble for anger, too strong for fear, and too happy to permit the presence of trouble.

—Christian D. Larson

PEP² IN ACTION—POSITIVE SELF-ESTEEM: JHOON RHEE

Jhoon Rhee was born and raised in South Korea. He immigrated to the United States in 1957, bringing with him the Korean form of martial arts known as Tae Kwon Do, which earned him the title of father of Tae Kwon Do in the United States. He is a world-renowned tenth-degree black belt. He has taught many notables, including Muhammad Ali, Jack Anderson, Tony Robbins, Jack Valenti, and over 100 congressmen, as well as thousands of young people all over the world. He has been inducted into the Black Belt Hall of Fame, is the author of five Tae Kwon Do books, has acted in two martial arts films, was the recipient of the 1976 Bicentennial Sports Award, and has served as a presidential appointee to the National Council of Vocational Education. He is also the inventor of martial arts safety equipment and the founder of the martial arts ballet. Most recently, Master Rhee, as his students call him, has

become a major influence on inner-city youth in the Washington, D.C., metropolitan area. He also has been a major force for positive change in the Soviet Union.

WR: Master Rhee, in my book I talk about six key principles: positive self-esteem, purpose, energy, education, positive attitude, and perseverance. We are getting together today to learn from you how these six principles, and the self-esteem principle in particular, have helped you succeed in life, love and business.

JR: When I was six years old, a five-year-old girl beat me up. I cried and went home hoping my mother would comfort me. My mother asked me why I was crying. When I told her, she scolded me and beat me up some more. That really destroyed my self-esteem. And so, I made a commitment to do something about it. I started lifting weights. I also wanted to learn how to defend myself. Unfortunately, the little town of Suwon, South Korea, where I grew up, did not have any place to learn self-defense. However, when I was a teenager, I moved to Seoul, and there, next door to my uncle's home, where I lived while I attended middle school, was a school of self-defense. I was 13 when I joined that martial arts school, and I have been practicing Tae Kwon Do ever since.

WR: How did you get from Seoul, South Korea, to America?

JR: I watched a lot of American movies when I was young. And so, at age 13 I established a goal to go to America. That goal grew on me. After I finished serving in the Korean army I immigrated to the United States in 1957 and enrolled in Southwest Texas State Teachers College in San Marcos, Texas. From there, I went to the University of Texas to study engineering. However, my plans were changed once again, in 1962, when during a summer stay in Washington, D.C., I was encouraged to open a Tae Kwon Do school. I have been teaching Tae Kwon Do ever since.

WR: You have received a lot of media attention because of your positive work with children and young people in the Washington, D.C., area. What do you teach these youngsters?

JR: I emphasize to my students that to have confidence you must have three ingredients: (1) knowledge in the mind, (2) honesty in the heart, and (3) strength in the body. You have to have knowledge to be confident. When you know what to do your self-esteem automatically rises. The same is true of the second ingredient, honesty in the heart. When you are consistently honest and have nothing to hide you never have a guilt complex, and you never have to think twice about what to say. These two ingredients are the foundation for positive self-esteem. But that may not always be enough. After all, we live in a wicked society, and no matter how good you may feel about yourself, sometimes wicked people will attack you and try to harm you. Hence the third ingredient, strength in the body. This is strength to defend yourself. These three ingredients really give you a tremendous positive self-image and positive self-esteem.

Martial arts is doing a lot of good for our young people. I used to have over 25 studios in the Dominican Republic about 20 years ago. Many of our students were very poor ghetto children. While I was teaching there we created 11 black belts. Since then, I have found out that of the 11 black belts, 10 became extremely successful. For example, one became a businessman, one a professor, one a dentist, one a lawyer, one an economist, and one a medical doctor. I couldn't believe it! I did not realize what Tae Kwon Do can do for ghetto children. That experience convinced me that a healthy self-image and positive self-esteem are really the keys to success. When you know in your mind clearly what you can do then you have the ability to take action. On the other hand, anything you have only vaguely or abstractly in your mind is very hard to implement. We must understand that the purpose of knowledge is to take action. No matter how much you know, if you sit and do nothing, nothing happens. So I say the purpose of knowledge is to take action, and the purpose of truth is to live. Not just know. We have a lot of social, political, and religious leaders who are unable to influence their followers. The reason is that many of them are not living up to the principles they are preaching. Setting an example, living the example for the children, should be the way to lead them so that they live by the three principles. Once they develop this knowledge and translate it into action they will become confident, have high levels of self-esteem, and become successful.

WR: That is a very interesting perspective. That is similar to my assertion that knowledge is nice but it is simply not good enough unless you translate it into change of behavior.

JR: Right! I always ask what the purpose of knowledge and ideas is. The purpose is to take action! Of course, unless you take action, nothing happens. That is why you have PhDs driving cabs. They have knowledge but they do not transform it into action.

WR: Of course, there is one more step that must be taken. Changes in behavior must be transformed into positive habits. You and I, and every other human being, are driven by habits. Therefore, developing positive habits is really important.

JR: I am glad that you mentioned that. I tell my students that whenever they take action the action by habit is the best one. When I was learning English I did not memorize things only in my brain. I memorized a whole bunch of short sentences with my lips. Each tissue of your body has memory. That is what habit forming is. So, when someone is coming at me to attack, I raise my arms. That happens automatically because my arms have memorized the action and respond automatically. [While talking, Rhee demonstrated this at such a speed that it was almost imperceptible. I was glad that I was not closer, or I am sure that I would have been knocked out.] That is what I tell my students. The brain is small; don't try to pile all that information in that small space. Send it out to the whole body to create more space in the brain for other information.

WR: You are making a very powerful observation. What you have just said is increasingly being demonstrated in the scientific literature. Evidence is accumulating that demonstrates that the mind is connected to the body through all types of different mechanisms and chemical pathways. That means that the immune system, the stomach, the intestines, and other vital organs actually have the capability to know.

JR: I tell my students that each cell has eyes, ears, and everything. Whenever someone says "I'm tired," every cell listens and that person begins to feel tired. If one says "I'm not tired," then all the cells obey and feel energized.

WR: I am glad that you have brought that up. That is really the entire thrust of this book, hence the title, *MAKE it a WINNING Life*. You and I make choices, and most of us choose to lose. Ironically, winning and losing take about the same amount of energy. But people do not recognize that this is a choice. Most feel it happens because of their environment, their parents, their spouse, their boss, or their place of birth. They feel that they really have very little control over their destiny. Of course, nothing could be further from the truth. Your life story, and your students' life stories as well, demonstrate that all of us have the ability to *MAKE it a WINNING life, if we want it badly enough.*

JR: Nothing happens by accident. Everything has meaning. You see things happening now that look like accidents. But two or more years later you will find a reason. Everything has a reason. I don't know if you know the four affirmations that all my students must repeat daily. They are as follows:

- I'm smart because I always learn something good every day.
- I'm perfect because I never make mistakes knowingly.
- I like myself because I always take action to make things happen.
- I am happy I'm me because I always choose to be happy.

WR: Those are very powerful and can serve as a compelling, positive driving force for your students.

JR: The driving force is happiness. And happiness is *the* universal purpose of human life. Many political leaders talk about the importance of universal human values. But they just talk about it. They really do not know what it is. Universal human values cannot be determined until you determine what the universal purpose of human life is, because purpose always determines value. For example, these eyeglasses have a purpose, so they have value. Let's say one is broken, and there's no way to replace it. So we throw them out. They no longer have value. When I ask what the purpose of life is nobody can answer, except five- or six-year-old kids. They know. They can answer, but adults cannot. As we grow up, we make our society so complicated that the purpose of life is hidden. It is so far out that some of us assume that we can only discover it after we die. Once we determine the universal purpose of life, then we can have universal human values.

WR: You are saying that the purpose of life is to be happy?

JR: That's right. Some people say their purpose in life is to worship God. But if worshipping makes you miserable you will not continue to worship. You worship God to bring you peace and happiness. Every second of our lives every human being is driven by two primary forces. We are either trying to pursue pleasure or avoid pain. My dog does it; every insect does it. The reason people don't want to get up at 6 in the morning on Saturday is that staying in bed provides more pleasure than getting up. Even on Monday we don't want to get up. But if we don't, we get a lot of pain later. We lose pay, or maybe even our job, so we get up. After all, if we get up we make money, and money can buy us a lot of pleasure. Every second of our lives we are calculating and manipulating our behavior to make sure that we avoid pain and seek more happiness. The purpose of life is to be happy, and so any value that contributes to happiness is a positive, universal value.

Any value that goes against that purpose is an evil value that takes away from happiness.

But then, what is the key to happiness? It is love. Unless you love you never get loved. Love never comes from things; it comes from other human beings. But what triggers love? As far as I'm concerned, there are two kinds of stimuli: physical beauty and heart beauty. You can take care of your skin beauty by cosmetics. But what is the cosmetic for your heart beauty? It is truth. When you are truthful, you become beautiful. When you are beautiful, you are loved. When you are loved, you are happy. So the three universal human values are *truth, beauty,* and *love.* What are the evil values? They are the opposite of truth, beauty, and love. Lying is one. When you lie you become ugly, and when you are ugly you are hated. When you are hated you are sad or in pain. If everybody in the world would live by these principles all human beings would have a meeting of the minds and common, universal values. There would be one common law for the happy way of life for all 5.5 billion people on earth. This is the universal law for happy living for everyone.

WR: That is a powerful perspective that dovetails with the *purpose* principle in my book. I have found that having a purpose, a set of overarching goals, serves as the driving force in people's lives. That purpose provides the internal motivation that makes us want to get out of bed and helps us persevere when the going gets tough. You are adding to this perspective a universal purpose, one that is shared by all human beings. That purpose is the universal value of happiness. I find that very exciting.

JR: I tell children: "You have a choice. You want to be happy? Be truthful. You want to be unhappy? Go ahead, lie." I try to stimulate children's minds.

WR: The other thing you talk about is skin beauty versus beauty in the heart. One of the people I interviewed for the book is W Mitchell. Mitchell has no skin beauty. In fact, it is difficult for most people to look at him because he is so terribly disfigured. But once you get to know him you discover his "beauty of the heart" and find out that he is one of the most beautiful people in the world. He is a master at leveraging his numerous handicaps. For example, when he ran for Congress his slogan was "I'm not just another pretty face."

JR: What a way to turn a disadvantage into an advantage, to take a handicap and make it into a strength.

WR: We agree on another principle, the principle of *perseverance*. You call it discipline and use the martial arts as a vehicle to teach this to your students. The words you use are *strength in the body*. Talk a little more about that.

JR: To become a champion in martial arts you must have physical endurance. When you do push-ups you must always do one more than your maximum. [At this point, Rhee, who is 60 years *young,* 5 feet, 6 inches tall, and 135 pounds, demonstrated what he was talking about by doing 100 push-ups in *1 minute!*] As a human champion, you must have a sense of perseverance, which equates to physical endurance in the martial arts and persistence in business. In fact, it is one of seven qualities of a human champion, qualities that have corresponding values in the martial arts, life, and business. The others are quickness, alertness, and market awareness; timing, punctuality, and meeting deadlines; power, knowledge, and financial success; balance, rationality, and stability; flexibility, gentleness, and adaptability; and last but not least, posture, honesty, and business integrity. Let's consider the quality of balance. In martial arts, when you try to kick with one leg, you have to have balance. You have to have flexibility. [Rhee demonstrated a leg kick that propelled his leg 180 degrees into the air so that his foot was directly over his head.] I do 500 push-ups in the morning and 500 in the evening; that's 1,000 per day. I have worked myself up to this. I could not do this at age 54. That is why there is hope for humanity. I try to set an example for my followers. I believe in leading by example. For example, when I ask an audiences of six- and seven-year old children and their parents whether it is good for children to smoke, they say no. Then I ask whether it is good for parents to smoke. They say no again. Whenever children see parents smoking, they think, "If they do it, why shouldn't I?" Adults must set a good example for their children. Politicians, teachers, preachers, and all other adults must lead by example. They must be flexible and open-minded. Don't say to someone, "If you don't believe in my religion you'll go to hell." The purpose of religion is to honor God, not to go to heaven. That is a marketing scheme.

Taking action is the key. It is not because we do not know truth. You find truth in your conscience. Your conscience tells you exactly what to do and not to do. Just follow your conscience and everyone will be a divine human being.

When I went to the Soviet Union I told the Soviet people that freedom is being introduced into their country for the first time in their generation. Freedom without discipline is chaos. Teaching the definition of freedom is tough to do even in our country. What is freedom? It is not taught well in our schools. OK, I'm free! Does that mean I can break all the windows in school? To me freedom means that you can do those things that are approved by your conscience. Behavior approved by your animal instincts is license. Undisciplined freedom is license. You make a choice. Your conscience knows exactly what is and is not right.

WR: In our society there are a lot of people who appear to lack that value system, that sense of conscience that guides their actions in a positive way. Somehow, somewhere along the line, it has just been totally lost. How would they make positive decisions?

JR: The reason they lost it is that they have never been taught the purpose of life. Once they are taught the purpose of life they say, "Oh, I see. It makes sense." Teach them how to become happy. Teach them when they are young. We have to start young to mold their minds into the universal laws of happiness: truth, beauty, and love.

WR: In our materialistic society a lot of people equate happiness with things.

JR: Happiness comes from emotions and from human relationships, not from things. That is why people make you miserable or make you happy.

WR: There's an old saying, I'm sure you've heard it before, that success is a journey, not a destination.

JR: That's right. I teach children how to be happy, then teach them how to enjoy the passage. Happiness is not the destination, it is the journey.

WR: In our conversation, you have not talked much about the physical aspects of martial arts. As the father of Tae Kwon Do in America, I expected you to talk more about what most of us associate with martial arts—the kicking, screaming, hollering, and decimating of your opponent. Why haven't you talked about that?

JR: The skill to defend yourself is a byproduct of the universal laws for happiness. What I teach people is a philosophy of life. Once you have mastered that, learning the skills of martial arts is easy, because the skill to defend yourself is merely an action. In other words, emotion creates motion as much as motion creates emotion. We have two basic tools in martial arts teaching. The first is *chario*, which means attention, paying undivided attention. This physiology will create a state of mind in which you can pay 100 percent attention, even to the point that if a bee sits on your nose and stings you you will not move a muscle. The physical act of standing at attention produces a mental state of alertness. Next is *kyungye,* which means respect. This is demonstrated by bowing, which creates a sense of humility and respect. If you teach children at a young age how to pay undivided attention and instill a sense of respect for teachers, parents, and adults, then you have laid the foundation for all learning, whether it is carpentry, cooking, playing the piano, history, or martial arts.

WR: I think you have a unique opportunity. To most young people martial arts is very macho. It has a certain kind of allure. It is the stuff they have seen in the Kung Fu movies. Instead of kicking and screaming, however, they must first learn philosophy, how to pay attention, and how to respect their elders. In other words, you use martial arts as the vehicle for teaching young people important lifetime success skills.

JR: I am in a unique position because of my physical activity. That is my passion; my philosophy just really stems from that. The things I am talking about do not come from reading, they come from my lifetime of experience.

WR: I must tell you that it has been a long time since I have met a 60-year-old who is as vibrant and physically fit as you are. I have thoroughly enjoyed our interview, and wish you lots of success with your crusade of making this world a better place.

JR: Thank you very much.

WR: Thank you, Master Rhee. Keep spreading the universal value message all over the world, and continue to *MAKE it a WINNING life.*

SUMMARY: A TRIP BACK TO THE FUTURE

- Self-esteem is the deep-down, inner feeling of your own self-worth.
- You are an incredibly sophisticated creation that is literally priceless and that therefore deserves your 100-plus percent respect, nurturance, and admiration.
- To assess your level of self-esteem, observe how you talk to yourself when you mess up and how you treat others in your life. People with

high levels of self-esteem forgive themselves readily and routinely make others look good.

- You are what you think you are.
- Your perception is your reality.
- You can maximize your potential by
  —taking advantage of the secret to success,
  —accepting 100 percent responsibility for your life,
  —using positive affirmations, and
  —acting like a winner.
- You can act like a winner by
  —practicing the double win,
  —giving yourself away,
  —catching others doing things *right,*
  —setting and competing against your own internal standards,
  —accepting value paid,
  —acting and looking your best at all times, and
  —letting your body say positive things about you.

SUCCESS ACTION STEPS

- ❏ The next time you mess up, listen to your self-talk. If your self-talk is negative, figure out how you can reframe your internal conversation to make it positive or future oriented. For example, focus your mental energies on what lessons you have learned, and then conclude your conversation by saying, "The next time. . . . ."
- ❏ The next time you interact with someone, visualize the words *Make me feel important!* in big, bold letters across his forehead. Assume that you are interacting with the most important person in the world, and act accordingly.
- ❏ Talk about others whenever you have the opportunity to say something positive. Otherwise, keep your mouth shut.
- ❏ Copy Exhibit 3-7 and place a copy on your refrigerator at home and a copy on every bulletin board at work.
- ❏ The next time you point a finger at someone note that there are three fingers pointing back at you!
- ❏ Make up an attractive sign that reads: "If it is to be, it is up to me." Put it where you can see it repeatedly throughout the day.
- ❏ The next time you negotiate with someone, force yourself to generate at least six options before you talk about solutions.

❑ Remember: "You can get anything in life you want if you will just help enough other people get what they want."
❑ Tomorrow, before leaving the breakfast, lunch, or dinner table, find something positive to say to your spouse. Make this a habit by doing it consistently for the next 21 days!
❑ Today, when you interact with your family members, use your abundant mental energies to find something positive that they have done. Then compliment them!
❑ Tonight, kiss your children good night and tell them how proud you are to be their parent. Repeat this or a similar positive action until it is a habit. (If you don't have children, find someone else you deeply care for and get into the habit of telling them how proud you are to be their sister, brother, child, friend, etc.)
❑ This weekend, pick up the telephone and make peace with one of your "enemies." Repeat it until you no longer have any enemies.
❑ This week, enrich someone's life by sharing something, no matter how small, with them. Repeat this for the other 51 weeks this year— and for the rest of your life.
❑ Right now, commit to never wanting to be like someone else. Instead, get passionate about being the best you can be.
❑ The next time someone pays you a compliment, note what and how you answer. If you make excuses, plan to generate another new habit, the habit of accepting value paid, by saying "thank you."
❑ Take a look at yourself in a full-length mirror before going to work tomorrow. Pretend that you are meeting the person in the mirror for the first time. Making a judgment on looks alone, would you hire the person you see? If the answer is no, devour a book on how to dress for success.

NOTES

1. D. Waitley, *The Psychology of Winning* (Chicago: Nightingale-Conant, 1979).
2. This information was compiled from various medical references.
3. E. Nightingale, *The New Lead the Field* (Chicago: Nightingale-Conant, 1986). Audiotape program.
4. Ibid.
5. "Busybodies & Crybabies: What's Happening to the American Character?" *Time* 138 (August 12, 1991): 14–23.
6. J. Leo, "The It's-Not-My-Fault Syndrome," *U.S. News & World Report* (June 18, 1990): 16.
7. J. Birnbaum. "Crybabies: Eternal Victims," *Time* 138 (August 12, 1991): 16–18.
8. J. Leo, "The It's-Not-My-Fault Syndrome."
9. Ibid.

10. J. Birnbaum, "Crybabies," p. 17.

11. Ibid.

12. D. Dunn, *Try Giving Yourself Away,* 3d ed. (New York: Prentice-Hall, 1970).

13. D. McGregor, *The Human Side of Enterprise* (New York: McGraw-Hill, 1960), pp. 33–57).

14. W. J. Rinke, *The Winning Foodservice Manager: Strategies for Doing More with Less*, 2d ed. (Rockville, MD: Achievement Publishers, 1990).

15. D. Waitley, *The Psychology of Winning*.

16. N. Hill, *Think and Grow Rich* (New York: Fawcett Crest, 1987).

ANSWERS TO MENTAL STRETCHING EXERCISES
Page 41

Did you answer 1 to both questions? If you did, you answered correctly. The rest are really birthday anniversaries. If you are older than 30, or whatever age you stopped counting, you may want to speak French on your next birthday and tell your friends that you are having a "anniversaire" party (that's French for birthday party).

Page 60

Did you get 5,000? That's what most people get. However, you might want to do it again, since that is *not* the right answer. What did you get this time? Frustrated? Perhaps you should use a calculator. Now you get 4,100, the correct answer.

ANSWERS TO BRAIN TEASERS
Page 47

1. Deep-sea fishing
2. It's right at the end of your nose
3. Stand-up comic
4. Four degrees below zero
5. Little house on the prairie
6. What goes up must come down
7. High jinks
8. Figure of speech
9. About face

Purpose

Until one is committed there is hesitating, the chance to draw back, always ineffectiveness. Concerning all acts of initiative (and creation), there is one elementary truth, the ignorance of which kills countless ideas and splendid plans: The moment one definitely commits oneself, Providence moves too. All sorts of things occur to help one that would never otherwise have occurred. A whole stream of events issues from the decision, raising in one's favor all manner of unforeseen incidents and meetings and material assistance which no man could have dreamed would have come his way.

—Johann Wolfgang von Goethe

Once you have recognized the importance of the first *P* (positive self-esteem) in PEP[2], you have begun to lay the foundation for your success. You have assembled a high-quality rocket supported by a launch site and maintenance buildings that are essential to beginning your journey to success. To ensure that your journey is focused, however, you will need a control center. That is, you will need a purpose. Charles Garfield referred to this as a mission.[1] He also found that all peak performers go beyond goals and become results focused. This is the second part of your success rocket. Without a sophisticated and well-functioning control center, even the best-built rocket will wander aimlessly until it burns itself out and falls from the sky. Your control center, then, is your purpose, your vision, your dreams, and your values, translated into specific goals and objectives that will keep you on track during your journey to success (see Exhibit 4-1).

PREVIEW OF COMING ATTRACTIONS

In this chapter, you will first take a brief quiz to assess how well your life is focused. Then we will discuss why you should be concerned with a purpose and goals anyway. After you are convinced that without goals there can be no planned success, I will provide you with a system that will help you chart your success journey. This system begins with you identifying your dreams and then translating your dreams into reality through a four-step process. Following that, we will focus on why fear is a potential

Exhibit 4-1 Your PEP² Rocket—Part 2: The Control Center (Purpose)

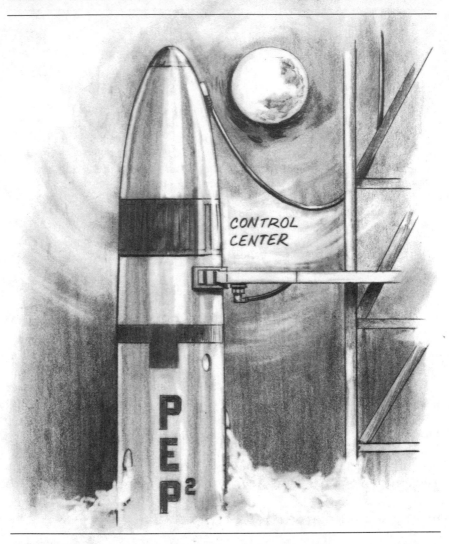

roadblock and identify six specific strategies that will help you overcome fear.

HOW WELL IS YOUR LIFE FOCUSED RIGHT NOW?

To determine how well your lifetime goals are focused, complete the Purpose Assessment Quiz (PAQ) in Exhibit 4-2.

Exhibit 4-2 Purpose Assessment Quiz (PAQ)

Instructions

Circle the *one best answer* for each question unless instructed otherwise.

1. Once I know what my lifetime goals are I don't have to bother writing them down.
   a. True
   b. False

2. I purposely provide for quiet time so that I can dream about what I plan to do with the rest of my life.
   a. Never
   b. Have done that once in my life
   c. About once every five years
   d. At least once every year

3. Generally speaking, we hold ourselves back more than anything or anyone else does.
   a. True
   b. False

4. **Circle all that apply** to you:
   a. I wouldn't recognize a lifetime goal if it hit me over the head.
   b. No one close to me has ever established clearly defined, written lifetime goals.
   c. The only place I have ever been exposed to goals and objectives is at work.
   d. Several important people in my life, as my boss, my parents, my spouse, or other family members, are in the habit of establishing clearly defined, written lifetime goals for themselves.

5. My lifetime goals are:
   a. Nonexistent
   b. In my head
   c. Written down
   d. Written down and internalized

6. If you awakened me in the middle of the night and asked me what my lifetime goals are, I would:
   a. Kill you
   b. Scream
   c. Not know what you were talking about
   d. Be able to tell you

7. Only losers fear failure.
   a. True
   b. False

8. My lifetime goals are (**circle all that apply**):
   a. Written down and placed in a location that ensures that I see them at least twice each day
   b. Running through my head like a perpetual movie loop most of the time

Exhibit 4-2 continued

    c. Supported by written objectives that are specific, measurable, attainable, relevant, and trackable

    d. Accompanied by detailed, written action plans that have been benchmarked in my calendar

9. My daily schedule is determined by:
    a. Any task or requirement that comes along
    b. What the boss or spouse tells me to do
    c. My daily "to do" list
    d. My daily "to do" list, which has been prioritized in accordance with my lifetime goals and objectives

10. When embarking on an innovative venture, it is generally better to ignore other people's advice.
    a. True
    b. False

_____ Total

Scoring Instructions

Each answer earns the number of points shown below. Mark the number of points earned next to each item. Total the points to determine your score.

1a.	0	3a.	5	5a.	−2	6c.	0	8c.	5	10a.	5
1b.	5	3b.	0	5b.	3	6d.	10	8d.	10	10b.	0
2a.	−5	4a.	−2	5c.	5	7a.	0	9a.	−3		
2b.	2	4b.	5	5d.	10	7b.	5	9b.	2		
2c.	5	4c.	5	6a.	−5	8a.	5	9c.	5		
2d.	10	4d.	10	6b.	0	8b.	5	9d.	10		

Interpretation of Your Score

≥ 91   *Outstanding.* You have got it down pat! In fact, you are a goal-setting genius. Please call me—I would like to coauthor a book on goal setting with you.

81–90   *Very Good.* You really know how to keep yourself on track.

71–80   *Good.* You have got the basics. Now it is time to build on those to get you off to a flying start.

61–70   *Average.* You will want to pay attention to this chapter because it will provide you with the tools that will help you focus your lifetime goals.

≤ 60   I'm really pleased for you because you will get more than your money's worth from this book.

PURPOSE AND GOALS: WHO NEEDS THEM ANYWAY?

That is a very interesting question. Why should you worry about purpose and goals? Who needs them anyway? *You do* if you want to succeed! Why? Because, to repeat our rocket analogy, a person without a purpose is like a rocket without a guidance system. Think of the Apollo moon mission. What do you think would have happened if a bunch of smart engineers and scientists had gotten together and said, "Let's get together, use all of our talents, find us a bunch of money, build the best rocket money can buy, shoot it in the air, and see if it gets close to the moon"? What would their probability of success have been? Or, what if you get the best basketball players in the world together, have them train until they play like champions, and then tell them to play the best game of basketball they can, only once they get to the court they find that neither side has baskets? You are probably thinking to yourself that these are absolutely absurd questions. Some of you probably are even getting a bit upset that I would insult your intelligence with such silly questions. If that is the case, then why are you, assuming you are like most of the people in the United States, running your life that way??? In study after study it has been demonstrated that only about 3 percent of the U.S. population have clearly defined, written lifetime goals. In other words, most of us are operating like rockets without control systems.

Insight Break

Those who do not have goals are doomed forever to work for those who do.

—Brian Tracy

Alice, Is That You?

Do you remember the story of Alice in Wonderland? Remember when Alice got to the fork in the road and asked the cat sitting nearby which road she should take? The cat asked in return where she wanted to get to. Alice answered that she did not know. The cat replied that in that case any road would get her there. Just like Alice, most of us have no idea of where we want to go. We get up every morning because someone said that we *have* to go to work; we trudge through the day with busy work, majoring in minors, taking care of all the things that *have* to be done; and then we go home and spend some time with the family, eat dinner, and plop down in front of the boob tube, letting it insult our intelligence and anesthetize our innately inquisitive minds, so that tomorrow when that alarm clock rings we are sufficiently numb to begin another day of stress relieving instead of goal achieving. In other words, most of us are wandering generalities, passive systems that react to the challenges that life presents us, much like the proverbial sailboat without a rudder. The question is, what is the probability of that sailboat hitting a harbor—not even a specific harbor, just any harbor? The answer of course is that it is unlikely; it is at best a chance occurrence, happening at the mercy of the winds, the elements, and luck. Tragically, most of us spend more time planning a holiday party, a vacation, or a Sunday excursion than we do planning our life! Before we find out why you should bother with this goal-setting stuff, you may want to grab a cup of coffee, sit up, and pay attention.

WHY BOTHER?

If most people do just fine without a purpose or goals, why should you bother to be any different? The reason is that YOU want to succeed! (Otherwise, you would not have spent your hard-earned money on this book, nor would you have gotten this far reading it. Another sad truth is that most people just put books on the shelf to impress their friends. Putting a book on the shelf without reading it is like fixing a beautiful chef's salad and not eating it. Just like that salad, a book will not nourish you unless you consume it.)

But let me give you some more meat to go with that salad and, I hope, more motivation. In a 1953 study of Yale graduates, researchers sought to determine how many of those graduates had clearly defined, written lifetime goals. They found that only about 3 percent of the graduates studied had goals. (Keep in mind that we are talking about Yale here, not some college of questionable reputation.) What makes this study so remarkable, however, is that the researchers followed up some 20 years later to find out how well the graduates did. Using career advancement and income as their measure of success, they found that the 3 percent of graduates who had clearly defined, written lifetime goals had accomplished more than the remaining 97 percent of graduates combined.[2] In other words, success in life is a function of having a system, and that system is goal setting!

Insight Break

Man can bear any what if he has a big enough why.
—Friedrich Nietzsche

PROVE IT TO YOURSELF

Are you still not convinced? It is important that I make a believer out of you, so let me let you convince yourself. Put down the book, close your eyes, and think of those things for which you have had what I call a "fire in the belly." These are the things that, as far as you are concerned, unequivocally will be accomplished before you "look at the radishes from the other side." It could be a specific academic degree, a spouse, a certain income, or a vacation in some exotic part of the world. Or maybe it is a house or a certain type of automobile. It is important that you think only of those things that you have a burning desire for—not "someday I'll" goals. That is, not things such as someday I'll spend more time with my family, someday I'll take that dream vacation, someday I'll buy my own house. Those are "I'll-ands" that you will never get off. I want you to visualize only "fire-in-the belly" goals. Do that now.

My Lifetime Goals

Because I will not know what you came up with as your goals, I will share with you some of my early lifetime goals.

My Lifetime Goal Number 1

I have had my first two "fire-in-the-belly" goals for as long as I can remember. My earliest lifetime goal was to drive a Mercedes. If memory serves me right, this one originated with my father. Because he lost everything in World War II, my father could barely find enough food to keep us from starving during the postwar period in Germany. During the time that we were slowly but surely pulling ourselves up by our bootstraps, my father kept impressing on me that people who have arrived "have a fat belly, smoke a fat cigar, and drive a big Mercedes." Although I opted not to strive for the first two, I always wanted to own a Mercedes. That goal provided me with an incentive to work hard, which I have done since I was 14 years old; to save aggressively (at least 10 percent of net income); to invest conservatively (mostly in real estate); and to live frugally and spend wisely (meaning spending on things that give the most "bang [translate as pleasure] for the buck"). As a result, about six years ago, I finally bought myself a new Mercedes Benz 300. And, in case you are wondering, no, I did not buy it to impress my friends. I bought it to impress myself! Actually *impress* is not the right word. The best explanation I have is that it provides me with a deep, meaningful sense of satisfaction that probably only I understand.

My Lifetime Goal Number 2

My second lifetime goal, which also goes back to my German upbringing, was to obtain a doctorate. Since no one in my family went beyond a high school education, I am not quite sure when or how this goal originated. What I can remember is that while growing up I was always abundantly impressed with people who were referred to as "Herr Doktor" or "Herr Professor" (Herr means Mr.), the salutation that is appropriate for individuals who hold a doctorate or who are professors. (The German people just go wild with titles and formality. They not only refer to everyone except their very closest friends by their formal designation, that is Herr [Mr.] or Frau [Mrs. or Ms.], they also add to it any additional titles that an individual has. A lieutenant colonel in the army becomes Herr Oberleutnant, a doctor becomes Herr Doktor, and a professor becomes Herr Professor. Today, I have all of those titles and use none of them. I much prefer that people, including my graduate students at Johns Hopkins University, call me Wolf. (I think that has to do with my self-esteem, which no longer requires me to use those things to make me feel good about myself. That is only part of the explanation, though. The other part is that titles make me feel older than I want to be.)

My Lifetime Goal Number 3

My third lifetime goal, which I have had for quite some time as well, was to earn $100,000 per year. Why this was so important to me also goes back to my childhood. Being born in Germany during the depths of the Depression to parents who had to dedicate all of their resources and energies to just feeding themselves and staying alive caused me to value, perhaps even overvalue, money. Money could buy food, clothing, living space, furniture, transportation, and all the other things that most of us take for granted, but that were mostly out of reach or only minimally available during my childhood. Money became increasingly more important to me after I left school and began working. That feeling was magnified when, after immigrating to the United States and going to college, I opted for security by staying in the military for 20 years. That decision, whether right or wrong, prevented me, at least while I was in the military, from making the kind of money I had always dreamed about. My inability to realize this goal during my military career caused my desire to smolder for 20 years. When I finally retired, it was as if someone had thrown gasoline on those smoldering desires; they became intense, extremely hot flames. This intensity helped me achieve my third lifetime goal only two and one-half years after retiring from the military.

Now, of course, I have established new lifetime goals. And even though they are important to me, I must confess that they do not have quite the same intensity as my original goals. Which, I suppose, proves that for many of us, adversity is the road to greatness, and abundance the road to apathy.

Your Burning Desires

But enough about me. What about your burning desires—the ones you identified before I started babbling about my goals? I bet that two things are true. First, it probably took you very little time to think of them. In fact, you are probably visualizing them all of the time. Second, you probably are currently on your way to attaining your goals, or you may have accomplished them already.

Insight Break

You have to stand for something. If you don't stand for something, you'll fall for anything.

—Denis Waitley

THE SYSTEM TO SUCCESS

What I am trying to say is that your purpose, supported by effective goal setting, represents a *system*. Once you have mastered this system, it will get you what you want. Just like the self-guided "smart bombs" that proved decisive in the 1991 Persian Gulf war, once it locks on its target, it will get there. Over mountains, through valleys, and around obstacles, it will, provided the target is within range, hit a bull's-eye sooner or later. An effective goal-setting system will do the same for you if you have identified a target that is within reach (your goal), locked in on that target (the fire in the belly), developed a plan, and are committed to stick with it (that is the perseverance in PEP^2—see Chapter 8).

At this point you are probably saying, "Enough already, I am convinced, just show me how to do it." Right on! It is great to see you get excited.

Mental Stretch Break

Excited or not, what you need to do first is to engage your creative energy because you and I are getting ready to dream a little dream. (Actually, it is a very big dream.) Your task, as before, is to translate each figure in Exhibit 4-3 into a word or short phrase. (See end of chapter for answers.)

Exhibit 4-3 Brain Teasers

1	2	3
POCHICKENT POCHICKENT POCHICKENT POCHICKENT	ii ii ◯◯	$\dfrac{GI}{CCC}$
4	5	6
ꓷ ∩	RIGHT=RIGHT	he's / himself
7	8	9
ECAP PACE	s d r k i n house	one *other* one *other* one *other* one *other* one *other* one *other*

DREAM A BIG DREAM

In his classic book, *Think and Grow Rich,* Napoleon Hill identified three key steps to success: conceive, believe, achieve.[3] (I call it the reverse ABC of goal setting.) He was absolutely right. All goals must start with a dream. You must first be able to conceive, visualize if you will, what it is that you want to accomplish. There are all kinds of books and many sophisticated systems that have been developed to assist with the process of goal setting. Even though I think many are excellent, I have made a commitment to KISS it, so here is my simplified methodology for goal setting.

You will need the following: a writing pad (or you can copy Exhibit 4-4 to help guide you), several 3 x 5 cards, a pen or pencil, and a quiet setting. (This is high-tech stuff, isn't it?) The best way to make sure that you have a quiet setting is to get up about one or two hours before everyone else on your next day off—let's say this coming Sunday. (Yes, do it *this coming* Sunday; you have procrastinated long enough. I know, I know. I didn't tell you that it was going to be this hard.) After you get up, take a brisk shower, get dressed, and pour yourself your favorite beverage. Put on some soft classical or easy-listening music. Now sit in your easy chair with your pencil and your writing pad. Take a deep breath, do some breathing exercises to help you relax, and partially close your eyes. Now dream about what you want to accomplish in your brief moment on this planet that we call earth. Do not, at this time, constrain yourself by anything. Ignore what others have told you can or cannot do; forget any past failures and setbacks; and ignore your current troubles and any handicaps, real or perceived. Dream what you want to accomplish, focusing on those things that are critically important to you. You will recognize them when you think of them; your heart rate will increase, you will breathe more rapidly, and you will feel that burning desire. At this point, do not worry about whether these are personal or professional goals.

Insight Break

When you reach for the stars, you may not quite get one, but you won't come up with a handful of mud either.

—Leo Burnett

To help you with this process, ask yourself questions such as the following: What goals would I set for myself if I had a 100 percent guarantee that I could not fail? What is my ideal life style? What do I stand for? What is really important to me? What epitaph do I want on my tombstone? What do I want my children or my loved ones to say about me when I am gone?

Exhibit 4-4 Dream Sheet

List as many "big" goals as you can think of in the following categories. Write them in the first person, using the present tense. Imagine that you cannot fail, no matter how lofty your goal. Project yourself into the future. Pick a date or an age, and visualize what is happening to you at that point in time. For example, in the financial category, you might write: "It is the year 2000 and I am earning $100,000 per year." Try to come up with at least one goal for each of the categories. However, do not worry if you cannot come up with something in every category or if you have several in some. It is important that you remember to think big. After all, this is your *dream sheet*.

Professional

Financial

Family

Social

Community

Spiritual

Personal

Where do I really want to live? (This is not necessarily in the part of the country, or even in the country, where you are currently living.) What is my ideal income level? What is my ideal career goal? Not what luck or circumstance has served up for me so far, but rather, what I really love to do. Write these things down as they occur to you; pay no attention to order, magnitude, possibilities, fears, limitations, or obstacles. Your objective is to dream and to capture your dreams. If you find it difficult to dream and write at the same time, you may want to talk into a recorder and then write them after you have captured all of your dreams. Copy the dream sheet in Exhibit 4-4 to assist you with this process. (If you are married or have a significant other with whom you are planning to spend the rest of your life, have your significant other go through the same process.)

Translating Dreams into Reality: Step 1

After you and your significant other have filled out your dream sheets, put them aside until the next weekend. At that time, both of you should spend one or two hours working with them. Begin by evaluating your dream sheet to determine how important each goal is to you. You may want to rate each goal on a scale from 1 to 10, with 1 meaning "This is a pipe dream that would be nice to accomplish" and 10 meaning "This goal is critical to me, it will change my life, and I am willing to pay any price to achieve it." Numbers between 1 and 10 indicate that you feel less strongly.

After you have rated every goal (I know it is difficult to do), strike all goals with a rating of less than 6. Then compare your dream sheet with your significant other's. Note the goals that both of you assigned high ratings to. As the next step, prioritize all of your goals from 1 to whatever, with 1 being your most important goal. The 1s should have received a score of 10 in the previous ranking. Weight those that you and your significant other both assigned high ratings to more heavily when prioritizing. Write your highest priority goals (at least 3 but not more than 5) on two 3 x 5 cards. Place one of these cards near your bathroom mirror, where you brush your teeth twice a day, or any other place where you will automatically see it at least *twice a day.* Take the other card to your office, school, or work. Place it where you will see it several times throughout the day. Place your goal card on your desk or work surface so that it is in your view when you look up from your work or when you are on the telephone. Also, have it nearby when you decide what you plan to accomplish for each day (your "to do" list).

If you have done things correctly, the goals you identified in step 1 are your lifetime dreams. (A completed dream sheet may look somewhat like the one in Exhibit 4-5. Note, however, that your dream sheet should look very different. For goals to work, they have to be uniquely yours.)

Exhibit 4-5 Completed Dream Sheet

List as many "big" goals as you can think of in the following categories. Write them in the first person, using the present tense. Imagine that you cannot fail, no matter how lofty your goal. Project yourself into the future. Pick a date or an age, and visualize what is happening to you at that point in time. For example, in the financial category, you might write: "It is the year 2000 and I am earning $100,000 per year." Try to come up with at least one goal for each of the categories. However, do not worry if you cannot come up with something in every category or if you have several in some. It is important that you think big. After all, this is your *dream sheet.*

Professional
- It is May 1995 and I am receiving my master's degree in business from the University of Maryland or Johns Hopkins University.
- It is 2000 and I am receiving my doctorate in business from a major university.
- It is 2002 and I am the director of a successful publications department. I have a highly skilled, hard-working, and loyal staff. I am involved in several professional organizations and am well-known and respected in my field.

Financial
- It is 1995 and I have saved and invested $50,000. I add 20% of my earnings each year.
- It is 2002 and I own my "dream" home — a large, multi-story house built to my specifications, surrounded by several acres of landscaped grounds.
- It is 2026 and I am financially secure so that I can do what I want — work part time or not work, as I wish.

Family
- It is 2001. I have a happy, solid, successful marriage. My husband and I have complementary goals and desires and work together toward them. We have two healthy, happy, and bright children.
- It is 2025. My children are grown, with children of their own. Everyone gathers at our house often. We are happy to be together as a family.

Social
- It is any time. I have a few very good friends with whom I am close and comfortable and on whom I can rely. I have a wider circle of friends with whom I socialize regularly. I also have an extensive network of acquaintances and contacts with whom I interact as the interest or need arises.

Community
- It is 2004 and I am an active member of my children's PTA.
- It is 2010. I am president of a volunteer action group committed to a major cause.

Spiritual
- It is any time. I have a strong relationship with God, a fulfilling spiritual life, and a sound knowledge and practice of the Bible and Christian principles. I am actively involved in my church.

Personal
- It is 1993. I weigh 112 pounds. I am engaged in a regular exercise program and keep myself in good physical condition.
- I travel to a foreign country or a different part of the United States for at least two weeks each year.

Insight Break

Inch by inch is a cinch, yard by yard is hard.

—Unknown

Translating Dreams into Reality: Step 2

To accomplish the lifetime goals you identified in step 1, you need an incremental plan of action. Such a plan should define several intermediate and short-term objectives for each of your lifetime goals. If all works the way it is supposed to, you will have attained a lifetime goal once you have successfully completed all of the objectives leading to it. To ensure that your objectives work for you, I recommend that you follow Ken Blanchard's advice[4] and make each objective S M A R T: specific, measurable, attainable, relevant, and trackable. To facilitate this, list each lifetime goal identified in step 1 on the goal tracking form in Exhibit 4-6.

While you are at it, I suggest that you identify the benefits that you and your family will experience when you reach your goal. I have provided a space for this information on the goal tracking form so that each time you review it you can remind yourself why you are inflicting this pain on yourself and your family.

Insight Break

When you don't know where you are going, it is hard to tell when you get there.

—Yogi Berra

Translating Dreams into Reality: Step 3

Now that you have identified the long-term and intermediate objectives that you must accomplish in order to attain your lifetime goals, you need to identify the appropriate action plans that will help you get to where you want to go. Each objective may require a number of action steps. Identify each action step, state when you plan to evaluate your progress, and estimate the date that you plan to accomplish each action step. Write this

Exhibit 4-6 Goal Tracking Form

LIFETIME GOAL _____

Goal Priority _____ Projected Goal Attainment Date _____

Today's Date _____

BENEFITS _____

_____

	Objective	Action Steps	Evaluation Date	Attainment Date
1.	_____	_____	_____	_____
		_____	_____	_____
		_____	_____	_____
		_____	_____	_____
Reward	_____			
2.	_____	_____	_____	_____
		_____	_____	_____
		_____	_____	_____
		_____	_____	_____
Reward	_____			
3.	_____	_____	_____	_____
		_____	_____	_____
		_____	_____	_____
		_____	_____	_____
Reward	_____			
4.	_____	_____	_____	_____
		_____	_____	_____
		_____	_____	_____
		_____	_____	_____
Reward	_____			

information in the spaces provided on the goal tracking form. Be sure to transfer these dates and action steps to your calendar to help you track your progress and to remind you when you must take the identified actions. Next, establish an appropriate reward for yourself, your spouse, and your family when you complete a specific objective. Be sure to always celebrate your successes, and have your family participate, so that all of you not only pay the price but also have something to look forward to that will help you stay on track. Update your goal tracking form on a specific day each week. Most people prefer Monday because it allows them to make plans for the entire week. The completed goal tracking form in Exhibit 4-7 may help you visualize this process.

Insight Break

Better to do something imperfectly than to do nothing flawlessly.
—Robert H. Schuller

Translating Dreams into Reality: Step 4, or How to Eat an Elephant

Having all these objectives to accomplish may seem a bit overwhelming. It might feel like the feeling you would get if you had to eat an elephant. Let me provide you with a system that will help you eat that proverbial elephant. To introduce it, let me share a bit of management folklore known as the $25,000 idea.

The story, as far as I can tell, was first told by Alec Mackenzie in *The Time Trap*.[5] Folklore has it that an efficiency consultant named Ivy Lee was meeting with Charles Schwab, the president of a steel mill. Schwab was interested in finding out how he could increase performance and productivity. Lee told Schwab that he could provide him with advice to better manage the company. Schwab, however, was not interested. He simply wanted to find out how to get more done within the time available, and he was willing to pay anything within reason for such advice. Lee said that he could increase Schwab's efficiency by at least 50 percent provided that he could have about 20 minutes of Schwab's time. When Schwab consented, Lee gave him a blank piece of paper and told him to write down the six most important things that he wanted to accomplish the next day. Schwab thought about it and completed the task in about three minutes. Then Lee instructed him to order these things from most important to least impor-

Exhibit 4-7 Completed Goal Tracking Form

LIFETIME GOAL   It is May 1995 and I am receiving my master's degree in business from the University of Maryland or Johns Hopkins University

Goal Priority ___1___   Projected Goal Attainment Date May 1995

Today's Date Aug. 15, 1991

BENEFITS Knowledge, greater self-esteem, improved work performance, increased promotional/employment opportunities

	Objective	Action Steps	Evaluation Date	Attainment Date
1.	meet all prerequisites for admission	meet with advisor	Aug. 22, 1991	Aug. 31, 1991
		request letters of recommendation	Oct. 15, 1991	Nov. 1, 1991
		gather transcripts	Oct. 15, 1991	Nov. 1, 1991
		complete required refresher courses	Sept. 28, 1991	Dec. 2, 1991

Reward nice dinner out with husband

2.	get accepted into master's program	complete application	Nov. 1, 1991	Nov. 18, 1991
		submit application	Nov. 25, 1991	Dec. 2, 1991
		schedule interview	Dec. 9, 1991	Dec. 16, 1991
		develop master schedule/register	Dec. 30, 1991	Jan. 10, 1992

Reward new leather briefcase

3.	complete core requirements	complete 2 core courses	March 1992	May 1992
		complete 4 core courses	Oct. 1992	Dec. 1992
		complete 6 core courses	March 1993	May 1993
		complete 8 core courses	June 1993	Aug. 1993

Reward Weekend "getaway" with husband

4.	Graduate	reevaluate/adjust master schedule	May 1993	Sept. 1993
		complete major courses	Jan. 1994	Aug. 1994
		complete remaining courses	Sept. 1994	May 1995
		complete application for graduation	Dec. 1994	Feb. 1995
		attend graduation ceremonies		May 1995

Reward one-week Caribbean cruise with husband

tant. That too took very little time. Lee then instructed Schwab to keep the list until the following morning, when he was to look at the first item and to work on it until it was completed. After that he was told to work on task number two, and so on, until the end of the day. Lee advised Schwab not to worry about those items on the list that he could not get done, and to repeat this process every working day. He told him to try this system for as long as he liked. Lee also told Schwab to have his employees try it, and if it worked to send him a check for whatever the idea was worth to him and the company. After several months, Lee received a check for $25,000 and a letter in which Schwab said that this was one of the most profitable ideas that he had ever been exposed to. It is reputed that the consistent application of this strategy helped to turn that small steel mill into Bethlehem Steel. The moral of this story is that to eat an elephant you have to take one bite at a time.

Insight Break

You've got to think about "big things" while you're doing small things so that all the small things go in the right direction.

—Alvin Toffler

Supplement your long-term goals with daily objectives in the form of a "to do" list. Just as Ivy Lee said, an effective way to accomplish this is to start each day by defining six important things you want to accomplish that day. Prioritize these from 1 to 6 by looking at your lifetime goals (remember, they are on your desk, on a 3 x 5 card) and your intermediate objectives (you may want to keep them in your calendar so that when you are in a meeting and getting bored you can review them and reenergize yourself). If an activity listed on your "to do" list contributes to your objectives and lifetime goals, assign it a high priority. If it does not, assign it a low priority or do not put it on the "to do" list at all (unless, of course, it is a part of your job or your boss has asked you to do it). Start by accomplishing number 1, number 2, etc., until the day is over. If you get interrupted during the day, review your list to make sure that you have not lured yourself away from the critical item or items on top of your list (the critical few). That takes a lot of willpower because, as you well know, it is so much more comfortable to keep yourself occupied with busywork (the irrelevant many). My strategy is to be tenacious about the top items on the list, with the result that most of the time—to the chagrin of my wife and two daughters—I don't call it a day until they are done. I am, however, much more flexible about the less important items, and often carry them forward to the next day. Remember to do as many of the top objectives as you can, but don't fret about those you were unable to get done. Repeat the same process tomorrow, and every working day for the rest of your life, and watch yourself moving toward the attainment of your lifetime goals like a true winner.

Mental Stretch Break

Before we look at the obstacles that will get in your way, let's do a brief exercise that will help you reengage the right side of your brain. After all, you will need all the creative energy you can muster to stay the course. Count the triangles in Exhibit 4-8. Hint: There are more than you think. (See end of chapter for answer.)

Exhibit 4-8 Triangles Exercise

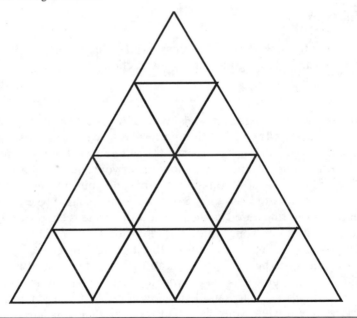

FEAR OF FAILURE

Now you have your road map to success. But before we go on to the next chapter, let's take a look at the roadblocks that will stand in your way or attempt to prevent you from staying the course. I have found that fear of failure gets in people's way more than anything else. This is the unique human ability to direct our mental energies to what might go *wrong*, instead of what might go *right*.

Insight Break

A man who fears suffering is already suffering from what he fears.
—Montaigne, *Essays* III. xiii

Fear: The Good, the Bad, and the Ugly

First, let me acknowledge that fear can be very helpful; it can even keep you alive. The fight/flight response gets you out of a burning building in a hurry or gives you exceptional strength in an emergency. Fear is also what prevents you from leaning on your horn while following a group of Hell's Angels and restrains you from telling your boss where to go until you have found a new job. More frequently, however, fear affects your life in negative ways. It can interfere with your ability to attain your lifetime goals or prevent you from doing the things you really would like to do. Or you may experience irrational fear, such as being fearful of something that you have no firsthand knowledge of. (Note that I said irrational, not unreal, because perception is reality.)

For example, my wife, my superwoman, the young lady with a black belt in shopping, has had, for as long as I can remember, two major fears. One is the fear of swimming in deep water; the other is a fear of dogs, specifically dogs she has not met before. (Note I said dogs, not Wolfs.) The latter fear is based on a childhood experience and is therefore not irrational. The former, however, is an irrational fear. One, she has never drowned before (not that I would want her to), nor has she ever had a bad experience in deep water. Two, she knows how to swim. I am not saying that she is an Olympic long-distance swimmer, but she can swim quite well in shallow water for at least 20 minutes. That is why I call this an irrational fear.

Let's not just pick on my wife. According to *The Book of Lists*,[6] the ten most common human fears are as follows:

1. speaking before a group
2. heights
3. insects and bugs

4. financial problems
5. deep water
6. sickness
7. death
8. flying
9. loneliness
10. dogs

These are not just irrational, they are funny. After all, how can anything so certain and finite as death be fear number 7, preceded by so many things that have seldom, if ever, with the exception of numbers 4 and 6, caused anyone irreparable harm?

You are probably thinking well, what's wrong with that? Actually, many things. For one, we program our biocomputer, our subconscious, all of the time. From our earlier discussion you remember that our subconscious accepts everything we put into it as if it were reality. To make matters worse, none of us has the ability to move away from that which we do not want to have happen. Instead, we move toward that which we think about most of the time. So, if we think about being unable to swim in deep water we will be unable to swim in deep water. If we are fearful of operating a computer we will fulfill what we put into our mind and not do a very good job with a computer. If we are concerned about losing our job we will begin to take actions that increase our chances of bringing that undesired outcome to pass. In other words, whatever image *psycho,* the mind, harbors, *soma,* the body, will carry out. Every time you have said to yourself: "I knew I was going to . . .

—miss that shot,
—miss that promotion,
—not make that sale,
—be turned down by my date, or
—not find a parking space,"

you have demonstrated this principle to yourself.

Fear versus Desire: It's Your Choice

A dramatic example of how none of us has the ability to move away from the reverse of an idea is the story, told by Warren Bennis,[7] of legendary aerialist Karl Wallenda. Wallenda walked the tightrope throughout his life, always without a safety net. He walked the tightrope in the circus, from one skyscraper to another, and across some of the most challenging chasms in the United States, including the Grand Canyon. According to Wallenda, "walking the tightrope is living, everything else is just waiting." Until that fateful day in 1981 when he fell to his death in San Juan, Puerto Rico, Wallenda had never fallen. His wife was asked in an interview why, after 71 years, her husband had fallen to his death. She answered that Wallenda had never worried about falling, only about walking, until shortly before his fall, when he became obsessed with "not falling," even to the point of personally checking the guy wires, something he had never done before.

The Wallenda story can serve as a powerful reminder to all of us that we have a built-in tendency to generally move in the direction of what we think about most of the time. You can make the conscious decision to make those thoughts winning thoughts or losing thoughts. The choice is yours!

Humor Break

On a recent airline trip, my neighbor struck up a conversation. Finally, he asked me what I did for a living. When I told him that I am a professional speaker, he retorted, "You don't look like a professional speaker." I answered, "That's because today is my day off."

Fear: How to Kill It Dead

Recognizing irrational fear is a good beginning. But it is even more important to figure out what to do about it. Here are six strategies that will help you keep fear in the closet where it belongs.

Acknowledge It

Acknowledging that fear of failure is normal allows us to see ourselves as normal human beings instead of chickens. It provides us with the mechanism for getting off our case. For most of us, we are the ones that hold us back more than anything or anyone else does. Not too long ago, I shared a taxi with a young man on my way from Chicago's O'Hare airport to downtown Chicago. He told me that he worked for CBS and was on his way to Chicago to make a big presentation to the CBS board of directors. When I told him that I was a professional speaker, management consultant, and author he got excited. He immediately began to quiz me on how he could be a more effective presenter for this big meeting he had coming up. I asked him what he wanted to improve. After some prying, he told me he wanted to be less nervous. I asked him why he wanted to do that. When he gave me a funny look that said, "Wonder what kind of professional speaker this guy is?," I explained that speakers who are not nervous are terrible speakers because they are deadly. I assured him that being nervous is a benefit, provided the nervous energy is channeled in the right direction. After coaching him, I left him with a thought that he eagerly wrote down: "Every speaker has butterflies. Excellent speakers make the butterflies fly in formation." One week later he sent me a note together with an order for my book and audiotape program. In his note he told me that he had made his butterflies fly in formation and that he had made the best presentation of his life. You too can do common things uncommonly well if you acknowledge that you are an imperfect human being—a human being who is constantly striving to get better every day of your life.

Insight Break

I believe that anyone can conquer fear by doing the things he fears to do, provided he keeps doing them until he gets a record of successful experiences behind him.

—Eleanor Roosevelt

Ignore Others

I have found over the years that the minute I announce an innovative idea, a new business venture, a great idea for an outing, or anything else that is different, there are always innumerable people who will tell me that it won't work, can't be done, is not feasible, or is too risky. The naysayer song goes on and on. If you have worked in any traditional organization or bureaucracy, I know that you too have heard that song many times. That type of advice used to slow me down. It made me cautious, made me rethink my original thoughts, caused me to worry, and led me to focus on all the reasons why something could not work, dissipating my energy to the point that I could no longer see all the reasons why it *could* work. Before I knew it, I joined the also-rans and gave up on what might have been a million-dollar idea. Not anymore. I have developed a simple but powerful strategy to silence the naysayers. What I do now is to simply say, "I appreciate your concern. Have you yourself done this before?" If the answer is no, I thank the person for his interest and ignore the advice. If the answer is yes, I listen attentively so that I can learn from his mistakes. I firmly believe that only the people who have taken the journey and who have experienced the risks are able to provide meaningful advice. Most of the rest want to be sure that you remain one level below them so that they can feel OK. After all, if you succeed too much it might kill whatever self-esteem they have.

Insight Break

You can do anything you want to do, *if* you want to do it badly enough.
—Wolf J. Rinke

Do the Thing You Fear and the Death of Fear Is Certain

Think about what you fear the most, and do it. Probably the biggest confidence builder in your life is doing the thing you fear. It may be quitting your current job, jumping out of an airplane (do put on a parachute first, and, while you are at it, get some decent instructions too), living in the wilderness, scuba diving, or giving a speech. Do your homework, get yourself mentally and physically conditioned, and break the task into small, doable steps, if possible, so that you can benefit from the principle of incremental success. For example, tightrope walkers start low to the ground. After they have it mastered at that height, they go up a little bit at a time. When they get dangerously high, they add a safety net. Only after they have mastered the task to the point that they could do it in their sleep do they remove the safety net. After experiencing incremental successes at whatever you are afraid of, you will be able do it, and you will no longer be afraid of it. Most importantly, it will empower you and put you in charge of your life, providing you with the confidence of a supremely successful human being.

A great example is my superwoman, Marcela, who you will remember was fearful of swimming in deep water, even though she knows how to swim. One day not too long ago, while we were at the beach, the weather got windy and we decided to flee to the hotel pool. The pool was of modest dimensions and fairly empty, of people that is. I suggested that Marcela swim widthwise first at the shallow end. With each crossing, I suggested that she move over about one yard toward the deep end. Before she knew it, she was crossing the small pool effortlessly at the deep end. After all, there was little for her to worry about: She was able to cross the pool in three to four strokes, the pool was not very deep, there were few people around to "laugh at her" (actually, everyone had better things to do), and I was available to rescue her if the need arose. The next step was to celebrate her success, which I did by telling her how proud I was of her. After that, we had to replicate that success in our large community pool. Here too, Marcela started on the narrower side; then, after building her confidence there, she proceeded to the deep end. Now Marcela swims in a 100-meter Olympic pool and has essentially killed her fear of swimming in deep water. For those of you who are keeping track, the fear of dogs still persists, but we are working on that as well.

Insight Break

It is better to try and fail than not to try and succeed.

—Unknown

Conduct a Worst-Case Analysis

One of the strategies that helped me to overcome my fear of failure is doing a worst-case analysis. Whenever I am presented with a challenge that scares me, I ask myself, What is the worst thing that can possibly happen? After I identify that, I ask myself, Can I live with that? If the answer is yes, I forget the worst case, visualize myself succeeding, and go for it.

Replace Fear with Desire

You and I and all other human beings are motivated by two very powerful human emotions: fear and desire. Both are extremely powerful and both work equally well, although in opposite directions. To overcome fear, we must recognize that the human mind can only hold one major emotion or thought at a time. To take advantage of this phenomenon, we must get in the habit of substituting desire for fear when we speak to ourselves and to others. Instead of programming our mind with the things we do not want to have happen we must use the same creative energy to tell ourselves what it is that we want to have happen. Telling ourselves what we want should be supplemented with visualizing what we desire in clear, vivid, dramatic pictures. Once you have formulated that picture in your mind, you should think of all the positive consequences associated with succeeding. That way you will be focusing on the rewards of success instead of the penalties of failure.

Humor Break

Fearful of having a bad day? For comparison, here are ways to know when you are having a bad day:
— Your husband says, "Good morning, Jane," and your name is Maria.
— You put both contact lenses in the same eye and wonder why you are not seeing well.
— Your boss tells you not to bother to take off your coat.

PIN It, Don't NIP It

A powerful basic strategy, which I learned many years ago from Karl Albrecht,[8] is the PIN technique. This strategy will help you focus on the positive instead of the negative, see the opportunity instead of the risks, and generally minimize stinking thinking. Internalizing and consistently applying the PIN technique has helped me to transform from a pessimist into an eternal optimist. This strategy has been so effective that, not long ago, someone said to me, "Wolf, you are such an optimist that you would go after Jaws in a rowboat and take along knife, fork, and tartar sauce." Well, be that as it may, it is a powerful strategy with significant implications for this book and, most importantly, for you *if* you choose to adopt it.

The PIN technique consists of a three-step mental process that first focuses on what is positive *(P)*, then on what is interesting or innovative *(I)*, and only finally on what is negative *(N)*. By PINing it, instead of NIPing it, you will provide yourself with the ability to focus your vast mental energies on positive thoughts instead of squandering them on negative and nonproductive ideas. NIPing it closes the proverbial mental shade, whereas PINing it allows you to go beyond your customary response pattern and provides you with a technique that will let you see the hidden opportunities and focus on desire instead of fear.

As a bonus, the consistent application of the PIN technique will enable you to enhance your self-esteem. It facilitates creativity and provides a powerful basis for establishing a positive climate in your home or organization, a climate in which people are willing to take calculated risks and feel free to experiment, thereby empowering them and their team members to *MAKE it a WINNING life.*

PEP² IN ACTION—PURPOSE:
CAPTAIN GERALD L. COFFEE, U.S. NAVY (RET.)

Retired U.S. Navy Captain Gerald L. Coffee is a living testament to the power of the human spirit to survive and triumph over the most adverse circumstances. In early 1966, while he was flying combat missions over North Vietnam, his aircraft was downed by enemy fire. He parachuted to safety, but he was captured immediately. For the next seven years he was held as a prisoner of war (POW) in the Communist prisons of North Vietnam.

After he returned to the United States in 1973, Coffee earned a master's degree in political science from the University of California, Berkeley, and subsequently graduated from the National Defense University in Washington, D.C. He continued his military service and became the commander of his own aircraft squadron. He retired from active duty in 1985.

His military awards and decorations include the Silver Star, two awards of the Legion of Merit, the Distinguished Flying Cross, two awards of the Bronze Star, the Air Medal, two awards of the Purple Heart, the Combat Action Ribbon, and the Vietnam Service Medal with 13 stars. He is the author of Beyond Survival, *published by G.P. Putnam's Sons, and has received numerous awards for his contribution to Americanism through public speaking, including the George Washington Honor Medal presented by the Freedom Foundation at Valley Forge, Pennsylvania, and the Council of Peers Award of Excellence, the highest recognition for professionalism in speaking, awarded by the National Speakers Association.*

Coffee's experiences during his seven years as a POW have enabled him to help others who face adversity, complexity, and change in their lives. His lessons in survival have affected thousands; they can do the same for you.

WR: Please give us a brief overview of how you became a POW. In particular, share how the principle of *purpose* helped sustain and guide you during those seven grueling years.

GC: As a young Navy pilot, just 32, I was flying a combat-reconnaissance mission over North Vietnam from the aircraft carrier USS *Kitty Hawk* when I was shot down. I was seriously wounded during the ejection from my aircraft at a very high speed, and I was captured immediately. My crewman was killed during the battle for our capture, which involved our own airplanes strafing the boats that picked us up out of the water near the shore. I was taken to Hanoi and held in the old French prison the Vietnamese called Hoa Lo, which means fiery forge. I was held in that prison, and other prisons around Hanoi, for the next seven years and nine days. I was shot down in February 1966 and released in February 1973.

As a military officer, of course, I had received training as to the pursuit of my duty and resistance of exploitation by the enemy for military information and propaganda. It became apparent very early on that the only reason that the Vietnamese maintained us as prisoners and kept us alive was for the purpose of exploitation. They looked at us as resources to be exploited. In Communism, propaganda is every bit as important as logistics, supply, and combat readiness. As American fighting men, we had a code of conduct that, in six brief articles, prescribes our behavior in those circumstances. One of those articles says that when we are captured we are bound to give only our name, rank, serial number, and date of birth. The code also tells us that we must evade answering all other questions to the best of our ability. The primary purpose of the code of conduct is to help POWs not just to survive, but to go beyond survival and pursue our duty to resist the enemy's efforts and to minimize whatever net gain they could achieve by having us there at their total mercy for what turned out to be such a long, long time. My purpose, however, became much broader after a few months. I went through the classic symptoms of denial and withdrawal and anger about what had befallen me. In my prayers I said, "Why me, God?" The real turning point for me was when my prayers turned from "Why me, God?" to "Show me, God. Show me what I'm supposed to do with this. What are you preparing me for? How am I supposed to use this experience? What is it all for?" After that reorientation of my thinking, there was indeed purpose to my life again. There was purpose to the experience, to the circumstance, and I determined to make the entire experience count for something positive, something from which I could learn and grow and emerge with insight and capabilities and credibility that I could never otherwise have accomplished in my regular career as a naval officer and pilot.

Our primary purpose was to resist, but as I mentioned, my scope of purpose broadened considerably after I became committed to use the experience to become a better and stronger person, a better naval officer, a better American citizen, Christian, husband, father, friend—a commitment to myself to use the experience to improve myself, to come away with something of value. Most of my contemporaries did the same thing. We arrived at that conclusion, that sense of purpose, in various ways and in various time frames. In fact, we were so united in our purpose of resistance that that caused us to form a sense of mutual support and sustenance that really was fairly effective in the primary mission of resistance, but also was effective in increasing our survival rate. The survival rate was really comparatively high given the nature and the circumstances of our environment. That's how the issue of purpose came to be literally paramount in my experience as a POW.

WR: Did this uniting come to be even though you were in solitary confinement?

GC: Yes it did. We were able to devise ways of communicating with each other and to stay in touch and to maintain our adherence to our senior officer's policies and orders, all of which, of course, were based around the basic premise of the code of conduct. That combined sense of purpose to resist the efforts of the enemy to exploit us was a very strong uniting factor. And it was easier to have faith in myself once I established a sense of purpose. That sense of purpose, I think, was key to my survival. We went along from year to year, although we seldom looked at it that way; it was more day to day, week to week, month to month, and pretty soon, before we knew it, another year had gone by. But if I had bumbled along for years without a sense of purpose, I'm not sure that I would have survived physically and mentally. The sense of purpose is what gave us the drive to survive and to learn and to glean and to study, to learn from one another through that communication system we built, even though it was covert. If you were caught communicating you were punished severely. Our sense of purpose also pertained to learning about Communism, about the enemy, and what motivated them and how they worked. This sense of purpose included insights into our own country and freedom and the system of democracy. It included a spiritual aspect. A sense of purpose led me to learn more about myself spiritually and my overall role in the big scheme of things and to know God better. Of course, when we're stripped of all the material trappings by which we tend to identify ourselves, we come to know ourselves better than we would have otherwise. In that way, I was able to keep faith in myself, as were most of my contemporaries. And because we shared a combined sense of purpose we were able to keep faith in one another and to translate our whole involvement to the overall policy of containing Communism and thwarting what truly turned out to be a manifestation of the domino theory. Faith in God was all wrapped up in the purpose to learn about yourself and your relationship with your God.

WR: Your experiences remind me of thoughts expressed by Dr. Viktor Frankl in his book *Man's Search for Meaning*.

GC: That was the first book I read on my return in 1973.

WR: That was how I made the connection back to you. Frankl talked about his three years in concentration camps in Dachau and Auschwitz and how he noticed that the people who had no sense of purpose, who basically had given up mentally, were the ones who succumbed much more rapidly than the inmates who had a purpose for their existence. The former inmates had thrown in the towel, complaining to Frankl that they no longer expected anything from life. Frankl replied that they had it all wrong, that life was expecting something from them. He maintains that life asks something from each and every one of us, even if we are fortunate enough not to have to suffer such unbearable conditions. All of us are expected to contribute something during our brief journey on this earth. It is our responsibility to figure out what unique contribution we can make. That contribution is our overarching purpose. Frankl found that the inmates who had such a purpose had a much higher survival rate. How does that compare with your experience in Vietnam?

GC: It compares very consistently. As I mentioned, our survival rate was relatively high. Of the roughly 600 men shot down and captured in North Vietnam over an $8^{1}/_{2}$-year period, we may have lost 30 to 35 men in the prison system. That's not to say that there weren't perhaps dozens killed in the process of their capture, but once inside the prison system and part of our overall group, with that mutual sense of purpose and commitment, the survival rate was very high. The most basic sense of purpose in Vietnam was to maintain your sense of dignity, and then everything would kind of expand from there like rings in a pool of water. If you could just maintain your sense of dignity that was the first step in maintaining any sense of purpose. For example, gaining lessons from the experience and emerging with more insight was one way to maintain your sense of dignity, but it had to start with your basic sense of humanity and dignity. I lived with a man for a while in a tiny cell. His resistance technique was to go to an interrogation just as rumpled and disheveled and as meek and mussed and weak looking as he could, figuring that the Vietnamese would look at him with such disdain that they wouldn't expect much of him. That was one technique, and I think for him it was successful. But for me, it was so contrary to my basic sense of dignity that I couldn't do it. Remaining dignified might have caused me to get more of a backlash from the interrogators and guards, but ultimately I think they respected that more than creeping in like a mouse and giving the other impression. Plus, it contributed to my sense of dignity.

WR: That seems to go right back to the first principle that I talk about, which is self-esteem. That is, in the most extreme sense, the ability, even in that environment, to still feel good about yourself, from which you then gained that inner strength. Is that basically what you are saying?

GC: Yes, because for most of us the change was instantaneous and cataclysmic. One moment we were hotshot fighter pilots, then suddenly we found ourselves with virtually no control over what happened, except for what control we maintained inside of our minds. It was a tremendous challenge to be totally vulnerable and at the mercy of somebody else and with no way to express your sense of pride and professionalism and accomplishment and duty other than to translate all that energy and commitment and professionalism into resisting the efforts to exploit you, and, more basically, to maintain your sense of personal dignity. After reading through your six principles, I can almost plug each one into various aspects of that experience as a POW, in turn or simultaneously. I think the six principles that you have focused on are great.

WR: I have found that people without a purpose are like a ship without a rudder. Unfortunately, most of us don't take time to plan. Most of us spend more time planning a holiday party than we do planning our lives. We just go from one day to the next, in what I call autopilot. From personal experience I have found that my burning desires have propelled me forward in life. I think you made an excellent point that you don't have to subject yourself or be subjected to the extreme to which you were to necessarily gain that insight. You can learn it from others. That is really what you are teaching me and my readers, that you have to have that fire in the belly, because it will pull you like a magnet.

GC: I agree. And as often as not, that fire or sense of purpose is crystalized by some terribly adverse circumstance or personal tragedy. My mission in speaking and writing is to illustrate to people that you don't have to wait for some tragedy to befall you to gain that insight. We can survive incredibly difficult circumstances, and if we believe that, then we will be able to approach our day-to-day challenges with so much more confidence, purpose, and self-esteem.

WR: Don't you find, as I find with my children, that the abundance in our society that many of us take for granted sometimes really works against us?

Abundance extinguishes those fires in the belly. As a result, we just sit back and become complacent. We expect things to come easily. Then we wonder, and some even complain, how the Korean and the Vietnamese immigrants who come to the United States with nothing outperform us in everything from scholastic achievement to annual income. Why? Because they have a burning desire, that fire in the belly. And they know that they must pay the price if they are to fulfill their dreams.

GC: If what you say weren't true there would be no market for the book you're writing. That's exactly right. We take so terribly much for granted, especially the younger generation, I think. By and large, our society takes so much for granted, and it does come to us too easily. But there is inspiration everywhere. It doesn't have to come from a guy who spent seven years in prison. In every audience I find people who have survived, and not just survived but gone beyond survival to build upon personal adversities and tragedies that I can't even relate to. There's inspiration everywhere, heroes in our midst every day of our lives. We can draw so much inspiration and insight from the people around us.

WR: And that is often where we get that inner drive, that determination that you have been sharing with us. Deprivation or tragedy often provides us with the greatest impetus to forge forward.

GC: One of my friends posed to me the question, "What would you do if the world were perfect?" I was stymied by that until I came to the conclusion that *the world is perfect.* It doesn't matter what happens, it's meant to be, and I'm supposed to derive something from it. Whatever adversity happens to us, whatever difficulty or quandary we may be in in our personal or professional life, we need to look at that quandary and say, "OK, what's the purpose of this, what am I supposed to learn from this, how will I be different after I've handled it?" Looking at everything like that, looking for the purpose in it and how you're going to emerge more capable or tougher or in some way better can help all of us put things in better perspective.

WR: That's an excellent comment. It reminds me of the Chinese symbol for crisis, which has two meanings: danger and opportunity. You just have to turn it around and look for the opportunity. If you look long enough you will likely find it.

Let me change the subject and ask you about fear. In this chapter, I talk about how fear and worry often interfere with our ability to move forward in life. Certainly, you must have been fearful many times during those seven years. What is your perspective on the idea of fear holding us back from lots of opportunities that present themselves?

GC: At the time, I didn't have a lot of insight into the fears that I experienced. But since then, as a result of studying and in retrospect, I've come to understand much more about the dynamics of fear. I can look back now and say, "Oh yeah, that's what I was doing, and that's what happened." There's no question that fear was a significant emotion during those years. I mean there were peaks and valleys, and those valleys were pretty deep. And when you're in a circumstance where you have so little control over what others can do to you physically, it's a fearful situation. You do fear for your life. Strangely enough, you don't fear so much for yourself as for your neighbor. You knew that they could inflict pain upon you and your biggest fear was the pain for someone else that might result from that. Every one of us was prepared to give our lives; it wasn't fear for our lives. Sometimes if you could have died it would have been preferable. Nobody ever thought of suicide, but there were some instances when I would almost rather have died than go through what I was going through, and that's what you fear. You just have to recognize that it's a very natural, normal, and helpful emotion. It's almost axiomatic now the kinds of psychological readiness that fear stimulates. But also, emotionally just recognizing that fear is normal and not being down on yourself for being scared are important, as are recognizing that fear is a very natural human reaction and not letting it undermine your sense of self-esteem.

WR: And also not letting it undermine your basic values or your ability to move forward toward your goals. After sorting through the emotions, as you mentioned, we all go through specific steps when we are in fearful situations like that. The important thing is that we must ask, "Is this rational or irrational?" If it is irrational, then we must be able to recognize that and get on with it. One way to analyze fearful situations is to ask yourself what the worst thing that can possibly happen is. If you can live with that, then go do it. I have found that too often we avoid taking advantage of opportunities because of irrational fears. Most of us simply don't want to get out of our easy chair to answer the door when opportunity knocks. Most of the time we fear the downside, and that fear prevents us from even seeing the upside, let alone capitalizing on it.

GC: That's exactly right. Hence the name for my book, *Beyond Survival*. Our purpose was not just to survive, but to survive and return with honor. I tried to translate that to my daily life and in the things I say from the platform. It's not enough just to survive the things that come down the pike and challenge us. The thing we want to do is go beyond survival and to build upon them and use them as vehicles by which we become better and more enlightened, and stronger and more capable.

WR: I've thoroughly enjoyed our time together. I feel that all of us can learn many valuable lessons from your terrible experiences as a POW in Vietnam. I also feel that we are fortunate that you have been able to share those lessons with us. I would like to thank you for your wonderful insights, your patience, and your time. Most of all, I would like to thank you for teaching me and my readers the importance of keeping our focus on our purpose and lifetime goals so that all of us, just like you, will *MAKE it a WINNING life*.

SUMMARY: A TRIP BACK TO THE FUTURE

- Your purpose and goals represent the guidance system for your PEP^2 rocket. Without a purpose, you will wander aimlessly until you run out of fuel and self-destruct.
- Only a small percentage of the U.S. population have clearly defined, written, lifetime goals. Individuals with goals tend to be much more successful than those who do not have goals.
- Only those goals about which you are passionate will provide you with a road map to success.
- Goal setting represents *the* system to success.
- Implementing a goal-setting system consists of the following steps:
  —Commit your dreams to paper.
  —Prioritize your dreams.
  —Establish objectives that are SMART (specific, measurable, attainable, relevant, and trackable).
  —Establish specific long-range action plans to ensure attainment of each objective.
  —Establish a daily "to do" list in support of your goals, objectives, and action plans.
- Irrational fears often interfere with our ability to attain our lifetime goals. To ensure that this will not happen to you, it is suggested that you
  —acknowledge fear as a normal human response;
  —ignore those who have not traveled the road;
  —do the thing you fear;
  —conduct a worst-case analysis;
  —replace fear with desire; and
  —PIN it, don't NIP it.

SUCCESS ACTION STEPS

❏ Interview someone who you consider to be very successful. Find out whether this person has clearly defined, written lifetime goals. Have her explain to you how they are used and what roles they have played in her success. Also find out what other systems this person has put into place to propel herself to success.

❏ Go to your local library and check out autobiographies of people who you consider successful. Read at least one every three months.

❏ If you have not done so already, complete the dream sheet and goal tracking form in accordance with the directions given in this chapter.

❏ Review your goals with your mentor, your significant other, or some other close associate or friend. Have him help you identify networks and resources that will help you attain your goals.

❏ If you are not sure what action to take in a specific situation ask yourself, What would I do if I knew I could not fail? Remember that you can do anything you want to do *if* you want to do it badly enough!

❏ Make a list of things that you are fearful of. Compare this list with your lifetime goals. If any of your fears stand in your way of attaining your lifetime goals, develop an action plan to overcome them. Do the same for any other fears that prevent you from living the "good life," as you define it.

❏ Join a club or support group that is dedicated to one of your high-priority fears. For example, if you are afraid of public speaking, join the local Toastmasters group.

❏ Make it a habit to frequently contrast your daily "to do" list with your lifetime goals. Assign high priorities only to those items that will contribute to your lifetime goals or those that you must do because they are an integral part of your job or have been specifically assigned by your boss.

❏ Recognize that no one likes to fail.

❏ When taking on a new project, seek out those who have experience with this or similar projects. Listen to them and ignore others.

❏ When beginning a new project, visualize success by envisioning how you will feel when you have succeeded. When negatives, doubt, and fear attempt to take over, reenergize yourself by talking with someone who has experienced the taste of victory.

❏ For the next 21 days, make it a practice to apply the PIN technique whenever you are confronted with something to which you would normally react negatively. This might be a "weird" idea promulgated by a team member, a strange manner of dressing by your teenage child, or an unusual vacation idea promoted by your significant other.

Catch yourself any time you react negatively by consciously acknowledging it, and then reversing yourself by first focusing on the positive and interesting.

NOTES

1. C. Garfield, *Peak Performers: The New Heroes of American Business* (New York: Morrow, 1986).
2. Z. Ziglar, "Stalking Your Goals," *See You at the Top* (Chicago: Nightingale-Conant, 1985). Audiotape program.
3. N. Hill, *Think and Grow Rich* (New York: Fawcett Crest, 1987).
4. K. Blanchard, Leadership workshop sponsored by the Daniel Management Center, University of South Carolina, conducted at the University of Maryland, December 14, 1987.
5. R. A. Mackenzie, *The Time Trap* (New York: McGraw-Hill, 1972), pp. 51–53.
6. D. Wallechinsky, *The Book of Lists,* quoted in J.W. Newstrom and E.E. Scannell, *Games Trainers Play* (New York: McGraw Hill, 1980), p. 85.
7. W. Bennis, "Learning Some Basic Truisms About Leadership," *National Forum; The Phi Kappa Phi Journal* (Winter 1991): 12–15.
8. K. Albrecht, *Brain Power: Learn to Improve Your Thinking Skills* (Englewood Cliffs, NJ: Prentice-Hall, 1980).

ANSWER TO MENTAL STRETCHING EXERCISE
Page 94

How many triangles did you count: 16, 21, 24, or even 25?

The answer is 25. There are 16 individual triangles, 5 triangles of four triangles each, 3 triangles of nine triangles each, plus 1 large overall triangle.

ANSWERS TO BRAIN TEASERS
Page 84

1. A chicken in every pot
2. Circles under the eyes
3. GI overseas
4. Upside down
5. What's right is right
6. He's beside himself
7. Pace back and forth
8. A round of drinks on the house
9. Six of one and half a dozen of another

Energy

What this power is, I cannot say. All I know is that it exists . . . and it becomes available only when you are in that state of mind in which you know exactly what you want . . . and are fully determined not to quit until you get it.

—Alexander Graham Bell

Energy, the stuff Alexander Graham Bell is talking about, comes from doing the things you love to do, knowing where you are going (That is why you identified your lifetime goals in the previous chapter. You did establish your goals, didn't you?), and pursuing your goals with everything you've got. Think about your success rocket. So far we have done an exceptional job. We have put together the best rocket money can buy. We have assembled it with great care and precision, making sure the foundation, the launch site, your self-esteem, is the best it can be. Next we supplied your PEP² rocket with a superbly equipped control center, your goals. But, no matter how well we have done up to now, notice that your rocket is still sitting on the launching pad. It will sit there forever unless you add a critical ingredient, the fuel, your energy. It is time to start your journey, so let's put fuel into your PEP² rocket (see Exhibit 5-1).

PREVIEW OF COMING ATTRACTIONS

That fuel, especially in the second stage, the booster stage, is absolutely essential if the rocket is to make it into orbit. Your life is just like that rocket. To boost yourself to success you must have a consistently high level of self-esteem, and you must commit yourself to your goals with every fiber of your being. Once you have identified your goals, you must take action and energize yourself so that you can perform at full throttle, wide open, fully committed, with no holds barred, until you get your success rocket

Exhibit 5-1 Your PEP² Rocket—Part 3: Fuel (Energy)

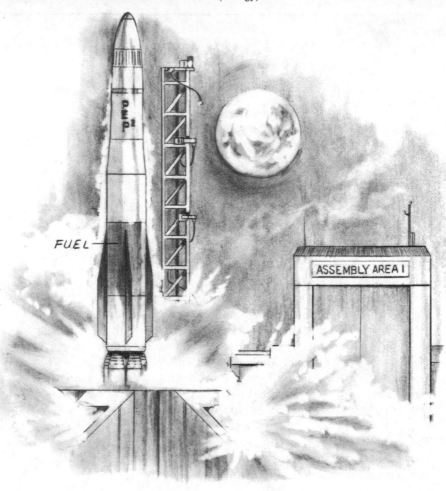

into orbit, a place where you can live comfortably, the air is pure, the view is spectacular, the competition is virtually eliminated, and life is not just easier, it is healthier, more enjoyable, and, most of all, more fun. Once you have arrived at that stage, you can jettison the first stage of your success rocket, throttle back somewhat, and begin to focus your energies on those things that you absolutely love to do.

Once we have you at that stage, we will shift gears and consider that all human beings, including you, are a composite of both strengths and weaknesses. Then I will convince you that to succeed in the game of life, love, and business, you must get rid of your weaknesses and build on your strengths. I will also assure you that you are never too old to succeed and show you how you can get a natural high without taking any drugs. This chapter will conclude by identifying six powerful strategies that will channel your energies and provide you with an achievement focus. But I'm getting ahead of myself here. First, assess your current energy level by completing the Energy Assessment Scale (EAS) in Exhibit 5-2.

Insight Break

The mass of men lead lives of quiet desperation.

—Henry David Thoreau

ENERGY AND POSITIVE SELF-MOTIVATION: WHAT IS THE CONNECTION?

Now that you have identified how well you do in the energy department, it is time to figure out what I mean by *energy* and how it relates to keeping yourself motivated. Energy and positive self-motivation are directly related. In fact, they are very similar, but energy fits better into the rocket analogy. Both energy and motivation can be divided into two major categories: internal and external. External motivation is what management theorist Fred Herzberg[1] (of satisfier and dissatisfier fame) referred to as KITA, or a kick in the ass (sorry, but that is how he said it). KITA comes in a variety of forms, including pay, vacation, a rug on the floor, and perks. KITA can indeed provide you with temporary movement, or help charge your battery. What you really want, however, is to first install a battery. That is obviously very important, because if you don't have one, it can't be charged. To provide yourself with a battery, you must begin with internal motivation; that is, it must come from within. Internal motivation is critical to success. It is the element that separates winners from the "also-rans." Because you are interested in succeeding, let's figure out what it will take to provide you with that internal motivation or, to stick with my model, what it will take to provide you with energy. We will begin by finding out what you love to do so you can build on your strengths.

Exhibit 5-2 Energy Assessment Scale (EAS)

Instructions

Using the scale below, circle the number that most closely indicates the frequency with which each statement applies to you *or* the degree to which you agree or disagree with each statement. (People have different preferences and opinions; therefore, there are no right or wrong answers.)

Never	Almost Never	Infrequently	Almost Always	Always
1	2	3	4	5
Strongly Disagree	Disagree	Neither Agree Nor Disagree	Agree	Strongly Agree

1. I get most of my energy from how I feel inside.   1 2 3 4 5 _____

2. I wish I had fewer flaws.   1 2 3 4 5 _____

3. The way to excel in life is to find a career that allows me to build on my strengths.   1 2 3 4 5 _____

4. Unless I fix my weaknesses, I will have a tough time succeeding in life.   1 2 3 4 5 _____

5. People who love their work and cannot wait to get to it about 80 percent of the time will succeed.   1 2 3 4 5 _____

6. I get energized from pursuing my goals.   1 2 3 4 5 _____

7. My potential income will be influenced more by the profession I choose than by how much I like what I do.   1 2 3 4 5 _____

8. I get on my case when things do not work out the way I had planned.   1 2 3 4 5 _____

9. I would not work if I did not have to.   1 2 3 4 5 _____

10. I worry about things that have happened in the past.   1 2 3 4 5 _____

11. I make it a practice to forget my weaknesses, except those that interfere with my ability to attain my lifetime goals.   1 2 3 4 5 _____

12. The primary trait I look for in the people I befriend is a positive attitude.   1 2 3 4 5 _____

13. Most of my mental energies are occupied by what I want to have happen in the future.   1 2 3 4 5 _____

14. I get very angry at my loved ones and/or employees when they make a mistake that I have repeatedly told them not to make.   1 2 3 4 5 _____

15. Greater results are obtained from getting started than from doing things perfectly.   1 2 3 4 5 _____

Exhibit 5-2 continued

16. A great boss is one who knows how to make a lot of money. 1 2 3 4 5 _____

17. Worrying takes up quite a bit of my time. 1 2 3 4 5 _____

18. I am able to readily forgive others when they mess up. 1 2 3 4 5 _____

19. I make it a practice to associate with people who are less successful than I am. 1 2 3 4 5 _____

20. I worry about those things over which I have control. 1 2 3 4 5 _____

Total _____

Scoring Instructions

Score items 1, 3, 5, 6, 11, 12, 13, 15, 18, and 20 in acordance with the number that you circled. For example, if you circled a 2 for question 1, you earned 2 points, which you should write on the line next to question 1.

Reverse-score items 2, 4, 7, 8, 9, 10, 14, 16, 17, and 19. This means that you have to turn the scale around to score these items, so that 1 = 5, 2 = 4, 3 = 3, 4 = 2, and 5 = 1.

Examples:

1. I get most of my energy from .... 1 2 3 4 ⑤ = 5
2. I wish I had fewer flaws .... 1 2 3 ④ 5 = 2
3. The way to excel in life is .... 1 2 3 ④ 5 = 4

Total your points.

Interpretation of Your Score

91–100 *Excellent.* You are a veritable energizer. I bet people like themselves best when they hang out with you.

81–90 *Great.* You are great at energizing yourself and others.

71–80 *Very Good.* Build on what you already know and you will be on the road to becoming full of PEP[2].

61–70 *OK.* But I bet I will be able to help you do much better.

<60 It is time to pay attention so you can discover how to energize yourself.

Insight Break

Do not let what you cannot do interfere with what you can do.

—John Wooden

IDENTIFY YOUR STRENGTHS

To rocket yourself to success, you first must determine what you are good at. Like it or not, there are no perfect human beings. (It took me only about 30 years to internalize that truism; I guess you would call me a slow learner.) Of the 5.5 billion people on earth, none are perfect (with the exception of your mother-in-law, right?). Every human being is a composite of strengths and weaknesses. Most of us spend a lot of time focusing on our weaknesses, focusing on the things we do *not* want to be, and wishing that we were more like someone else. (That is actually very silly because, believe it or not, there are several people who wish they were more like you.) You should not squander your valuable mental energies with such nonsense.

Take another of your days off, say three Sundays from now. (Why three weeks from now? Because during the next two weeks you are going to identify your lifetime goals and the action plans to go along with them. You do remember making that commitment, don't you?) On that day, do the following:

1. Get a blank sheet of paper.
2. Divide the paper in half.
3. Label the left side "Strengths," the right side "Weaknesses."
4. Put on some classical music. (No heavy metal please, even if you like heavy metal music. Research has demonstrated that classical music can enhance your thinking ability, but "hard" music will diminish it.)
5. Get yourself a cup of your favorite brew.
6. Make yourself comfortable and think of all the things that you are proud of. What do you do very well? What things give you a lot of joy and satisfaction? What is it that comes easily to you? Work hard at this; do not give up until you have filled just about the entire column.
7. Do the same thing for the other side. List your weaknesses. Be honest with yourself, be tough, and be candid. Generate as many things as possible. Think of all the things that you wish were different about you, that you would like to do better, or that you want to change.

Now, let's get to work and find out what you can do with this valuable information you have just generated.

BUILD ON YOUR STRENGTHS

The first thing you should do is take a look at the side of the sheet that lists your strengths. If you currently are in a job or, better yet, are in a career track, you should ask yourself whether your current job or your anticipated career capitalizes or will capitalize on your strengths. Will the things that you identified as strengths help you excel in your position or chosen career? Are these the skills and attributes of others who have succeeded in such a career? If the answer is yes, you are likely in the right career and should stick with it. Two things are very likely: (1) you love your job, and (2) you will be successful in it! More about that in just a moment.

What if you do not have a job or are not in a career track? In other words, what if you don't know what you want to do when you grow up? Don't let that bother you. In today's rapidly changing world, people make several career changes in their lifetime. It took me only about 30 years to figure out what I really love to do. (I guess I grew up slowly too.) Take a look at your strengths and list all the careers, jobs, or positions that you can think of that will provide you with an opportunity to build on your strengths. You should be able to come up with at least a dozen. If you can't, show your list of strengths (not weaknesses) to your parents, close personal friends, teachers, or anyone else who you would consider a mentor. Ask your mentors to help you generate a list of possible careers that would allow you to build on your strengths. If you know very little about a particular career, I suggest that you meet with one to three individuals who have succeeded in that career. Find out from them what has helped them to succeed. Match that list to your strengths. If you have a close overlap you have probably identified a powerful career for you. You can narrow it down even further by working or volunteering in a field temporarily so that you can see if your "dream" job or career is really right for you.

Insight Break

What lies behind us and what lies before us are tiny matters compared to what lies within us.

—Ralph Waldo Emerson

QUIT YOUR JOB

Is there a significant mismatch between your strengths and what your current job demands of you? If there is, you probably do not particularly care for your job. If this is the case, you are not alone. Jacqueline McMakin, author of *Working from the Heart*, maintains that four out of five people in America are unhappy with what they do.[2] A national survey conducted by Donald Kanter and Philip Mirvis, authors of *The Cynical American*, found that 78 percent of American workers feel cynical about their work.[3] This, according to Kanter and Mirvis, leads to low performance, decreased productivity, and low-quality goods and services. In short, if you dislike what you do you will never be excellent at it, no matter how long you work at it or how much energy you devote to it. I recommend to my success workshop attendees that if they do not love their job or career, which I define as actually looking forward to work four out of five days, they should get out of it, and get out of it now! Why 80 percent of the time? Because jobs or careers are just like people. There is no perfect job; every job has some aspects that you will not care for.

For example, I love public speaking. At times I have so much fun at it that I wonder why I am being paid so well for it. It almost seems that I should be paying the audience. (Please let that be our secret. I wouldn't want meeting planners to know that I feel this way; they might try to negotiate my fee too aggressively.) But there is a downside to public speaking. It is traveling, especially airline travel (better known as cattle herding), and being away from my superwoman and my two wonderful daughters. So, for me, traveling is the other 20 percent. That 20 percent is the price you have to pay to do the things you really love to do.

Why is all this important? Because *only people who love what they do, most of the time, will succeed.* The ultimate goal is to find work that seems like play to you. Finding a profession that lets you play will allow you to function at full throttle, giving it all you have to give. Ultimately, if you adhere to the other PEP[2] principles, you will succeed at it, and you will be compensated handsomely for it. People who love their work make more money, much more money, than those in the same job who hate it.

Mental Stretch Break

As I am about to ask you a trick, I mean quiz, question, it might be a good idea to have you reengage the right side of your brain. Move only three circles in Exhibit 5-3 to turn your success triangle right side up. (See end of chapter for answer.)

Exhibit 5-3 Is Your Success Triangle Upside Down?

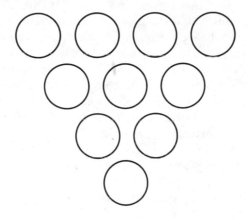

ARE YOU SELF-EMPLOYED?

I have a question that I like to ask audiences in my success seminars: I say, "Raise your hand if you are self-employed." Very few people raise their hands. I then smile and repeat the instruction, telling them that it is a trick question, and I ask them to reconsider. Usually, at that point a few more hands go up. There is a reason for the question. It is to make people realize that all of us are indeed self-employed. We all work for only one person—ourselves. We work so that we can earn money that can be converted into all kinds of neat things that provide us with pleasure.

Others, of course, believe that they *have* to work. I would like to dispute that. I not only *want* to work, I *love* to work. Whenever I talk about loving your job, I think of one of my heroes, George Burns. There is a man who loves his work. Here he is, 95 years "young," still putting on shows all over the world, truly enjoying what he does. The question is, does George Burns do what he does because he *has* to do it? You know, like you *have* to go to work? I would submit to you that George Burns does what he does because he *wants* to do it. Who at age 95, with the amount of money in the bank that George Burns has, *has* to go to work? After all, what is he going to do with all that money? Even if you gold-plated it, there is only so much money you can spend on a coffin. The question then is, why does George Burns still work? The answer is, because he loves what he does so much that it keeps him alive. (In fact, George Burns is booked for his 100th birthday party in London, England.)

That is the type of work you want to find—work that is more like play *to you* than work. Note that the emphasis is on "to you." You see, what is easy for George Burns to do would be extremely demanding for someone who does not enjoy being in front of people. When you think of what you would love to do, please do not think only of glamour jobs. I have known physicians, lawyers, entertainers, public speakers, professors, and other so-called glamour professionals who absolutely hated their jobs. None, by the way, were exceptionally successful. On the other hand, I have known restauranteurs, teachers, writers, auto mechanics, entrepreneurs, janitors, nurses, hair stylists, managers, and others in much less glamorous profes-sions who absolutely loved their jobs. And yes, you guessed right. Almost without fail, these people were successful. In some cases, they made more money than those people in the glamour professions. The only work that is truly "glamorous" is the work that you love to do.

Insight Break

If a man is called to be a street sweeper, he should sweep streets even as Michelangelo painted, or Beethoven composed music, or Shakespeare wrote poetry.

He should sweep streets so well that all the hosts of heaven and earth will pause to say, here lived a great street sweeper who did his job well.

—Martin Luther King, Jr.

THROW AWAY YOUR WEAKNESSES

What about the weaknesses that you have identified? Well, hold on to your hat. I'm going to recommend that you throw them away! All of them? you ask. No, not quite. What you need to do is to get out the list of lifetime goals that you have identified during the last two weekends. Now evaluate which of your weaknesses interfere with you being able to attain your lifetime goals and which weaknesses will interfere with you being able to excel in your chosen profession. They may be the same. For these weak-nesses, you should establish an action plan to help you to overcome them and, ideally, to translate those weaknesses into strengths.

For example, if you dislike public speaking (Is hate a better word?) join a local Toastmasters group, and practice as often as you can. Speaking is like most skills—the more you practice, the more at ease you feel, and the better you get. If you are your own worst enemy, commit to becoming your own best friend (Think of it. If *you* are not your friend, how can you expect anyone else to be?), catch yourself doing things *right,* and reward yourself every time you do. If you do not believe in yourself, or if you have a fear of failure, set yourself up for success by breaking complex tasks into small, incremental steps so that you can catch yourself succeeding. If you worry too much, ask yourself whether your chances for success are improved if you worry about a specific issue. If the answer is yes, keep worrying. If the answer is no, quit worrying and focus your mental energies on your goals instead. If you do not believe in yourself, ask yourself who you can believe in, and prepare an action plan to invest in yourself so that you become such a valuable commodity that you have no choice but to believe in yourself. (By the way, these are the weaknesses listed most frequently by my graduate students in the business courses I teach at Johns Hopkins University.)

Now, what about the weaknesses that will not affect the attainment of your lifetime goals? Throw them away! Yes, throw them away. One of my clients had such difficulty with this that he recorded his weaknesses onto an audiotape. Then he took a hammer and smashed the audiotape into pieces. This physical act helped him to get rid of those weaknesses once and for all. You're right, this did not actually get rid of the weaknesses, but it did help him to forgive himself for not being perfect and allowed him to make peace with an imperfect self. This, in and of itself, will make you more serene and comfortable with who you are instead of who you think you ought to be. Remember, there are no perfect human beings, and if you can forgive yourself for your weaknesses you will be more at peace with yourself. This in turn will allow you to "get off your case" and let you be your own best friend.

Humor Break

Language is a funny thing. To illustrate what I mean, here are several items that have been reported by insurance claims agents. They supposedly are from actual claims. The source is unknown. Enjoy!

The accident happened when the right front door of a car came around the corner without giving a signal.

Coming home, I drove into the wrong house and collided with a tree I don't have.

I had been driving my car for 40 years when I fell asleep at the wheel and had an accident.

The guy was all over the road. I had to swerve a number of times before I hit him.

BUT I'M TOO OLD

There you go again with that *but* word, that nice word that lets you rationalize away any chance for change and possible success. Whenever I talk about building on your success, someone invariably has enough courage to rationalize why that is a really silly idea. "After all," they say, "I've been in this job for 25 years. Why should I change now?" Or they say, "I've spent over 20 years specializing in this profession and now you want me to change." That is wrong from the start: I don't want you to change, I want you to *want* to change. It is more that just semantics. My favorite, though, is "I'm too old!" I really take exception to that one because you are never too old unless you decide that you are too old. For example, age did not seem to stop *Bedtime for Bonzo* actor Ronald Reagan from becoming President of the United States. By the way, he continues to speak, write, and work. Age did not stop Kentucky Fried Chicken's Colonel Sanders, who started that "small" franchise at age 65, with his first retirement check of less than $100. Age doesn't seem to be stopping explorer Jacques Cousteau, who said to a television interviewer, "Don't ask me what I have accomplished during the past 75 years, ask me what I'm going to accomplish during the next 75." And age isn't stopping Mark Spitz, winner of seven gold medals in the 1972 Olympics, from training at age 40-plus (considered "old age" in competitive athletics) for the 1992 Olympics in Barcelona, Spain. Nor did it stop Carl Lewis from breaking his own previous record and becoming the "World's Fastest Human" by running the 100-meter dash in an unbelievable 9.86 seconds in 1991 at age 30. (I know 30 sounds like he is a spring chicken, but keep in mind that he beat his own 24-year-old protegé, Leroy Burrell.)

Insight Break

You have enormous untapped power that you will probably never tap, because most people never run far enough on their first wind to ever find they have a second.

—Golda Meir

GETTING HIGH, WITHOUT GETTING STONED

The human brain, that 3 1/2 pounds of walnut-shaped, pinkish-grey tissue that resides between your ears, is one of the most fantastic creations known to humankind. It is, as some have said, the most complex living structure on earth, the most powerful biocomputer that has ever been, or ever will be, built. This biocomputer communicates by means of electrical and chemical messages, with impulses shuttled among nerve cells (neurons) at the incredible rate of 80 times per second. Talk about nanosecond speed! Now add to it that we have about (are you ready for this?) 100 billion neurons in our brain, and you will begin to understand why it has been said that our mental capacity is absolutely limitless.

But the brain does so much more for us. It lets us decide how we feel, helping us on one extreme to feel depressed and on the other to feel high, so high that it seems as if we were high on drugs. And on drugs you will be, except that these are the body's internally produced natural drugs. Dr. Solomon Snyder of Johns Hopkins University discovered some 20 years ago that the brain has built-in receptors for opiates such as heroin and morphine, which the body produces in the form of endorphins.[4] More recently, researchers from the National Institute of Mental Health have discovered that the body generates marijuana-like substances called cannabinoids. Although much of these findings is still speculative, these researchers reported that these chemicals exist naturally in the human body.[5] They have been able to definitively identify a receptor located on the outside of brain cells that is designed to grab a molecule of delta-9-tetrahydrocannabinol (THC), the active ingredient in marijuana. (In other words, we are all potheads.) Kidding aside, these researchers are simply validating what long-distance runners have experienced (called a runner's high) and explaining the extraordinary physical capabilities that we sometimes hear about in the news, such as a woman lifting an automobile off a child's body.

But what are you to do if you are not a long-distance runner or are fortunate not to be in an emergency situation that requires you to demonstrate superhuman strength? How can you turn on those natural substances to keep yourself high and generate extraordinary energy on an ongoing basis? From personal experience, I say the way to do this is to be actively and fully engaged in the pursuit of your "fire-in-the-belly" lifetime goals and to find something, whether you call it work, job, or career, that you absolutely love to do.

Earlier, I shared a bit of my background with you, so you already know that I dedicated 20 years of my life to the U.S. Army Medical Department. Although I enjoyed that experience, it was not one that let me fully build on my strengths. After I had fulfilled my basic commitment, the Army kept making attractive offers that I felt I just could not refuse. First it was an assignment in Germany, then a master's degree, and then a doctorate. Before I knew it, I had been in 13 years, with only 7 years to go before I could retire with a minimal pension. It was just too difficult to give up that retirement check. This is a decision I do not regret, at least not most of the time. And when I do, I remind myself that regretting, no matter how well I do it, will not make time go back, so I refuse to squander my mental energies in that fashion.

In 1988, at the first available opportunity, I "retired," and dedicated myself to those things that would allow me to build on my strengths. Since then I have been pursuing the goals that I have dreamed of. Taking calculated risks. Starting one entrepreneurial venture after the other. Doing the things that I love to do. The outcome is nothing short of euphoria. I have been, since my retirement on October 1, 1988, on a perpetual high. (No, I have never snorted anything. I've never even tried marijuana. In fact, about the strongest thing that I take is an aspirin on those rare occasions that I have a headache.) Being able to control my own destiny, to pursue the goals I want to pursue, to take the actions I want to take, to chase the dreams I have been dreaming, to make independent decisions, and to take action instead of talking about it, has provided me with a sense that, for the first time in my life, my self-imposed chains have been cut, leaving me in total charge of my own destiny.

These experiences have convinced me that nothing is as energizing as pursuing your dreams, living your goals, and doing what you enjoy best. Am I succeeding? That depends on how you define success. I see myself succeeding beyond all stretches of my imagination. Here are some of the reasons why. I have the opportunity to influence many people in positive ways. I enrich many people's lives. There is nothing more gratifying. I am helping many people, organizations, and companies succeed. I have an exceptional marriage (23 years to the same woman). I continue to be an excellent father (at least that's what Marcela and I think) to two beautiful daughters. I have started two highly profitable companies. I hold other corporate advisory positions and several volunteer leadership appointments. I am a member of the part-time faculty of Johns Hopkins University and the University of Maryland. I am doubling my income every six months. And, most importantly, I am having more fun in a year than most people do in a lifetime. Do you consider that a success? I do!

Insight Break

A bore is a fellow who opens his mouth and puts his feats in it.
—Henry Ford

I needed that insight to get back to what is really important—you.

At this point, you are probably thinking, so what does that have to do with anything? Actually, nothing. I shared this with you not to bore or impress you, but to convince you that absolutely nothing is more energizing than pursuing your goals and doing what you love to do! If that is not what you are doing now, identify your lifetime goals, establish that action plan, and begin to chase your dreams. Do what you love to do, and experience what it feels like to be on a natural high.

Mental Stretch Break

Before we look at several other specific strategies that will help you keep your energy level high and propel you forward on your journey to success, let's do a brief mental stretching exercise. Translate each figure in Exhibit 5-4 into a short word or phrase. (See end of chapter for answers.)

Exhibit 5-4 Brain Teasers

1 TIK	**2** A B E DUMR	**3** *nude* **naked** Goldilocks UNCLOTHED
4 morning	**5** *GROUND*	**6** EZ iiii
7 ti • me	**8** ri poorch	**9** 3 5 7 9 11 13 VS. u

Now let's look at several specific action strategies that you can use to keep yourself motivated and energized.

FOCUS ON ACHIEVEMENT

Focusing on achievement (1) begins with the recognition that anything started is half done, (2) is followed by an intense bottom-line orientation (a focus on outcome, not process), and (3) is accompanied by persistence (more about that in Chapter 8). The importance of this was verified by Charles Garfield, who found that one of the five key traits of peak performers is that they are intensely results oriented.[6] The following six strategies will help you focus on achievement.

Have a Ready, Fire, Aim Perspective

Any accomplishment, no matter how large or how small, requires that you BEGIN. Once you have begun, however, you must make small, midcourse corrections. If you keep your eye on your purpose and your goal and persevere, you will ultimately get there. Conversely, even with the best plans or the best intentions in the world, if you don't start, I can guarantee you that you will never get there. (I guess Aristotle figured that out some years ago when he said, "Well begun is half done.")

Humor Break

It seems that an attendee at one of my workshops, "Winning Management: Strategies for Doing More with Less," went back to her company and was ready to apply what she had learned. Frustrated with how slow her team members were, she gave them a rip-roaring speech using the Ready, Fire, Aim analogy. She went one step further and hung signs all over the office that read: "DO IT NOW." Several months after the presentation she asked me to consult with her because things were not working out. I asked her what had happened. "Well," she said, "the talk went over fine, but after I had hung up the signs, things started happening left and right." I asked her what was wrong with that. She answered, "Plenty. Three days after the signs went up, my supervisor took off with my accountant, my salesman stole $1000 worth of products, my secretary eloped with my best manager, and my general manager took off with the petty cash."

Directly related to that bit of levity is the idea of doing it now, regardless of your current level of competence. Let me share an example to make this point. Recently, at the conclusion of one of my presentations, someone came up to me and asked how he could become as effective at public speaking as I am. I asked him about his area of expertise and suggested that he start speaking at every opportunity. He protested, "I couldn't do that. I'm just not good enough at public speaking." I responded that he was probably right. I pointed out that, as for myself, I am not nearly as effective at public speaking today as I will be five years from now. But, because I don't know how to get from here to there without dying and coming back (an alternative that I discard because it is fraught with uncertainty), I will do one presentation at a time, constantly striving to do each one better than the last. I suggested that if I kept that up, making about 100 talks per year, I would definitely be a better speaker in five years than I am today. The point is, to get good at anything, we must do our homework, and then we must practice, practice, practice, practice, and practice. But, whatever we do, we must do it now, because to get to anywhere we must start from where we are.

Take Advantage of the Pygmalion Effect

The power of the Pygmalion effect, also referred to as the self-fulfilling prophecy, was established by Rosenthal and Jacobson in a series of scientific studies in which school children were randomly divided into so-called bright and dull groups on the basis of *bogus* IQ test data.[7] The children were told which group they were in. After a time, even though both groups of children received the same instruction, the group labeled "bright" began to outperform the "dull" group. To further test the power of this phenomenon, the children were told that a mistake was made, that the dull students were really the bright ones and vice versa. The students' academic performance began to reverse itself. This trend continued into the next grade even when the students were taught by teachers who did not take part in the original experiment. What makes these findings so astounding is that there were no real differences between students in the two groups.

Similar findings have been reported in a wide variety of publications, including the management literature,[8] and in popular movies and plays such as *My Fair Lady*, in which Professor Higgins bet that he could transform the common flower girl Eliza Doolittle into a "lady." Professor Higgins won that improbable wager, partially because of hard work, but mainly because of his unwavering belief in Eliza. Such a belief in yourself can provide you with equally dramatic results.

Insight Break

Only excellence will stir your soul.

—Wolf J. Rinke

Commit to Excellence

Excellence spells excitement. Just think of the pride and excitement you felt when you completed a project to which you gave everything you had to give. Then think of how you felt when you had to cut corners. Only excellence motivates, excites, and fully satisfies you. In addition, only excellent work will result in excellent compensation. This has been referred to as the law of compensation, which basically says that in the long run you and I will be paid in accordance with the service we provide to others. Although at times this seems quite inequitable, at least to those who receive low compensation, it appears to be true over the long run. For example, Bill Cosby will be paid in excess of $100 million per year for his television work. Is that fair? Well, if you are Bill Cosby, I am sure it is quite fair. After all, he is providing a lot of joy and pleasure to an incredible number of people. The network seems to think it is fair. After all, they did not have to agree to renew his contract. Probably, from the network's perspective it is more than fair, it is profitable, meaning that Bill Cosby will bring in far more money than he is paid. Is it fair to you? Only you know that. To me, it is not a question of fairness but rather a given. That is, fair or not, that is how the game is played. Instead of changing the rules of the game, I am trying to take advantage of them by polishing my skills so that one day I will have increased my value to others so that I too will be provided with "unfair compensation." (Why else do you think I'm sitting here at the word processor on a beautiful fall weekend?)

Insight Break

Excellence can be attained if you
- care more than others think is wise;
- risk more than others think is safe;
- dream more than others think is practical; and
- expect more than others think is possible.

—Unknown

Associate with Winners

Make it a practice to hang out with, observe, and emulate other winners. You will become like those you associate with. (My grandmother used to say that if you go to bed with dogs, you will wake up with fleas.) Nothing is more devastating than being around people who have "stinking thinking." If they work for you, fire them. Or, better yet, send them to the competition! Nothing can zap your energy and drain your vitality more than people who have hardening of the *categories.* Your friends, family members, and mentors are role models for you. They will affect your thought patterns, your enthusiasm, and your positive attitude. So, whatever you do, be sure to pick your spouse and friends carefully. This is particularly important because you can't pick your parents. Your life is like a mirror. It reflects your own attitudes, which are influenced by those around you. This can be either positive or negative; it is your choice.

Pick Your Place of Work Carefully

Hanging out with winners extends to where you are employed. After all, most of us spend at least one-third of the best years of our lives at work. That is why you need to find a place of employment that has a positive organizational culture. A company culture is fairly easy to figure out. How are people talking to each other? Are they upbeat, positive, energetic, and generally positively inclined toward their bosses, their coworkers, and the organization as a whole? Check for stinking thinking by noting how many signs tell you what you are *not* supposed to do, how thick the policy manual is, and how many policies identify things that are *not* allowed. During an interview, ask the person conducting the interview to show you the corporate vision or philosophy. If she does not know what that means, ask for the organization's mission statement. If the interviewer still does not know what you are talking about, forget it. Such a company does not know where it is going, and in that case, you cannot help get it there. If there is a vision statement or philosophy, see what it says about the organization's commitment to developing its human resources. If nothing is said, it is very likely that the organization will not be in business for very long, because people are the only resource that has the potential to *a*ppreciate. Virtually all other resources *de*preciate. Life is too short for you to join a shortsighted organization that is dedicated to having you depreciate. The natural aging process does that just fine on its own; it doesn't need a helping hand. Also look for a company or organization that is willing to pay you in accordance with how you *per*form, instead of how you *con*form or how many hours you warm a chair. Look for a company that is committed to innovation and calculated risk taking, and one that provides ample promotion opportunities to people who want to succeed.

Pick Your Boss Carefully

Working with a positive boss is very important for the reasons I mentioned regarding associating with winners. But there are more. First of all, who in his right mind would work for a boss spelled backward. (Did you get it? Are you chuckling? If not, you might need another stretch break or need to tune your funny bone.) *Boss* backward spells "double SOB." The right boss is a person who is, first and foremost, full of PEP^2. She is also interested in *your* personal and professional development, knows how to practice the double win, and is on her way to the top. Great bosses are also excellent mentors; they tell it like it is, provide you with straight advice, use their abundant mental energies to catch you doing things *right,* are intent on making *you* look good, are committed to helping you succeed, and can take you along to the top. (If you are working for such a person now, I suggest that you cultivate and nurture that relationship. It is worth its weight in gold.)

Humor Break

A collection was being taken for a going away present for a domineering boss.
Contributor: "Is he going away?"
Collector: "No, but it's worth a try."

Quit Worrying

Worrying is like succeeding in reverse. If you worry, you are vividly imagining all of the things you do *not* want to have happen. Talking about worrying and how not to do it reminds me of two experts. One is my mother-in-law, the other is Jeselle, my oldest daughter. Of the two, I think mother-in-law gets the first prize. Her ability to worry about things that *might* happen never ceases to amaze me. When I was dating her daughter, any time we were a bit late she was able to generate the most vivid details of what heinous things had happened to us. The detail and richness of her imagination always fascinated me. I have noticed that as she has gotten older these abilities have improved even more. For example, at the beginning of the Persian Gulf war, Jeselle and a friend decided to get away from winter and fly to visit Jeselle's grandparents in sunny Clearwater, Florida. After I had dropped them off at the airport I called to let the grandparents know that they were on their way. After speaking with my mother-in-law, I was left with the clear impression that one of Saddam Hussein's terrorist squads had just visited the Tampa airport. Mother-in-law was sure that they would not be able to make it to the airport to pick up my daughter. There were so many restrictions mother-in-law was sure that they would not even be able to park their car, let alone get to the terminal. The fact that I had just successfully dropped Jeselle and her friend off at Baltimore-Washington International Airport did not faze her at all. Besides, she was deeply concerned and questioned my judgment in sending my daughter to Clearwater during such unstable times. After all, it could be bombed. (Keep in mind that we live on the outskirts of Washington, D.C., a much more likely terrorist target.) She then proceeded to vividly and in every detail describe for me all the things that could go wrong.

Jeselle, although much younger, is almost as skilled at worrying. Since starting college recently, she has been worrying incessantly about being unable to keep up her grades. Mind you, at this point she has taken a total of three exams. She did flunk her first accounting exam, which, granted, is not a good way to start a college experience. She did well on the other two exams, though, getting an 88 and an 86. The number of negative "what ifs" she has generated has been absolutely astonishing, all focusing on the things she does *not* want to have happen. Hard as I try to teach her otherwise, it seems that she simply enjoys worrying. Perhaps she does it to compensate for her father and mother, who are both probably too optimistic. I am so optimistic that I put a dime into the parking meter when my wife and I go shopping. (Are you chuckling? If not, your wife must not like to shop until she drops.) (Late-breaking news: Since I first wrote this, Jeselle has finished her first semester and received her first college report card. Her grades were all As and Bs, with an average grade of 3.46.)

Neither my mother-in-law nor my daughter are particularly unusual. Nightingale[9] once studied what people worry about and discovered the following worry patterns:

- Things that will never happen   40 percent
- Things that have already happened   30 percent
- Needless worry about health   12 percent
- Miscellaneous petty worries   10 percent
- Legitimate worries   8 percent

You are probably wondering what is wrong with worrying. Actually, nothing is wrong if you worry about the things over which you have control, that is, those things that you can do something about. As noted above, only 8 percent of all worries are legitimate, meaning that they are under your control and you should do something about them. What about the other 92 percent? They do not meet what I call the worry litmus test: What will happen or change if I worry real well? An example is me worrying about what will happen if you, and the million other people who I hope have decided to buy this book, do not like it very much. For me to worry about that while you are reading it is a bit too late. The time to do something about it is now while I am writing it. (That is exactly what I am doing. I am creating excellence as best as I know how, and I am doing it right now.) But once the book is published, that type of thinking is counterproductive. I call it worthless worry, because it simply will not change a thing. (To ensure that I do not engage in worthless worry, I have included a feedback form in the back of the book so that I can incorporate your suggestions in my next edition. Please take a moment NOW and let me know what you think about this book. I and readers of future editions will appreciate it very much.)

Insight Break

When I look back on all these worries, I remember the story of the old man who said on his deathbed that he had a lot of trouble in his life, most of which never happened.

—Winston Churchill

Another example, which as a parent or parent-to-be, you will be able to relate to, is worrying about my daughter coming home late. Let's say her curfew is 11:00 p.m., and it is now 11:30 p.m. What will happen if I worry, as best as I know how, about her being late? Yup, pardner, that's right, nothing! Any time the answer is nothing, it is a worthless worry, and I recommend that you quit doing it. Let's take this example a bit further. What if I wake up at 3:00 a.m., go to her room, and discover that she is still not home? Now it is time for me to worry. Or is it? It is time for me to wake up my wife and find out if my daughter possibly called while I was asleep. If she has not called, then this worry needs to be translated into *action*. This action might consist of calling the parents of the friends that she was to be with, calling the police, and so on. For additional worry busters, see Exhibit 5-5.

We must distinguish between the things over which we can exercise

Exhibit 5-5 Worry Busters

How to get rid of worries in eight "easy" steps:

Step 1: Clarify what it is that you are worried about. If you have difficulty doing this in your head, write it down.

Step 2: Ask yourself if there is anything at all you can do to affect the situation. If the answer is no, it is a worthless worry, and you should immediately go to step 8. If the answer is yes, go to the next step.

Step 3: Identify the worst possible outcome.

Step 4: Ask yourself if you can live with the worst possible outcome. If the answer is yes, go to step 6. If the answer is no, go to the next step.

Step 5: Do everything in your power to get out of the situation now.

Step 6: Develop an action plan that will get you out of the situation or that will minimize the negative consequences associated with it.

Step 7: Take action.

Step 8: Quit worrying. Either it is too late or worrying will not make a difference.

control and those things over which we have no control. The latter, I think you will agree, covers a multitude of sins, including your skin color, your parents, your innate abilities or disabilities, the weather, everything—yes, I mean everything—that has happened in the past, little aches and pains, things that others might do, and things that others might say. We must learn to give up worrying about the things over which we have no control. How can you do that? You can do it by focusing your mental energies on what you are doing in the present. Focus on whatever you are doing right now with everything you have so that you can deliver excellence, consistently, every time, all of the time. That even applies to reading this book. You see, often you and I are present only part of the time, no matter what we are doing. Only half of our mental energies are focused on what is before us; the other half is focused on something else—an upcoming trip, the next weekend, a date, the football game, or whatever it is that we look forward to. When we do that, we are cheating ourselves because we are doing neither activity well. Single-mindedness—focusing intensely on what is before us, without being distracted—is a very important skill that we must hone all of the time.

The remainder of your mental energies should be focused on what it is that you want to have happen in the future—your vision, your goals, your dreams, your desires—and the action plans that will help you get there. If you do this well, your conscious and subconscious will be so filled with positive things that there will be virtually no room for worthless worrying.

Humor Break

Why Worry?
  There are only two things to worry about;
  either you are well or you are sick.
  If you are well, there is nothing to worry about.
  If you are sick, there are two things to worry about;
  either you will get well or you will die.
  If you get well, there is nothing to worry about.
  If you die, there are only two things to worry about;
  either you will go to Heaven or you will go to Hell.
  If you go to Heaven, there is nothing to worry about.
  If you go to Hell, you will be so busy shaking hands with friends,
  you will not have time to worry.

—Unknown

Focus on the Future

Talking about focusing on the future reminds me of an example I like to share with my audiences to help them become future oriented. To make my point, I like to use the proverbial spilled milk example because everyone can readily relate to it. I ask people what happens when their son spills his milk after they have repeatedly told him to be careful not to spill it. (If you do not have a child, think back to your own childhood. This helps you develop your visualization skills.) Most parents say that they get mighty upset. Some rant and rave, calling their son a stupid, clumsy, bumbling fool. I then ask the participants whether this response works—whether it has a positive impact on the bottom line. If they rant and rave long enough, does the milk pick itself up and jump back into the glass? I have yet to come across anyone who has been able to accomplish that. What is accomplished, however, is very destructive. By punishing the actor instead of the act (that is, by not separating the inappropriate behavior from the person), you significantly diminish your son's self-esteem.

The same result will occur if you do not forgive yourself for mistakes that you have made. Losing is part of winning, and making mistakes is part of succeeding. If you do make a mistake, don't fret about it. Try again, or refocus. Winners learn from the past, as opposed to living in the past, and they focus all of their mental energies on the now, the only moment of time over which we have any control. Winners also forgive themselves for making mistakes because they recognize that progress requires that they make a reasonable number of mistakes. Without failures you have status quo, which means that in this powershift era, you will be out of business or out of a job in the very near future. Always direct your mental energies on what you plan to achieve. All of us have a built-in tendency to generally move in the direction of what we think about most of the time. You can make those thoughts winning thoughts or losing thoughts. The choice is yours!

Insight Break

If you want to double your success rate, triple your failure rate.

—Wolf J. Rinke

Before introducing you to a real winner, I want to share a great poem by Edgar A. Guest that illustrates an achievement focus in action (see Exhibit 5-6).

Exhibit 5-6 It Couldn't Be Done

Somebody said that it couldn't be done,
   But he with a chuckle replied
That "maybe it couldn't, but he would be one
   Who wouldn't say so till he'd tried."
So he buckled right in with the trace of a grin
   On his face. If he worried he hid it.
He started to sing as he tackled the thing
   That couldn't be done, and he did it.

Somebody scoffed: "Oh, you'll never do that;
   At least no one ever has done it.
But he took off his coat and he took off his hat,
   And the first thing we knew he'd begun it.
With a lift of his chin and a bit of a grin,
   Without any doubting or quiddit,
He started to sing as he tackled the thing
   That couldn't be done, and he did it.

There are thousands to tell you it cannot be done,
   There are thousands to prophesy failure;
There are thousands to point out to you, one by one,
   The dangers that wait to assail you.
But just buckle in with a bit of a grin,
   Just take off your coat and go to it;
Just start to sing as you tackle the thing
   That "cannot be done," and you'll do it.

—Edgar A. Guest

Source: The Best Loved Poems of the American People. Compiled and selected by Hazel Felleman, Doubleday & Co. New York, 1936, p. 89.

PEP² IN ACTION—ENERGY:
DR. EUNICE RUTH HULL BENNETT

Ruth Bennett was born January 25, 1897, in Tobias, Nebraska. In 1908, she moved to Central City, Nebraska, where she completed high school in 1914. She attended nearby Friends College and decided to go into medicine in her senior year. She became engaged to Claude Bennett in 1916.

After three years of teaching, interspersed with finishing her pre-med studies at Penn College, Iowa, and the University of Chicago, she entered the University of Nebraska College of Medicine in 1921. She received her medical degree in 1925. An internship at the New England Hospital for Women and Children in Boston followed. She then spent two years as medical officer at the Massachusetts Reformatory Prison for Women.

In 1928, she made her first journey to India and began what became her true hobby, traveling. She arrived in India in November after a long, arduous journey that took her across America to Vancouver, British Columbia, Canada, with stops in Japan, Shanghai, Hong Kong, Canton, and Singapore. She was in charge of the medical work of the American Friends Mission in Chhatarpur, Bumdelkhand, India, for seven years. To return to the United States in 1935, she traveled westward from Bombay by ship through the Red Sea and the Mediterranean, across France by train, across the English Channel, and then onward by sailing vessel from Liverpool, England, to Boston.

Claude Bennett had waited patiently while she was in India. Although they had seen each other occasionally between 1917 and 1928, their courtship continued primarily by correspondence. On February 17, 1936, she retired from medicine for the first time and married Claude Bennett. The newly married couple took up residence near Ovid, Colorado.

A few weeks later, she was offered a temporary post with the Northampton (Massachusetts) State Hospital for Nervous and Mental Patients. Her husband stayed in Colorado to tend the farm and Bennett moved to Massachusetts. Soon after, she learned she was pregnant. She continued practicing medicine until it was time to give birth to their son, Claude Fraser Bennett, on December 6, 1936.

Shortly after the birth of her son, the Medical Department of the Mission in India asked her to serve a three-year term. Her husband was also invited, but he decided to remain in Colorado. Bennett's son was nearly nine months old when they sailed from New York to India. After a three-year tour in Bumdelkhand, India, Bennett and her son returned to the United States via Columbo, Penang, Singapore, Batavia, Balakpappan, Cebu, Victoria, Manila, Honolulu, and Los Angeles, then continued east by train home to Sedgwick County, Colorado.

During the next 20 years, she substituted for local physicians and practiced in the eye department of a field hospital during World War II. At 65, she retired once again, but soon found herself on the staff of Fairview State Hospital in Costa Mesa, California. Her husband spent winters with her in California; summer vacations were spent on the farm in Colorado. Once again she retired, this time at age 70; however, this was her mandatory retirement.

She returned to Colorado, where her husband died of a severe stroke on March 16, 1975. To help her deal with the loss, Bennett moved to Sandy Spring, Maryland, near her son and his family. She resides in a very pleasant retirement community called Friends House, from where she continues to actively pursue her hobby, traveling.

WR: In my book, I talk about six success principles. For each, I am interviewing someone who embodies that principle. I read your story in the newspaper and wanted to interview you because you appear to possess an inordinate amount of *energy*. I admire people who do all the things you do at your age and still keep themselves motivated. Many of the people I talk to have excuses. In fact, many people who are much younger than you have a lot of excuses. One of the excuses is "I'm too old." How old are you now?

RB: I'm 94. I turned 94 in January. I was born in 1897.

WR: You've seen a lot of things in those years. One of the things that struck me is that at age 94 you are still running marathons.

RB: Yes, in Maryland in 1989 and 1990 I had a walking competition. In the Senior Olympics I received the bronze medal in 1989. In 1990 I got a silver medal and a gold medal. The silver was a bonus because I walked faster than the woman who won the gold medal in the 80-to-85 group. There were no other participants in the 85-to-90-plus age group, so naturally I won. And they clocked me—I walked 2 seconds faster than I had the year before. Because I won the gold medal, I'm invited to the National Senior Olympics in Syracuse, New York, this year.

WR: I gather that you love to travel. What modes of travel do you prefer?

RB: Bus, train, plane, automobile, anything—elephant and camel in India.

WR: Tell me more about your recent trips.

RB: In February and March 1990 [at age 93], I went to Antarctica. In July, I traveled to the Amazon. I landed at Maraus, which is halfway up the Amazon, and took a cruise ship from there to Iquitos, Peru. I traveled in parts of Brazil, Colombia, and Peru all in one day. We got off the cruise ship in Iquitos and flew over the Rockies to Lima and then flew home.

WR: How long a trip was that?

RB: Two and a half weeks.

WR: And you just do that, you're not worried about anything?

RB: Why should I be? If you do things you like, then you have nothing to worry about. You don't care if you die if you're doing what you like.

WR: One of the things I talk about in the book is what one has to do if one wants to succeed in life. I suggest to my readers that they have to figure out what their strengths are, what they really like to do, because the way to succeed is to focus on your strengths and forget about your weaknesses.

RB: I suppose one does that naturally if they're doing what they like.

WR: Please tell me a little bit more about your trip to Antarctica. I'm fascinated that you are still making what must have been a long and arduous journey.

RB: We flew from Miami, Florida to Santiago, Chile, then took another flight to Punta Arenas, which is on the tip of Chile. There we boarded a cruise ship and crossed the Drake Passage, which is always very stormy. But I don't ever get seasick. On my first trip across the Pacific, the first time I'd ever been across an ocean, I thought I would get seasick, but I didn't. I've never been seasick. I'd like to be, just to see how it is. Have you been?

WR: I was a sailor as a young man. Initially, I got sick, but once there's something to occupy your mind you forget about being seasick. That's what happened to me. What is the next trip that you are planning?

RB: I hope to travel the Arctic Ocean, perhaps from Finland—I'm not sure where we start from—along the shore of Siberia to the other side and then maybe come back on a train through Siberia.

WR: When you travel, do you go alone or with friends?

RB: Usually by myself because most people here at Friends House don't like to travel. Sometimes I go with family. For instance, when I went to Russia, my grandchildren were both in high school and their social sciences teacher arranged that anyone who read a prescribed book and took this tour during spring vacation and wrote a report would get half credit. Parents were invited. I was the only grandparent on the trip.

WR: So, with all the traveling that you do at 94 years old—young, I should say, old is not a good word for you—how do you get that energy, that self-motivation, to keep yourself going?

RB: I do what I like. All my life I've done what I like. It's been hard on other people sometimes.

WR: It sounds to me that you have built on your strengths and forgotten about your weaknesses all your life. You went to medical school when medical school for women was not very common—that was in 1921.

RB: I started in 1921 and graduated in 1925 from the University of Nebraska College of Medicine in Omaha.

WR: You went into missionary medicine. You went to India to practice medicine.

RB: Yes, after I graduated from college I interned in Boston at the Hospital for Women and Children, and then I went to work at a prison for 2 years before I went to India. I had to pay my medical college debts. In other words, I went to prison for debt, and was deported to India!

WR: Had you met your husband before you went to India?

RB: Yes, I met him in 1914, I guess. That's the first time I ever saw him. We were at a small college in Nebraska called Nebraska Central. I didn't date him until 1915. We were engaged in 1916 when I was 19 years old. We were married in 1936.

WR: Your husband waited 20 years to marry you?

RB: Yes, we were good friends. Before I went to India for 7 years, I told him, "If there's anything else in the world you want to do, don't wait for me." I was so pokey about setting the date. When I got back in August 1935, he was in Colorado. We were married on February 17, 1936. Our son was born in December 1936, 10 months later. We were married 39 years before my husband died in 1975.

WR: So you were engaged for 20 years and married for 39 years. How was your marriage?

RB: Wonderful! I still did everything I wanted to do.

WR: How about your husband? Did he do everything he wanted to do?

RB: I hope so. He often went with one of his brothers to look at land, especially in the Dakotas. I worked in Massachusetts after we were married and our son was born, and then the Board asked if I would go back to India because they needed somebody badly. So, with my husband's approbation, I said I would go. Our son was 10 months old when I arrived back in India. My husband did not go with me. My son went with me. My son doesn't remember too much about India. He was almost 4 when we came back.

WR: Your son lives in Silver Spring, Maryland, right?

RB: Yes. I see him and his family frequently. Last weekend we went by car to visit my granddaughter, who is studying drama at the University of Pittsburgh. We went to see her play.

WR: I'm just amazed that you do all those things at age 94. Just as a comparison, my parents, who are in their late 60s, live about three hours from us, but seldom come to visit because, according to them, the trip is too strenuous.

RB: My father's people, some of them are quite long-lived. My mother's people were not. Although my father said I looked more like my maternal grandmother.

WR: How long did you practice medicine?

RB: I have a 50-year plaque from the American Medical Society. I retired in 1975. I still did some volunteer work up until 1975.

WR: Do you practice for your marathons?

RB: I may go on the 29th of this month to a race, with friends from here. We go to a track to walk about three times a week. We walk a mile.

WR: When you met me today, I noticed that you walk just as fast as I do. I also noticed that you are wearing a button that says "Enjoy your age." You really seem, unlike so many elderly people, to enjoy your age. What's your secret?

RB: No secret except that I do as I like. I'm just happy to be alive, and I enjoy every minute and make the most of every minute. My father lived to be 91½. He had 12 siblings. Four of the men lived into their nineties. The youngest of the 12 lived to be 98. His daughter will be 100 in July.

WR: Mentally, you are extremely sharp. You remember dates better than I do. Are you still reading?

RB: Of course I am. My retina is very good. I have no deterioration. After my cataracts were removed in 1976, I wore contact lenses and battered my cornea with them. I could have a corneal transplant but it would take about a year to clear. If that should happen before I go on my next trip, I couldn't go. That would cause me to miss a new experience, and I love new experiences.

WR: I noticed several issues of the *Journal of the American Medical Association* on your end table. Do you still read *JAMA?*

RB: Yes, of course. That way I can keep up with the latest advances in medicine, something I enjoy very much.

WR: Have you been physically very active during your life?

RB: Yes, I've always liked to walk. In India, a group of us would go for walks.

WR: Do you take any special care regarding what you eat?

RB: I eat anything. I usually have ice cream for breakfast. I just eat what I like and what I want. I eat a lot of food.

WR: Have you ever smoked?

RB: I've never smoked because my brother, who was 8½ years older, started to smoke. He had a pitch pipe for the mandolin. I was told as a little girl never to touch it, but when no one was watching I picked up the pitch pipe and blew it. I can remember what a terrible taste it had because he had been smoking when he used the pitch pipe. Ever since then tobacco has been taboo. I don't even like to be in the presence of smokers now.

RB: Do you like alcohol?

WR: No, I don't touch the stuff.

WR: You have certainly given credence to what I talk about in my book. That is, that if you want to keep yourself motivated and energized on an ongoing basis you need to find something that you love to do and pursue that with a vengeance. That's how you get a natural high in life. You have certainly been able to master and live the energy principle to the nth degree. I would like to thank you for taking the time to share with me and my readers how we can keep ourselves energized and how we can at the same time live a long and enjoyable life.

Postscript: After the interview, Dr. Bennett offered me ice cream. Because I'm watching my calorie and cholesterol intake, I turned her down. She seemed truly disappointed. Instead, she took me for a walk around Friends House, and even though I'm a jogger, I must confess that I had to step on it to keep up with her.

SUMMARY: A TRIP BACK TO THE FUTURE

- Energy and positive self-motivation come from reaching for your dreams and doing the things you love to do.
- All people are a composite of both strengths and weaknesses.
- To have maximum energy, you must build on your strengths and get rid of your weaknesses.

- To succeed, you must find a job or career that lets you build on your strengths.
- Successful people love what they do.
- Fix the weaknesses that get in your way of attaining your lifetime goals. Forget the rest.
- You are never too old to succeed.
- Pursuing what you want and having fun at what you do will give you a natural high.
- Focusing on achievement is facilitated by six action strategies:
  —Have a ready, fire, aim perspective.
  —Take advantage of the Pygmalion effect.
  —Commit to excellence.
  —Associate with winners at work and play.
  —Quit worrying.
  —Focus on the future.

SUCCESS ACTION STEPS

❏ If you have not already done so, identify your strengths and weaknesses right now! Then prepare an action plan that will allow you to build on your strengths. Remedy any weaknesses that will interfere with attaining your lifetime goals. Forget the rest of your weaknesses.

❏ Ask yourself if you look forward to your job about 80 percent of the time. If not, review your strengths and identify a job or career that will provide you with the opportunity to build on your strengths.

❏ Get excited. Yes, you read correctly. Getting excited about what you do is just as much a choice as getting depressed. Do not give that choice to someone or something else!

❏ Think about the three things you love to do the most. If one of these three things is job related, stay with it, and you will succeed. If none is job related, engage in a freewheeling brainstorming session with your significant other, your mentor, or a close friend to come up with as many strategies as possible that would allow you to make a "hobby" into your profession. Capture all of these ideas on audiotape or paper and refer to them when you decide that your current job no longer compensates or fulfills you adequately, or when you are laid off, whichever comes first.

❏ Regardless of who employs you, remember that you ultimately work for only one person—YOU.

❏ Assume that the next project you are assigned will decide whether you get the next promotion. Now perform accordingly, because in the long run it does. Once you get the hang of it, do the same for the next assignment, and for every assignment to come.

❏ Regardless of where you currently work, give your employer *more* than he expects. Start right now. In the long run, you will be compensated according to the value you deliver.

❏ The next time that you are not sure how you should behave at work (for example, if you are not sure whether you should go home early, take a certain action, or specify a certain piece of equipment), ask yourself what you would do if the company belonged to you. Then act accordingly.

❏ Do you currently look up to your friends, colleagues, and boss? Do you learn something new from them all of the time? Are you proud to associate with them? Do they help you grow? If you said no to two of the four questions, it is time to find yourself some new friends, new colleagues, and, yes, even a new boss.

❏ Do you currently spend more than 10 percent of your time worrying? If yes, copy Exhibit 5-5, and refer to it the next time you worry.

❏ Listen to your self-talk. Is it generally focused on the past, the present, or the future? When you catch yourself focusing on the past, shift gears and focus your mental energies on what you are doing right now. If you are idle, focus on what you plan to do in the future.

NOTES

1. F. Herzberg, "One More Time: How Do You Motivate Employees?" in *People: Managing Your Most Important Asset* (Boston: Harvard Business Review, 1990), pp. 26–35.

2. J. McMakin and S. Dyer, *Working from the Heart* (San Diego, CA: Luramedia, 1989).

3. D. Kanter and P. Mirvis, *The Cynical American* (San Francisco: Jossey-Bass, 1989).

4. S. H. Snyder, "Planning for Serendipity," *Nature* 346 (August 1990): 508.

5. L. A. Matsuda, S. J. Lolait, M. J. Brownstein, A. C. Young, and T. I. Bonner, "Structure of a Cannabinoid Receptor and Functional Expression of the Cloned cDNA," *Nature* 346 (August 1990): 561–564.

6. C. Garfield, *Peak Performers: The New Heroes of American Business* (New York: Morrow, 1986).

7. R. Rosenthal and L. Jacobson, *Pygmalion in the Classroom* (New York: Holt, Rinehart & Winston, 1968), p. 11.

8. J. S. Livingston, "Pygmalion in Management," *Harvard Business Review* 66 (September–October 1988): 121–130.

9. E. Nightingale, *The New Lead the Field* (Chicago: Nightingale-Conant, 1986.) Audiotape program.

ANSWER TO MENTAL STRETCHING EXERCISE
Page 120

Exhibit 5-7 Solution: Is Your Success Triangle Upside Down?

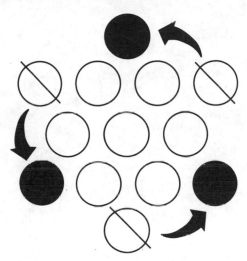

ANSWERS TO BRAIN TEASERS
Page 127

1. Arctic circle
2. Bermuda triangle
3. Goldilocks and the three bears
4. Top of the morning
5. Six feet underground
6. Easy on the eyes
7. A point in time
8. Take from the rich and give to the poor
9. The odds are against you

6

Education

The most important economic development of our lifetime has been the rise of a new system for creating wealth, based no longer on muscle but on mind.

—Alvin Toffler

Once your success rocket is in space, you must collect data and intelligence about the performance of its vital systems and about your actual course of travel. This information is constantly changing; therefore, it must be monitored continuously by the on-board computer. That computer represents your education and your commitment to lifelong learning and mental development (see Exhibit 6-1).

Just like your success rocket, which is traveling a constantly changing journey toward a hard-to-reach target, this book is about how to succeed in a tough and rapidly changing world. If we were to consider current success as a barometer of future success, we would find that most of today's successful men and women are engaged in "knowledge work." (These people are also known as "gold-collar" employees.) For example, an examination of *Forbes* magazine's list of the ten richest people in the United States reveals that seven of the ten made their fortunes in media, communications, and computer support industries such as software and services.[1] If Alvin Toffler is correct (and I don't see why he wouldn't be, he has been correct before) in the "powershift" era we now live in, future wealth and power will no longer be created from military might, money, and manufacturing.[2] They will instead be created from the exchange of data, information, and knowledge. Toffler says, "Today the most powerful wealth-amplifying tools are the symbols inside workers' heads."[3] The idea of becoming perpetual learning machines is not restricted to individuals. Peter Senge, author of *The Fifth Discipline: The Art and Practice of the Learning Organization,*[4] said it best when he quoted Ray Stata of Analog

149

Exhibit 6-1 Your PEP² Rocket—Part 4: The On-Board Computer (Education)

Devices, "The rate at which organizations learn may become the only sustainable source of competitive advantage."[5] This "intellectual capital" premise is echoed by the chief executives of such leading companies as Polaroid, Merck, IBM, and American Express.[6] This means that if you want to succeed in life or business in this "super-symbolic economy," as Toffler has labeled it,[7] you must be constantly engaged in education and lifelong learning.

Insight Break

Empires of the future are empires of the mind.

—Winston Churchill

PREVIEW OF COMING ATTRACTIONS

In this chapter, we will first determine how committed you are to lifelong learning. After that, I plan to convince you, once and for all, of the importance of lifelong learning and why it is absolutely critical that if you want to succeed that you make a habit of investing in the most precious resource you will ever own: yourself. From there, I will provide you with a five-step self-directed learning system and a seven-step process that will help you to think. Then, I will teach you how you can arrive at creative solutions by implementing the five-step holistic thinking model. And last, but not least, I will show you how you can get the most out of your next group learning activity. Of course, as always, I will do my best to keep you alert by keeping you amused and by periodically reengaging the right side of your brain.

LIFELONG LEARNING SKILL INVENTORY

Let's begin our discussion of education and self-development by assessing your commitment to lifelong learning. Complete the Lifelong Learning Skill Inventory in Exhibit 6-2.

LIFELONG LEARNING: ANOTHER SECRET INGREDIENT OF SUCCESS

To participate in the process of wealth creation in what Toffler calls a "knowledge economy,"[8] you must become a voracious lifelong learner.

Exhibit 6-2 Lifelong Learning Skill Inventory

Instructions

Using the scale below, circle the number that most closely indicates the frequency with which each statement applies to you. (People have different preferences and opinions; therefore, there are no right or wrong answers.)

1	2	3	4	5
Never	Almost Never	Infrequently	Almost Always	Always

1. I am committed to learning one new thing every day.   1 2 3 4 5 _____

2. I regularly read three or more professional publications related to my work or career.   1 2 3 4 5 _____

3. Learning new things is a painful experience for me.   1 2 3 4 5 _____

4. I read at least five hours per week.   1 2 3 4 5 _____

5. I listen to educational and/or motivational audiotape programs at least 50 percent of the time while in my car.   1 2 3 4 5 _____

6. I regularly read at least one professional publication totally unrelated to my work or career.   1 2 3 4 5 _____

7. I make it a point to be with people who think like I do.   1 2 3 4 5 _____

8. I view at least two educational programs or videotapes per year.   1 2 3 4 5 _____

9. I attend at least two educational seminars or workshops per year.   1 2 3 4 5 _____

10. I read at least one nonfiction book per year.   1 2 3 4 5 _____

11. I pursue at least two learning projects per year.   1 2 3 4 5 _____

12. I invest at least 2 percent of my annual income in my personal and professional development.   1 2 3 4 5 _____

13. I usually finish a learning project once I have started it.   1 2 3 4 5 _____

14. When in group settings, I avoid asking instructors questions if something is not clear to me.   1 2 3 4 5 _____

15. I feel that how well I learn something depends on how well it is taught.   1 2 3 4 5 _____

16. I create quiet time so that I can do some innovative thinking at least once a week.   1 2 3 4 5 _____

17. After I have attended a workshop or seminar I review my notes.   1 2 3 4 5 _____

Exhibit 6-2 continued

18. After I have attended a workshop or seminar I teach   1 2 3 4 5 _____
    or review at least one major concept I learned to or
    with someone else.

19. I sit as close as possible to the back when I attend   1 2 3 4 5 _____
    courses, seminars, or workshops.

20. I engage in activities that make me stretch my mind.   1 2 3 4 5 _____

                                                    Total   _____

Scoring Instructions

Score items 1, 2, 4, 5, 6, 8, 9, 10, 11, 12, 13, 16, 17, 18, and 20 in accordance with the
number that you circled. For example, if you circled a 2 for question 1, you earned 2
points, which you should write on the line next to question 1.

Reverse-score items 3, 7, 14, 15, and 19. This means that you have to turn the scale
around to score these items, so that 1 = 5, 2 = 4, 3 = 3, 4 = 2, and 5 = 1.

Examples:

1. I am committed to learning one .... 1 ② 3 4 5 = 2

2. I regularly read three or more professional .... 1 2 3 ④ 5 = 4

3. Learning new things is .... 1 ② 3 4 5 − 4

Total your points.

Interpretation of Your Score

91–100 *Excellent.* You are an expert lifelong learner. Anyone who scores this high is
        a bona fide learning machine that devours information like a paper shredder
        in overtime status at the Pentagon.

81–90   *Great.* You possess the skills to direct your own lifelong learning program.

71–80   *Above Average.* Add to your current skills and you will become a learning
        machine poised for success.

61–70   *Average.* This chapter will provide you with powerful self-directed learning
        skills that will move you ahead of the competition.

 <60   Aren't you glad that you are reading this book?

That is, you must go backward. What I mean by that is that you and I were designed to be perpetually inquisitive, innovative, and curious. You can't think back that far? Then take a look at your preschool age children or grandchildren. Why preschool age? Because once children begin school the education system starts to stifle and, in some cases, even kill those innate abilities. After all, little people are very smart. They quickly figure out that to succeed in school they need to regurgitate the *right* answer and avoid making mistakes. (Both of these skills decimate creative thinking.) Unfortunately, these creativity-killing skills are further reinforced once people "complete" their formal education and enter corporate America. The result is that even the best and brightest in corporate America simply do not know how to learn.[9] The antidote to this destruction of your innate abilities is to go back in time. You must literally relearn how to learn and internalize the belief that learning is a lifelong process.

In addition, because of the explosive growth in knowledge and technology, information obsolescence has become a way of life, such that the "half-life" of knowledge may, in certain professions, be only 2 to 3 years.[10] A formal education, such as an advanced degree, will provide you with a useful foundation to build on, but it provides little protection against obsolescence. In fact, it has been estimated that the usefulness of a degree is cut in half after about 10 to 12 years.[11] Extrapolating from that, and taking into consideration the knowledge and information explosion, I estimate that the usefulness of a degree earned today is cut in half in 2 to 4 years. Such rapid decay can only be overcome if you are engaged in updating and renewing your knowledge on a perpetual basis. In addition, education and continuing learning are important in themselves because studies have repeatedly demonstrated a clear link between level of education and success.

Therefore, engaging in an ongoing, planned continuing education program is absolutely critical if you want to succeed. But let me warn you, education is addictive. People's level of education has been closely linked to subsequent involvement in education and training. As a result, the educational "haves" continue to leave the "have nots" even further behind.

Insight Break

Superior performance depends on superior learning.
—Peter M. Senge

INVEST IN YOURSELF

Some people are caught in what Brian Tracy, president of the Institute for Executive Development, calls an "intelligence trap."[12] This occurs when people think that they know it all and therefore no longer need to learn. (In reality, the opposite is true: The more you learn, the more you realize just how little you know.) As a result of such shortsightedness, 45 percent of Americans do not read any books.[13] Compare that to Nielsen's finding that the average individual watches *7 hours and 2 minutes of television per day* (an incredible 49-plus hours per week)[14] and you will quickly realize why most of us get mentally further behind as we get ahead.

Looking at this from a positive perspective, though, you can see how easy it is to gain an advantage over your competition. After all, if you read only 1 book per year you will be doing better than 45 percent of the population. But that is simply not good enough for you because the people who read regularly read an average of 16 books per year.[15] In a knowledge economy, knowledge and information represent *the* system for wealth creation. To succeed in such an economy, you must invest in the most important resource you will ever own: yourself. You must be infinitely curious, be a voracious lifelong learner, and continually invest in yourself. A convenient measure is to ask yourself how many hours you currently spend at work each day. If you are working an average of eight hours per day, you are working barely long enough to survive. Anything in excess of the basic eight hours is an investment in yourself and your future, especially if you dedicate a portion of that "overtime" to self-development. That investment should take the form of reading (at least five hours per week—don't groan, that's only one hour each working day); listening to audiotape programs; viewing educational videotapes (your television and videocassette recorder may experience a shock, but educational tapes won't break them); and attending seminars, workshops, and college courses.

The American Society for Training and Development (ASTD) recommends that corporations spend 2 percent to 4 percent of their payroll dollars on training and development. Some successful U.S. companies are doing that and more. For example, in 1987, IBM spent an average of 5 percent of its payroll on formal training and development; Xerox, 4 percent; Texas Instruments, 3.5 percent; Honeywell, 3 percent; Motorola, 2.6 percent; and General Electric, 2 percent.[16] What does that mean in real time and money? For Xerox it means spending $2,500 per employee per year to attend six days of formal training. One reason that our competitors in Japan and Germany are currently outperforming us is that they spend in excess of 4 percent on formal training and development. Using ASTD's recommendation and what the winning companies are doing as a guide, I recommend that you invest 2 percent to 5 percent of your annual income in your personal and professional development. This investment will keep you on the cutting edge, place you in the top 1 percent of the population, and ensure that you achieve long-term success.

Mental Stretch Break

To help you think creatively, here is a different type of brain teaser. Place the numbers 1, 2, 3, 4, 5, 6, 7, 8, and 9 in the nine squares shown in Exhibit 6-3 so that the three numbers in any row or column (horizontally, vertically, and diagonally) equal 15. You may use each number only once. (See end of chapter for answer.)

Exhibit 6-3 Number Exercise

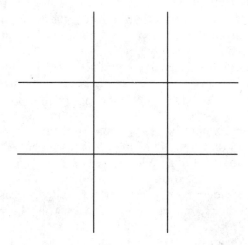

LEARN HOW TO LEARN

Toffler, in his earlier best seller, *Future Shock,* stated that the illiterate of the year 2000 will be the individual who does not possess the competence to learn, unlearn, and relearn.[17] That assertion was confirmed by a major study of U.S. employers that found that "knowing how to learn is the most basic of all skills because it is the key that unlocks future success."[18] As simple as that may sound, many adults avoid self-directed learning, primarily because our educational system has conditioned us to think that learning has to occur in a formal classroom environment. Nothing, of course, is further from the truth. Most of us are involved in all kinds of learning projects on an ongoing basis, such as learning to use a computer or operate a new kitchen appliance. According to a classic adult education study conducted by Allen Tough, adults undertake an average of eight learning projects per year.[19]

Insight Break

Real learning occurs after you think you know it all.

—Earl Nightingale

To foster these lifelong learning skills, I recommend that you accept full responsibility for your own learning and follow a five-step process to bring it about:

1. *Conduct a needs assessment.* Identify what you need or want to learn. Compare this list with what you already know. The differences between what you know and what you need or want to know are your learning needs.

2. *Define your objectives.* From the learning needs identified in step 1, define your learning objectives. Be sure they describe clearly what you want to learn and how you will know when you have achieved each objective. To the maximum extent possible, make these objectives SMART (see Chapter 4).

3. *Establish an action plan.* Determine the who, what, when, where, and how of meeting your educational needs. This includes identifying who can help you get to where you want to go, what money and material you will need to accomplish your objectives, when you want to have what accomplished (be sure to note specific benchmarks and target dates in your calendar), where you can find the type of knowledge that you are seeking, and how you will accomplish your learning objectives (for example, by engaging in self-directed study, attending a college course, listening to audiotapes in your car, or finding a mentor).

4. *Take action.* Here we go with that action stuff again. As you know, the best-made plans are absolutely no good unless they are executed. Now that you have your plan, all that is left to do is to go for it!

5. *Evaluate.* Determine whether you have satisfied the educational needs you identified in step 1. If not, start the process all over again.

If you are getting excited about the prospect of being in charge of your own learning, there is an excellent "how-to" guide to self-directed learning for both learners and teachers. It is *Self-Directed Learning* by Malcolm Knowles, the father of adult education.[20] It describes in detail everything you must know to engage yourself and others in the exciting journey of self-directed and contract learning.

Insight Break

Nothing pains people more than having to think.
—Martin Luther King, Jr.

LEARN HOW TO THINK

Yes, you read correctly. No, I have not gone totally mad. A sad reality is that most of us, assuming that you are an adult and have finished your formal education, simply do not think much anymore. Most of us are on what I call "autopilot." (Remember our discussion about habits in Chapter 1?) Think of the last time your spouse called just before you left your office to ask you to stop by the store on the way home to pick up a gallon of milk. You said, "No problem," headed to your car, got in, and drove off toward home. The next thing you knew, you were sitting in your driveway, ready to park the car. Then a faint memory stirred: Wasn't I supposed to do something before coming home? Then it hit you: Pick up a gallon of milk! This is just one example. Being on autopilot is very important to us at times, however, because it keeps us sane. You see, if you had to think about everything from scratch each time you had to do something, you would go mad. On the other hand, in this knowledge economy, responding to everything on autopilot will most certainly set you up for failure.

So, you ask, what am I to do? The following seven-step system, an expansion of a system I learned from the late Earl Nightingale, will help you to think.

1. On a specific day each week, arrive at the office one hour earlier than anyone else. If you are a night owl, stay one hour later. If you can't find a quiet hour at work, set aside an hour at home on the weekend.
2. Locate a writing tablet and pencil. (There's that high-tech equipment

again.) At the top of a page, write a major problem with which you have been struggling. If you should be so lucky that you have no major problems, write the following: How can I better serve and/or provide greater value to my customers? The next week, change the last word to "employer," "spouse," "employees," "children," "parents," or anyone else who relies on you.

3. In a free and uninhibited manner, totally ignoring feasibility, affordability, practicality, usefulness, and all other constraints that normally impede your thinking, write down as many ideas as you can generate. Include anything that might come close to addressing the issue written at the top of the page. Let go of all your preconceptions, inhibitions, and constraints. Just dream a big dream. Strive to fill up the page. Force yourself to come up with a minimum of 20 ideas.

4. Lay the tablet aside and stretch, get yourself a beverage, go to the bathroom, or take a brief walk.

5. Prioritize each item on the page, with number 1 being your most powerful and most useful idea. (Do you remember how you can decide which items should have the highest priority? Remember those 3 x 5 cards you generated in Chapter 4? The ones that list your lifetime goals? If not, go back to Chapter 4 and do a brief review.) All results that move you closer to the attainment of your lifetime goals represent high-priority items.

6. Transfer the number-one item to your action plan (see Chapter 4) and your daily to do list.

7. Now comes the hard part: Do it! Continue until you have implemented the top three ideas. After that, you will be ready to generate another list of ideas that will help you succeed. That is exactly what this system will do, because so few adults know how to think.

Now that you know how to think, let's move into the advanced stuff and learn how to think creatively. But, before you get nervous, review my definition of thinking creatively.

Insight Break

Thinking creatively means to put two or more known ideas together in a way that no one has ever thought about them before.

—Wolf J. Rinke

LEARN HOW TO THINK CREATIVELY

The assumption that creative thinking happens all by itself and to only a select few is erroneous. Although researchers have not fully agreed on the specific terminology, there is consensus that the creative thinking process consists of five major phases: preparation, manipulation, incubation, insight or illumination, and verification. I have termed this process holistic thinking to complement my theory of holistic education.[21] Regardless of what it is called, I tend to agree with Peter Drucker, who tells us that creativity is 1 percent genius and 99 percent hard work.[22] If you are not willing to work hard or are unwilling or unable to engage your emotions, feelings, and intuition (the right side of the brain), you will not be able to maximize your creative potential.

Step 1: Preparation

This is the step that is all hard work and no play. Here you have to do your homework, investigate, read, study, and otherwise totally immerse yourself in the problem before you. Let's pretend that you have just lost your job. What should you do? Begin by thinking of multiple options. Instead of focusing on the two obvious solutions, find a new job or draw unemployment compensation, find other options from which to choose. This is primarily a left-brain activity of assembling lots of material, information, and data. You might, for example, reevaluate your strengths, ask yourself what you have been dreaming about when not busy at work, identify what you like to do that really turns you on, or consider what hobbies you have cultivated that might lend themselves to making a living for you.

To illustrate this, during the later part of my 20 years in the military, I began to make a lot of presentations. I enjoyed this immensely. In fact, I enjoyed it so much that initially I did it at no charge. Each time I made a presentation, I found that I received three new requests. After some time, when I received more requests than I had vacation time, I began to charge a fee. All of a sudden I liked it even more, especially since demand continued to increase. That is how I turned a hobby into a lucrative profession.

Perhaps sailing is your hobby. Because of your love for the sport you have become extremely knowledgeable about it. In fact, you have been teaching your friends to sail for years and have loved every moment of it. Here are some new options that you should explore. You might want to become a sailing instructor, take people for charter cruises, or maybe write a sailing book. (That is how Dan Poynter, a self-publishing expert, got started when he wrote his first book about hang gliding.) Do not worry that it has nothing to do with your current occupation; most adults make several career changes throughout their lives. Of course, it could be woodworking, gardening, cooking, or anything else that you love to do. Whatever it is, this is the stage in which you must do your research. You need to find out what the supply and demand are for what you think you would like to do with the rest of your life. Go to your library, talk to your friends, talk to people who are currently in similar occupations or who are in atypical careers, study the literature, make calls to professional associations, consult with experts, investigate somewhat unrelated markets that are flourishing, and study anything else that you can find relating to market trends and consumers' buying habits. Although this is easy to describe, it usually requires significant time and effort. After you have become knowledgeable about the particular subject in question and have filled the left side of your brain with information, it is time to get creative.

Insight Break

Nothing is more dangerous than an idea when it is the only one you have.
—Emile Chartier

Step 2: Manipulation

To engage the right side of your brain, you must mentally manipulate and play with the information you have loaded into the left side of your brain. There are several ways to accomplish this:

- by making the familiar strange (Place a table upside down, with its legs in the air. What is it good for now?);
- by visualizing the opposite of what you want to happen and using that new situation as a steppingstone to innovative ideas (Thinking about how to encourage people to walk *on* the grass could lead to all kinds of wild ideas that would help keep people *off* the grass.);
- by changing your assumptions (What would you do if your goal was making your customers angry instead of pleasing them?); and
- by asking "what if" questions (What if we put fish food in our marine paint?).

Your goal here is to play mental games, games that will cause you to look at the problem as everyone else but to see something no one has seen before. Ideally, you want to involve as many people as possible in this process, because manipulation and idea generation are enhanced by such group processes as brainstorming,[23] the nominal group technique,[24] random association, synectics, hypothesizing, and other creative thinking techniques described by Adams,[25] Albrecht,[26] von Oech,[27] and Ruggiero.[28]

Now that you have engaged the right side of your brain, it is time to take it easy so that you can put both sides of your brain to work.

Step 3: Incubation

This is the stage in which your mind gets to play. The goal here is to relax your conscious effort, which you can accomplish by daydreaming, visualization, meditation, or any other unconscious thinking strategy that occurs below the level of awareness. Although this phase is the least understood, it is probably the most critical phase. It is also the phase that is most often frowned upon, especially by task-oriented (Type A) people, because direct observation would indicate that you are "goofing off." What the skeptics do not realize is that this is the phase that engages the right side of the brain, which assimilates the information into a whole and leads directly to insight or illumination.

To demonstrate the importance of this stage, think of the last time you met someone you knew but were unable to remember his name. As you continued the conversation you were frantically searching your memory for the name. You felt particularly foolish because it was "on the tip of your tongue." Your left hemisphere did have a record of the name, and your right hemisphere had a record of the face. You were, however, not processing the data effectively because your data "crunching" occurred in the left hemisphere without the benefit of the right hemisphere. Not until you said goodbye and walked away did you provide your brain with the opportunity to approach the problem holistically. After you stopped forcing it, your conscious efforts relaxed, the subconscious took over, and the incubation phase led directly to illumination: "Oh, my goodness, that was Brian Johnson. How could I ever have forgotten his name?"

You can preclude this from happening in the future by using positive affirmations. For example, the next time you are unable to verbalize what you have on the tip of your tongue, say to yourself or to the person you are having a conversation with, "I can't think of the name right now; let's just go on with our conversation, and I will think of it in a minute." In most cases you will! Certainly this will work more frequently than when you program your "computer" with a negative affirmation such as "I can never remember people's names."

Insight Break

The only man who can change his mind is the man who's got one.
                                        —Edward Noyes Westcott

Step 4: Illumination

In this phase of the holistic thinking model you will have a desired insight that will, in relation to the subject at hand, be your first conscious awareness of a new and valuable idea or association. It is this flash of inspiration, also known as the "aha response" or the Eureka effect, that most people refer to as creativity. All of us have these moments of insight. They often come at unusual times (in the middle of the night, while brushing your teeth, while driving to work, etc.) usually after extensive periods of conscious thought followed by some period of rest and relaxation. Because insights come unexpectedly, I suggest that you record these valuable thoughts immediately so that you can retain them. Having pencil and paper or a recorder nearby at all times is important because if the ideas are not committed to what I like to call external memory (for example, paper) they may be forgotten.

Step 5: Verification

The last phase in holistic thinking is the verification phase. This is primarily a left hemispheric activity that consists of implementing or testing the insight, organizing the facts, conducting a detailed review, and perhaps sharing it with others. This step is especially critical so that you can keep a record of your effectiveness, especially if you had to rely extensively on your intuition.

Mental Stretch Break

Now that you know how to think creatively, let's see how well you do with the following exercise.
You have before you a cake and a long, sharp knife (see Exhibit 6-4).

Your challenge is to cut the cake into as many pieces as possible with four straight cuts. Unlike the normal rules for cake cutting, these pieces do not have to be of equal size. Happy cutting. This exercise is a "piece of cake"! (See end of chapter for solutions.)

Exhibit 6-4 Cake-Cutting Exercise

LEARN WITH NO TIME DOWN

Most of us would like to know how we can get something for nothing. Get ready, because I am about to tell you how you can learn without taking away from your precious discretionary time. If I were to stretch it a bit, I could even claim that it will not cost you any time at all. Most of us drive an automobile. On average, Americans commute almost 4 hours per week, or 192 hours per year. That's a lot of time! What are you doing during that time? Are you managing the other drivers with your body language or using sign language to communicate with them? I used to do both, until one day, after I had been cut off several times by a nasty driver during a particularly terrible Washington, D.C., commute. I was angry and I let everyone know it. My secretary, being of a more temperate personality, suggested that I calm down. She reminded me that the other driver was probably unaware that I even existed. She went on to point out that that driver had been controlling my life ever since I walked in the office.

Humor Break

Friend to high-strung, super-charged entrepreneur: Have you ever had a heart attack?
Entrepreneur: No, but I'm a carrier.

I realized that managing other drivers with body language is somewhat like worrying. It does no good, no matter how well you do it. So I quit doing it. What I do instead is invest in myself by listening to motivational and educational audiotape programs while I drive. They keep me on the cutting edge, provide me with all kinds of new entrepreneurial venture ideas, and help me stay motivated even on days when I experience a temporary slump. I have become so addicted that my car looks like a tape library, a classroom on wheels. Because I drive about 20,000 miles per year, I estimate that I spend about 445 hours per year in my car. I listen to audiotapes about half that time. Since an average three-credit graduate course requires about 45 hours of class time, I get the equivalent of 15 graduate credits per year just by listening to educational and motivational audiotapes while driving in my car. That's like getting a new master's degree every three years. And I get that using time that would otherwise be totally wasted. (That is what I call a significant return on investment.) Another benefit is that it feels as if my driving time is cut in half, especially on long trips when I am by myself. The excitement of learning powerful new self-development strategies gets me so excited and involved that time just simply flies by. Before I know it, I have reached my destination. So that you can take advantage of this powerful strategy, I have listed several sources of excellent audiotape programs at the end of this chapter.[29] Turn to it, order at least one program, and start listening while driving. You will find yourself energized and on the road to success.

Insight Break

Some people are so busy chopping wood, they don't have time to sharpen their axe.

—Unknown

HOW TO GET THE MOST OUT OF YOUR NEXT LEARNING EXPERIENCE

Another powerful strategy that will help you stay ahead of your competition is attending seminars, workshops, and college courses. Interacting (in today's lingo, networking) with people who have the expertise that you are seeking and who have arrived where you are trying to get to can save you considerable time, money, and mistakes, and eliminate countless false trials. If you are currently employed, you are probably attending corporate-sponsored educational programs. (If you are not, you should get your employer to get with it; your competitors are doing so.)

Unfortunately, my experience has revealed that many people do not know how to get the most out of these learning experiences. In fact, unless it is training in a specific skill such as operating a computer, most people translate less than 10 percent of what they learn into action. One reason is that even if they listen and take notes, they usually do not review their notes or do anything else with their newly gained knowledge. I would like to acquaint you with a method for note taking that will help you to translate newly gained knowledge into action. I call this the CAT method, which I have adapted from a technique I learned from Ken Blanchard, coauthor of *The One-Minute Manager*.[30] Using this method requires you to divide your note paper into three sections as shown in Exhibit 6-5. Each of the three sections is discussed below.

Take Notes Like a CAT

C—Capture

Use this section to take notes during the presentation. This is the section in which you write fast and furiously, without concern for spelling, logic, or anything else. You must, of course, be able to decipher your own writing.

A—Apply

After the presentation, review and clarify the *Capture* information in this section. Unless you review your newly gained knowledge, you will forget about 87 percent after 24 hours. Focus on what information you want to keep and apply. Review this information on a regular basis for at least 21 days, or until it becomes a new habit. If it is too theoretical, modify it and try it out on family members or professional colleagues. Quiz each other on an ongoing basis.

Exhibit 6-5 Take Notes Like a CAT

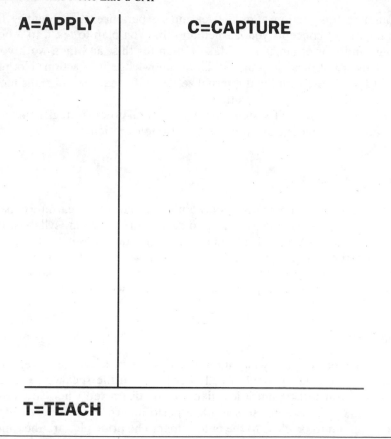

I have always been intrigued by how physicians are able to memorize and learn so much clinical data and medical knowledge. Working with physicians for many years gave me a chance to study how they do this. I found that physicians study, learn, and memorize just like you and I do, but with several major differences. Once they have learned new information, they apply it, but most importantly, they reinforce each other by continually "testing" and updating each other in a nondefensive manner. The rest of us need to use the same strategy, because in any discipline or profession, including yours, knowledge is not just changing at hyper-speed, it is literally unlimited, but our abilities to know and recall are finite. Find yourself a mentor or professional colleague and keep each other "on your toes."

T—Teach

Complete this section after the learning experience also. Identify the most important concepts you learned and that you plan to teach to others in your family or organization. Make a plan for this, and then work your plan. This is a critical step in translating knowledge into action. Nothing will help you understand and internalize new information and skills more effectively than teaching it to others.

In addition to the CAT system, there are several other strategies that will help you get the most from your next learning experience.

Know What You Want

Before you begin, know what you want to get out of the learning experience. One way to accomplish this is to review the program, syllabus, description, or at least the title ahead of time. Also take a look at the speaker's or instructor's credentials. Before the speaker begins, formulate at least one specific question that you want answered. This will make you goal focused and will help you pay closer attention to what is said.

Sit up Front

It is much easier to pay attention when you have a chance to read the speaker's body language and directly benefit from the speaker's enthusiasm. Also, you will be much less likely to be distracted when you sit up front. Think of it as going to see a live performance, where most people pay a premium to be close to the entertainer. The principles are the same, except in this case you will not have to pay any more to be close to the action.

Listen Actively

Listening actively means that you have asked yourself, What's in it for me? Your body is there already, why not get your mind in gear as well? If you do not want to do that, find an opportune moment and leave. Many people think that to do so is discourteous to the speaker, but I do not agree. The speaker is there to provide a service, and if that service does not meet your needs, you should feel free to leave during a stretch break or at any other time when it will not distract the other learners. Your time is too precious to be wasted.

Assume a Positive Attitude

If you work at it hard enough, you can get something out of *every* learning experience. The problem with some learners is that they use all of their mental energies trying to catch the speaker making a mistake, or worse, trying to prove to themselves that they are just as smart as the speaker is. Although it may be true, this is extremely nonproductive behavior. After all, you are not getting paid to prove the speaker wrong. Just because someone gets in front of an audience does not make her omnipotent. A much more productive strategy is for you to use your abundant mental energies to figure out what you or someone in your family or organization can do with the information. If you find yourself slipping into a critiquing mode, use the PIN technique that we discussed in Chapter 4 to pull yourself out of it. Never criticize unless you can do it better. No matter what, while you are sitting in the audience you will not have a chance to do it better. Your turn will come when you get yourself invited to be a speaker.

Insight Break

I keep six honest serving men
They taught me all I knew:
Their names are What and Why and When
And How and Where and Who.

—Rudyard Kipling

Ask Questions

If something is not clear, ask a question or ask for a practical example. If you do not understand it, there is probably at least one other person who is equally confused. If the speaker has not told you how he prefers to handle questions, that is his problem. Experienced speakers let the audience know whether they prefer to field questions during or after the presentation. In any case, you are the customer, so be assertive and ask. Remember, there are no dumb questions, only dumb answers.

Keep an Open Mind

It has been said that there is no such thing as an open mind, meaning that all of us are influenced by our values and belief systems. On the other hand, you can maintain a sense of curiosity and inquisitiveness that will allow you to be open to other people's ideas. (The PIN strategy works wonders for this as well.) This does not mean that you have to adopt others' ideas. It simply means that you use your abundant mental energies to avoid discarding information just because it seems "far out." Sometimes you can use unusual ideas as mental steppingstones to help you to come up with realistic and creative solutions.

Humor Break

Talking about keeping an open mind reminds me of a humorous anecdote.

This is a story about a young man who was hitchhiking through Tennessee. This must have been his lucky day. An elderly farmer offered him a ride in his beat-up truck. As they were riding through the countryside, the farmer's conversation soon turned to the subject of moonshine, obviously something the farmer knew quite a bit about. After a while, noting the young man's skepticism, the farmer reached behind the seat and produced a jug of what looked like dark brown syrup. When the young man protested that he didn't drink very much and didn't really want any, the farmer became insistent. Handing him the jug, the farmer said, "Take a sip. Take several sips. I insist!" The young man was equally insistent and continued to refuse. Finally, totally frustrated, the farmer brought the truck to a screeching halt. He reached behind the seat one more time, and produced a shotgun, which he pointed at the young man's head. "I said take a sip. Take several sips. I insist!" At this point, the young man answered, "OK, OK. I've got an open mind. I'll try this stuff." He took several hardy swallows, not knowing how incredibly strong the moonshine was. He began to gag. His eyes teared, his throat constricted, and he coughed relentlessly. The farmer looked at the young man with a big grin and said, "Awfully good, ain't it?" Unable to respond, the young man just nodded. The farmer then handed the young man the gun and said with a grin, "I'm glad you like it after all. Now you point the shotgun at me, and make me take a drink."

Now that you have reengaged your funny bone, you are ready to meet someone who has translated the education principle into a *WINNING* practice.

PEP² IN ACTION—EDUCATION:
BENJAMIN S. CARSON, SR., M.D.

Dr. Ben Carson, known to his colleagues as "gentle Ben" and to his patients as "Miracle Hands," gained national prominence in 1987 when he headed the 70-member surgical team that separated the Binder Siamese twins.

Carson was raised, together with his brother, in the inner city of Detroit, Michigan, by a mother with a third-grade education. His future did not look bright. He had no father and no other positive role models. He lacked motivation, had poor grades, and possessed a violent temper that caused him to almost kill his good friend. But he did have his mother, Sonya Carson, who had a vision for her two sons. She was determined that they would make something of themselves, even if their environment said otherwise. Carson was able to internalize that belief. With a strong belief in God, incredible willpower, and relentless hard work, Carson propelled himself to the top of his high school class. As a result, he won a full scholarship to Yale University. He continued his studies at the University of Michigan Medical School. At age 33 he became Director of Pediatric Neurosurgery at the Johns Hopkins Hospital in Baltimore, Maryland.

He is internationally renowned for his "gifted hands" and his ability to successfully perform extremely intricate and dangerous neurological surgeries, which have saved hundreds of children who had no other hope. Carson is also known for his numerous scientific papers, motivational presentations, and national television appearances, which have celebrated his skills, decency, compassion, intellect, and courage. In recognition of his contributions, he has received innumerable achievement awards as well as six honorary doctorates. He is an extraordinary human being who serves as an exceptional role model to others, regardless of race, sex, or occupation.

WR: I have identified six critical success principles that, based on my studies, appear to make a difference between winning and losing in the game of life. These six principles, collectively called the PEP² principles, are positive self-esteem, purpose, energy, education, positive attitude, and perseverance. One principle that appears to have made a significant difference in your life is *education*. You grew up in the inner city of Detroit, without a father, not unlike many Black families today. In that environment, there must be a feeling of hopelessness and frustration. Yet, you were able to get out of it. How did you do it?

BC: First of all, in the case of my brother and myself, I believe we were able to avoid that sense of hopelessness because of my mother, who, even though she had only a third-grade education and was out there struggling, working two or three jobs at a time, never felt that she was a victim. She always thought it was possible for a person to somehow determine his or her own status in life and that the only people who were victims were people who chose to be victims. And she did not choose to be one. She was always telling us, "Anything that anyone else can do, you can do better." Almost brainwashing us. Even when we were doing well, she was always encouraging us to do better. I guess the thing that really made the biggest difference was that at one point, after she prayed for divine guidance, she just said no more TV. All we were allowed to do was watch two or three preselected programs per week. Instead of watching TV we had to read two books per week and submit book reports to her. At that time she couldn't read, but we didn't know that. She subsequently got her GED and went to college and became an interior decorator after we were on our way.

I was very resistant to the whole idea of reading. I didn't like to read; I didn't want to do it. I wanted to play and watch TV like the other kids. But after a few weeks, I got really interested in books, because all of a sudden I could go anywhere, do anything, be anybody, and meet anybody between the covers of those books. It opened up a whole new vista, a whole new horizon, which was particularly important because we were so poor we could never go anywhere or do anything. All of a sudden I could go anywhere. After a few weeks, I couldn't wait to get home from school and get into those books. Of course, the more I read, the more perspective I developed. The world wasn't just that little community I lived in anymore. It was the city, it was the state, it was the country, it was the world. I felt I knew a lot about the people who live in Switzerland. I knew about the plants that grow on the Serengeti plain. I knew about volcanic ashes. I knew all of these things. I didn't feel that I belonged just to one little inner-city community anymore. And that's the way I started to view myself. I began not to worry so much about what the peer group had to say because I realized that they were simply products of that little microcosm of the world and that they did not have perspective and that they couldn't possibly understand. It may have seemed like I was setting myself up as a superior being, but it wasn't so much that as it was that I knew that they didn't have any perspective and I knew that people without perspective don't go anywhere. That's what changed it for me. I think my brother developed the same sort of perspective. We could look ahead and we could see ourselves 10, 15, 20, and 25 years down the road. And we knew, with that kind of perspective, that what we did today impacted significantly on what we were going to be doing 25 years from now.

WR: It seems that reading reinforced your mother's self-fulfilling prophecy. Many parents, including myself, tell their children, "You can do anything." But when they fail, they begin to doubt their parent's positive affirmations because they are not backed up by their actual experiences. In your case, reading positively reinforced what your mother was saying to you. Reading opened up your perspective. To quote from your book, *Gifted Hands*, "If you can read, you can learn just about anything."[31] That coincides with one of the mottoes I have adopted over the years, which is that I can do anything *if* I want to do it badly enough. And so can any other human being.

BC: The average human being has over 14 billion cells and connections in his or her brain. That's a lot of firepower. And it wasn't just put there to hold your ears apart. I think it was intended that we should be able to achieve intellectually. Yet most people go around almost like animals, allowing circumstances to control them rather than controlling circumstances. They go on without spending time to intellectualize, to contemplate, to think. It's very unusual for anyone to say, "I'm going to sit down for a while, and I'm just going to contemplate my life and where I'm going and what is the direction of my life." People will not invest one hour in a lifetime to do that.

WR: That is an interesting observation, especially since you have not had a chance to read my book. In the chapter that deals with the purpose principle, I make the observation that most people spend more time planning a holiday party than planning their life. We don't take the time to reflect on where we want to go. Reading and being able to transport yourself into other worlds gave you perspective and long-range goals.

BC: Not only that, but the important thing about reading is that you have to take those letters and make them into words, the words into sentences, and the sentences into concepts. You have to use your imagination. You don't have to do that when watching television. The other important thing is that when you read you learn how to spell because you see the words. You learn where things need to be capitalized, you learn how to punctuate, and you learn syntax and grammar. This, in turn, teaches you how to speak better. And when you learn how to speak better you find yourself able to move much further in society. People form their initial impression of you by how you communicate. If you haven't learned those skills, you can be smart and know a lot of facts, but you simply are not going to be able to convey your value as an individual, and many opportunities will escape you.

WR: Plus, people discount you. They discount you up front and say, "Well, he's not very smart, not very educated. Why should I waste my time?" All of a sudden you have this obstacle that you have to overcome. You know the old saying, "You never get a second chance to make a first impression." It's true. I tell people why waste your time, start off right the first time.

One quotation from your book that I would like you to talk about is "No knowledge is ever wasted."

BC: I think I said that after I talked about my pursuit of knowledge of art and classical music. When I was in the 10th grade, I had a backsliding episode. I got involved with peers. Clothes, basketball, and the group all became more important than studying. My grades plummeted. After overcoming that situation and recognizing again that if I wanted to control my destiny, I had to have a grasp of knowledge, I became an A student again in the 11th and 12th grades. I had a goal of being a contestant on "College Bowl." I was pretty good at most of the academic subjects but I didn't know much about classical music or art, so I decided that I needed to learn these things. I would go downtown and roam through the galleries until I knew every painting. I listened to classical music until I got to the point where I could name most pieces almost immediately. I never got to be on "College Bowl," but when it came time for residency selection, the fellow who was in charge was a tremendous classical music buff and was so enthralled by me and the knowledge I had of classical music that there was no way I wasn't getting into the program, because he had to have somebody to discuss the stuff with. The knowledge of classical music paid me back handsomely. I had to find a way to distinguish myself from all those other excellent applicants, and that was what did it. As a consequence, I say that no knowledge is ever wasted. Often young people, and this particularly occurs among minorities, will say, "Oh, that is irrelevant to my culture. I don't need to know that." My response is that if you want to influence your household, then you only need to know what's relevant to your household. If you want to influence your community, you need to know what's relevant to your community. If you want to influence your state, then you need to know what's relevant to your state. If you want to influence the world, then you need to know what's relevant to the world. It really doesn't matter what socioeconomic background you have. If you want to be an individual who is relevant to everyone, you must know what is relevant to everyone. It's as plain and simple as that. You make the choice. You decide how significant you want to be and then tailor your education accordingly.

WR: I think that is a beautiful concept. It is one that I emphasize over and over again in my book. I think that the difficulty in our society, speaking of the United States as a whole, is that everybody wants to succeed. Consider sports, for example. There are lots of role models, people who are successful by most people's standards to the nth degree, even to the point that it has gotten out of hand. But nobody wants to pay the price. We all look at someone who has succeeded as lucky. I'm sure you get that.

BC: You're absolutely right. You do have to pay the price. But I don't necessarily agree that many of the sports stars are successful. What you have to recognize is that only 7 in 1,000,000 make it as a starter in the NBA. And only 1 out of 10,000 in the music field makes it. The average career span in professional sports is only $2^{1}/_{2}$ to $3^{1}/_{2}$ years. Five to 10 years down the road, most of those people find themselves back on the streets. Now, over the course of a lifetime I would not consider that a successful career. But the media hypes these things up to the point where you have got millions and millions of young people wandering after these people, almost worshiping them, thinking this is the epitome of success, not realizing that the total picture is not one of success. The same thing occurs in the entertainment field. Even though 1 in 10,000 makes it, what you have to recognize is that of those who do make it, the majority of them are no longer in the public eye in 10 to 15 years. The majority are groveling around in some dingy nightclub trying to get people to remember who they are. And many of them can't even make it in nightclubs. Many of them end up selling clothes behind some counter in a department store. Not that selling clothes is bad, but it's a big drop from stardom. It's a miserable life when you haven't really done anything that contributes to society, when you haven't really done anything to potentiate your talents and you have to spend the rest of your life dreaming over a few years.

WR: Don't you think it is the easy-street concept again? It looks so easy. All I have to learn is to shoot baskets. If I get really good at it I will have it made.

BC: That's why lotteries make so much money. Even though the odds are ridiculous, people want to go out there and put their hard-earned cash down with the thought of striking it rich.

WR: I tell people that I am a winner automatically because I do not play the lottery. I invest in myself instead. Let's go back to the idea that our brain is not there just to keep our ears apart. Different studies related to brain power have identified that we use anywhere from $1/10$th of 1 percent up to a maximum of 10 percent of our capability. That is really sad.

BC: It is sad. I don't ever like to quantify what we use. I just like to say that we don't come anywhere close to our capacity. For the most part, we never go past stage 1. The thing about education that really bothers me a lot is how we are doing compared with the other industrialized countries of the world. We're last, particularly in science and math. Our emphasis is in the wrong place. We actually have made our youngsters think that science and math are difficult. They shudder when they think about higher mathematics and chemistry, when in fact these things are not difficult at all. But like everything else you must understand the building blocks in order to build. You wouldn't be able to spell if you didn't know the alphabet. You've got to learn the alphabet so you can spell. And you've got to learn certain principles to be able to deal fluently with science and mathematics. The way it's presented is such a hodgepodge that people tend to miss this and miss that. Very frequently, teachers do not have a grasp of it themselves and cannot break it down. If you break it down, it becomes quite simple. Make it real to the students' lives, and they will understand and learn it. That's another part of our problem. We do not place the correct emphasis on our teaching institutions. We do not give our young people the kind of teachers they need to have. We do not pay teachers enough to make the people who understand the material want to go into teaching. Until we recognize this, I really don't see it getting a whole lot better. Until we start deemphasizing sports and entertainment and start emphasizing intellectual achievement, why should our young people pride themselves on that? When you go into your average high school you see giant displays, and trophies—all-state this and all-state that. You might see some tiny list in a corner somewhere about who made National Honor Society or who is on the honor roll. If you're lucky, you'll see something about a science fair. It's completely out of whack. Just listen to television around the time of the Academy Awards; there is all this hoopla for weeks and weeks about who's going to get best picture, who's going to be best director, who's going to get best supporting actor—on and on. In-depth analysis, as if this stuff is really important. Then, when it comes time for the Nobel prizes, it's "So and so won the Nobel prize in physics. Now on to entertainment." It's ridiculous! I don't think people stop long enough to realize this.

WR: Not wanting to pay the price and delaying gratification—it comes back to that. The anology I always use is people who overeat for 30 years, then, all of a sudden, they look in the mirror and say, "Oh my, I'm fat!" Then they go on the latest diet. And if the diet doesn't get the weight off in 30 days, it's absolutely no good. Forget the fact that it took 30 years to put it on, they want it off *now*. It's the idea that we don't want to invest for the long term. Give me gratification and give it to me now. If I can't have it now, forget it!

BC: The concept of delayed gratification is another one I like to talk about because, again, here's where television has hurt us. So many of the pictures you look at emphasize the life styles of the rich and famous. All the *things* they have. One can get the impression that if you're not a millionaire by age 40, something's wrong with you. It puts inordinate amounts of pressure on young people. They think, "How can I get all these things? How can I have all of this?" Consequently, they don't think very seriously about those things that require a lot of in-depth work.

WR: It's like sowing and reaping. You must plant the seed and nurture it, and if you weed it, take care of it, and water it long enough, then sooner or later you'll be able to harvest. We don't want to do that. We just want the fruit. Let me ask you about creativity. You demystified it in your book. You said creativity is nothing more than learning to do something with a different perspective. Let's talk a little bit about that.

BC: When babies are born, according to child psychologists here at Johns Hopkins, 98 percent of them are creative. Now you ask yourself the question, Why is that? It's because they have to be creative. What is there to do when you're a baby? You'll notice how a baby is totally fascinated with a piece of cotton or a piece of paper. They're using their imagination— working with that thing. In this country, by the time young people reach the age of 18 or so, child psychologists say that only about 3 percent are creative. Why is that? What's happened to all that creativity? It's gone because they don't have to be creative. Everything is done for them, particularly in terms of entertainment. Our society is geared toward entertainment by television. You don't have to think.

People who are creative usually are creative because they need to be. They need something. And the reason they know they need something is because they stop and think about it. I need that, now how can I get it? Of course, the logical thing first of all is to say, Does it already exist? If the answer is no, then the next logical step is to figure out how to make it happen. If that means doing something new and different, at least you've stopped and identified what that something new and different is, which is half of coming up with it. If you don't stop and identify it, you're never going to come up with it. Again, it goes back to really being able to start to develop perspective in terms of where you're going and what you need. And until you can do that, creativity simply will not be a byproduct.

WR: In other words, you are suggesting that abundance inhibits our ability to be creative, because we get everything on a silver platter. The other difficulty we have in our society is that we're not rewarded for creativity. As a parent, I'm not sure that I've always done the best. When my girls were little, we demanded order, conformity, and obedience. Once you get into the world of business, they too, do not reward creativity. If you're creative you are accused of being in the clouds. If you ask people to come up with synonyms, nobody will ever put executive and creative together. In fact those may be antonyms. In general, we're really not rewarded for being creative.

BC: I used to walk around with a little notebook when I was a teenager putting down ideas of things I thought needed to be done. I remember the summer I worked for the Ford Motor Company I decided we needed air bags for automobiles. I worked the idea up, put it in the suggestion box, and, of course, no one responded. And years later, when the air bag came along, I always wondered if it was my idea.

WR: People have referred to you as having gifted hands. But you talk about the idea that too many people pigeonhole other people because they're just a secretary or they just have a little education. That's where we really think alike. I firmly believe that *every* human being has some sort of gift.

BC: It goes back to taking time to think. You have to be able to say to yourself, "What have I done right in life? What have I done wrong?" Go to somebody you respect and ask, "What do you think I'm good at?" You start seeing a pattern. You start recognizing what you're good at. Why not choose a career along those lines? If you decide to go into something you're not talented at you might be all right, you may get by, but you're not going to excel. Again, people don't stop to think. They do what mommy and daddy think they should do, or what their peer group says, or they go with the flow without stopping to analyze where it is they really want to go.

WR: In my book, I tell people that they should list their strengths and weaknesses. Then I tell them to look at their lists and consider whether what they want to do allows them to build on those strengths. If it does, and they stick with it (perseverance principle), then they will succeed. If not, no matter how hard they work, they are never going to excel at it.

BC: It's so natural, yet people don't stop and think about it. That's one of the major keys to success in any career.

WR: But on to something else. Black America today—particularly what happens to Black males in American today. The statistics are absolutely overwhelming. What words do you have for Black America?

BC: The fact of the matter is that America is a racist country. I always say if you walk into an auditorium of racist people, they have a problem, you don't. They're worried about you sitting next to them. You can sit any-where you want. This is the attitude that Black America has to adopt. They need to adopt these principles of success we've talked about. Build on your own strengths, look at where you want to go, and stop worrying about what someone else is doing. The opportunities exist in this country. It doesn't matter if everybody likes you. It doesn't matter if everybody smiles at you and says you're a great person. That's insignificant. What matters is what you can do, particularly to make yourself into a valuable individual, a person who other people respect for what you know and what you can do. Once that occurs, people become color blind. This whole concept of being owed something and putting energy into that is a waste of time. That energy should go toward developing your talent and developing your worth rather than worrying about what's owed you. Life is not fair. You make your own breaks by developing those talents that you have. That's what I would tell people. I want people to stop complaining so much and start thinking about positive things.

WR: What I'm hearing you say is exactly how I feel. It really doesn't matter whether you're male, female, black, blue, or orange. The bottom line is how you help people, what service you deliver to another human being. That is what is really going to make the difference in the long run.

BC: You've only got so much energy, so why waste it on all that negative stuff, the stuff you can't change.

WR: On behalf of myself and my readers, I want to thank you for a most inspirational interview. Keep talking to the young people of America. They need you. And most importantly, continue to *MAKE it a WINNING life!*

SUMMARY: A TRIP BACK TO THE FUTURE

- Future wealth and power will be created from the exchange of data, information, and knowledge.

- In a rapidly changing "knowledge economy," learning how to learn and internalizing the belief that learning is a lifelong process is a critical survival and success skill.
- People full of PEP[2] invest heavily in the most important resource they own: themselves.
- Investing in lifelong education has a positive impact on your "bottom line."
- Effective self-directed learners
  —prefer to learn alone;
  —complete learning projects;
  —accept responsibility for their own learning;
  —enjoy learning; and
  —like to solve problems.
- The five-step self-directed learning process is as follows:
  1. Conduct an educational needs assessment.
  2. Define learning objectives.
  3. Establish an action plan.
  4. Take action.
  5. Evaluate your effectiveness.
- Learning how to think is facilitated by a seven-step action system:
  1. Establish a routine time for thinking.
  2. Define a problem.
  3. Generate at least 20 solutions.
  4. Take a break.
  5. Prioritize the solutions.
  6. Establish an action plan.
  7. Take action.
- The creative (holistic) thinking process consists of five steps:
  1. preparation;
  2. incubation;
  3. manipulation;
  4. illumination; and
  5. verification.
- Listening to motivational and educational audiotape programs will reduce your nonproductive driving time and provide you with a competitive edge.
- Strategies to get the most out of group learning include
  —using the CAT note-taking system;
  —defining questions or learning objectives ahead of time;
  —sitting up front;
  —listening actively;

—maintaining a positive attitude;
—being inquisitive; and
—keeping an open mind.

SUCCESS ACTION STEPS

❏ Take an inventory of your "personal" investment strategy by making a list of the things you have done within the past 60 days that will help you appreciate in the long run. If you cannot list at least three things, make up an action plan to remedy this serious handicap.

❏ Calculate your annual gross income and multiply by 2 percent. This figure represents your self-development budget for the year. Develop an annual plan identifying continuing eduction and self-development activities you plan to engage in during the coming year. This could consist of books, audiotapes, seminars, workshops, college courses, or anything that will increase your worth. Put these activities on your calendar, and stick to your plan! Next year, increase your self-development budget to 3 percent, the following year to 4 percent, and the year after to 5 percent. Keep it there, and watch yourself rise to the top!

❏ For the next six months, set aside at least 2½ hours per week (that is only 2 percent of your available time [24 hours minus 8 hours for sleeping equals 16 hours of available time per day]) on your calendar to invest in your own excellence. Stick to it religiously.

❏ Within the next 30 days, set aside 3 hours to go to the public library to explore. You will be stunned by the impressive self-development resources available.

❏ Right now, turn to the audiotape sources (note 29) listed at the end of this chapter. Request ordering information from one source. When you receive it, order one audiotape program. Do not worry about your investment. All suppliers of quality merchandise provide you with a money-back guarantee. (If they don't, you should not be ordering from them.) After you receive the program, establish a new habit by listening to educational audiotapes at least one way of your commute every day for the next 21 days. Watch yourself outperform the competition without giving up any discretionary time.

❏ During the next two weeks, identify something that you have wanted to learn for a long time. Set up a learning action plan and a time line. Note progress benchmarks on your calendar to keep you on track and help you get there over the next 6 to 12 months.

NOTES

1. H. Seneker, D. Latiniotis, C. Button and V. Catonvesti, "The *Forbes* Four Hundred," *Forbes* 144 (October 23, 1989): 144–147.
2. A. Toffler, *Powershift: Knowledge, Wealth, and Violence at the Edge of the 21st Century* (New York: Bantam Books, 1990).
3. Ibid., p. 239.
4. P. Senge, *The Fifth Discipline: The Art and Practice of the Learning Organization* (New York: Doubleday/Currency, 1990).
5. P. Senge, "The Leader's New Work: Building Learning Organizations," *Sloan Management Review* 7 (Fall 1990): 7–23.
6. T. Stewart, "Brain Power," *Fortune* 123 (June 3, 1991): 44–60.
7. A. Toffler, *Powershift*, p. 238.
8. A. Toffler, *Powershift*, p. 10.
9. C. Argyris, "Teaching Smart People How to Learn," *Harvard Business Review* 69 (May–June 1991): 99–109.
10. C. Livneh, "Characteristics of Lifelong Learners in the Human Services Professions," *Adult Education Quarterly* 38 (Spring 1988): 149–159.
11. S. S. Dubin, "Obsolescence or Life-Long Education: A Choice for the Professional," *American Psychologist* 27 (May 1972): 486–498.
12. B. Tracy, "Seven Secrets of Self-Made Millionaires," *Insight* (Chicago: Nightingale-Conant, 1987). Audiotape program with accompanying written materials. Nightingale-Conant Corp., 7300 North Lehigh Avenue, Chicago, IL 60648.
13. J. Kremer, *1001 Ways to Market Your Books,* 3d ed. (Fairfield, IA: Ad-Lib Publications, 1990).
14. Based on 1988–1989 Nielsen Media Research Report on Television, as reported in *Information Please Almanac* (Boston: Houghton Mifflin, 1991).
15. J. Kremer, *1001 Ways to Market Your Books.*
16. Data based on 1987 statistics provided by the American Society for Training and Development Information Center, Alexandria, Virginia.
17. A. Toffler, *Future Shock* (New York: Random House, 1970).
18. A. P. Carnevale, L. J. Gainer, and A. S. Meltzer, *Workplace Basics: The Skills Employers Want* (Alexandria, VA: American Society for Training and Development, n.d.), p. 8.
19. A. Tough, *The Adult Learning Projects,* 2d ed. (Toronto: Ontario Institute for Studies in Education, 1979).
20. M. Knowles, *Self-Directed Learning: A Guide for Learners and Teachers* (Englewood Cliffs, NJ: Cambridge Books, 1988).
21. W. J. Rinke, "Holistic Education: Toward a Functional Approach to Adult Education," *Lifelong Learning: The Adult Years* 5 (April 1982): 12–14, 25, and W. J. Rinke, "Holistic Education: An Answer?" *Training and Development Journal* 39 (August 1985): 67–68.
22. P. Drucker, "The Discipline of Innovation," *Harvard Business Review* 63 (May–June 1985): 67–72.
23. A. F. Osborn, *Applied Imagination* (New York: Scribner, 1953).
24. A. L. Delbecq, A. H. Van de Ven, and D. H. Gustafson, *Group Decision-Making Techniques in Program Planning* (Chicago: Scott, Foresman, 1974).
25. J. L. Adams, *Conceptual Blockbusting,* 3d ed. (New York: Norton, 1986).

26. K. Albrecht, *Brain Power: Learn to Improve Your Thinking Skills* (Englewood Cliffs, NJ: Prentice-Hall, 1980).

27. R. von Oech, *A Whack on the Side of the Head: How to Unlock Your Mind to Innovation* (New York: Warner Books, 1983).

28. V. R. Ruggiero, *The Art of Thinking: A Guide to Critical and Creative Thought,* 2d ed. (New York: Harper, 1988).

29. Three excellent sources for educational and motivational audiotapes are:
    1. Nightingale-Conant Corp., 7300 North Lehigh Avenue, Chicago, IL 60648
    2. The Zig Ziglar Corp., 3300 Earhart, Suite 204, Carrolton, TX 75006
    3. Achievement Publishers, P.O. Box 1289, Olney, MD 20830-1289

30. K. Blanchard and S. Johnson, *The One-Minute Manager* (New York: Morrow, 1982).

31. B. Carson with C. Murphy, *Gifted Hands: The Ben Carson Story* (Grand Rapids, MI: Zondervan, 1990): 39.

ANSWERS TO MENTAL STRETCH EXERCISES
Page 156

The answer to the number puzzle in Exhibit 6-3 is readily found through experimentation once you realize that 5 is the center of the nine-number sequence. See Exhibit 6-6.

Exhibit 6-6 Solution: Number Exercise

2	**9**	**4**
7	**5**	**3**
6	**1**	**8**

Page 164

There are two optimum answers to the cake-cutting exercise.

Answer 1 involves cutting the cake as shown in Exhibit 6-7, which results in a total of 11 pieces.

Exhibit 6-7 Solution #1: Cake-Cutting Exercise

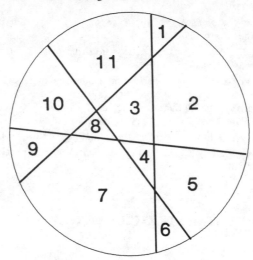

Answer 2, which is even better, assumes that the cake is three dimensional, which it is, even though I did not draw it that way. Now you can cut seven pieces with the first three cuts, and then cut the cake horizontally for the last cut. This will give you a total of 14 pieces, as shown in the Exhibit 6-8. I know these slices are a bit messy, but that's how it goes when you get into a creative thinking mode.

Exhibit 6-8 Solution #2: Cake-Cutting Exercise

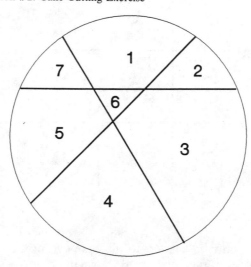

Wasn't that a "piece of cake"?

7

Positive Attitude

A positive attitude is like a bank account. You can't continually draw on it without making deposits.

—*Wolf J. Rinke*

Here we are, heading toward orbit. Your PEP² success rocket is moving ahead at full speed. Now all we have to do is sit back and enjoy, right? Well, not quite, because something happens when you get into orbit. The air gets much thinner. In fact, it is totally devoid of oxygen. This means that if we want to continue moving up we must add something to our fuel. That additive is the oxidizer, a positive attitude. Our journey is very demanding, with many disappointments, setbacks, and stresses. The only way we will make it to the highest level is to have an internal mechanism that will sustain us and help us stay on course (see Exhibit 7-1).

PREVIEW OF COMING ATTRACTIONS

We will first find out how well you PASS, meaning how well you do on the Positive Attitude Scope Scale (Exhibit 7-2). After that, you will be ready to learn what it takes to *make* every day a great day, how our attitudes are related to our mental and physical well-being, and why it is absolutely essential that you adopt and maintain a positive attitude if you want to succeed in the game of life, love, and business.

POSITIVE ATTITUDE: WHAT IS ALL THE FUSS ABOUT?

Attitudes are like the common cold—they are catching. The trouble is that negative attitudes are caught just as readily as positive attitudes. My study of people has suggested that negative people outnumber positive

Exhibit 7-1 Your PEP² Rocket—Part 5: Fueled and Oxidized (Positive Attitude)

OXIDIZER

people by about three to one. I also have found that the one characteristic virtually all people with PEP² have in common is a positive attitude. Contrary to what most of us believe, a positive attitude is created. It is not given by some mysterious force; instead, it is a state of mind. To be more precise, it is a state of your subconscious, which is under your control.

In my *MAKE it a WINNING life* seminars, I like to ask how many people

Exhibit 7-2 Positive Attitude Scope Scale (PASS)

Instructions

Using the scale below, circle the number that most closely indicates the frequency with which each statement applies to you *or* the degree to which you agree or disagree with each statement. (People have different preferences and opinions; therefore, there are no right or wrong answers.)

Never	Almost Never	Infrequently	Almost Always	Always
1	2	3	4	5
Strongly Disagree	Disagree	Neither Agree Nor Disagree	Agree	Strongly Agree

1. Every day is a great day for me.   1 2 3 4 5 _____

2. Attitude is more important than aptitude.   1 2 3 4 5 _____

3. When I meet people for the first time, I tend to notice their shortcomings.   1 2 3 4 5 _____

4. I like all people.   1 2 3 4 5 _____

5. I have clearly defined, written lifetime goals.   1 2 3 4 5 _____

6. I think life is incredibly exciting.   1 2 3 4 5 _____

7. I tend to be a perfectionist.   1 2 3 4 5 _____

8. People tend to like themselves best when they are with me.   1 2 3 4 5 _____

9. I experience at least four minor illnesses throughout the year.   1 2 3 4 5 _____

10. I find myself laughing and chuckling several times every day.   1 2 3 4 5 _____

11. When I go to bed at night, I tell myself that tomorrow will be a great day.   1 2 3 4 5 _____

12. I believe I control my health.   1 2 3 4 5 _____

13. I engage in an aerobic exercise program at least three times per week.   1 2 3 4 5 _____

14. When I get up in the morning, I think about the problems that I have to solve that day.   1 2 3 4 5 _____

15. I find that many people try to take advantage of me.   1 2 3 4 5 _____

16. I believe that things work out for the best in the long run.   1 2 3 4 5 _____

17. When I make a mistake, I tend to get on my case.   1 2 3 4 5 _____

18. I tend to worry.   1 2 3 4 5 _____

Exhibit 7-2 continued

19. I expect to win in life, and usually do.	1 2 3 4 5	_____
20. People who know me would describe me as an optimist.	1 2 3 4 5	_____

Total _____

Scoring Instructions

Score items 1, 2, 4, 5, 6, 8, 10, 11, 12, 13, 16, 19, and 20 in accordance with the number that you circled. For example, if you circled a 2 for question 1, you earned 2 points, which you should write on the line next to question 1.

Reverse-score items 3, 7, 9, 14, 15, 17, and 18. This means that you have to turn the scale around to score these items, so that 1 = 5, 2 = 4, 3 = 3, 4 = 2, and 5 = 1.

Examples:

1. Every day is .... 1 2 3 4 ⑤ = 5
2. Attitude is more important .... 1 ② 3 4 5 = 2
3. When I meet people .... 1 ② 3 4 5 = 4

Total your points.

Interpretation of Your Score

91–100 *Exceptional.* You PASS with flying colors. Most people consider you to be an eternal optimist and a fun person to be around.

81–90 *Excellent.* This is a very high PASSing score. When life hands you a lemon, you get busy making lemonade. No one will love this book more than you.

71–80 *Very Good.* You have PASSed. You have the ability to give yourself a checkup from the neck up. This chapter will provide you with additional tools.

61–70 *Fair.* You just missed a PASSing score. I would guess that you look through the keyhole with both eyes.

<60 Your glass tends to be half empty. It is time to sit up and pay attention to the principles outlined in this chapter. They will make the difference between winning and losing in life, love, and business.

would like to have a great day, every day, for the rest of their lives. Typically all hands go up. Next I ask how many believe it is possible to have a great day every day. Typically only about one-third to one-half of the hands go up. Unfortunately, most people do not realize that they have given up a very precious freedom—the freedom to decide what kind of day and what kind of life they are going to have! They have given that basic choice to someone else—their spouse, their boss, their children, their doctor, anyone, so long as it is not themselves. These folks, who are mostly externals, have not accepted the reality that they, and only they, are in charge of programming their own subconscious.

But you know who is in charge of that subconscious mind. (If you don't, reread Chapter 3.) I suppose it is somewhat like happiness, which was best described by Abraham Lincoln when he said, "Most of us are about as happy as we make up our minds to be." Your attitude, good or bad, is your choice. Don't steal from yourself—always choose to *make* it a winning attitude.

Insight Break

The greatest discovery of my generation is that human beings, by changing the inner attitude of their minds, can change the outer aspects of their lives.

—William James

ATTITUDE OR APTITUDE: WHICH IS MORE IMPORTANT?

If you had to choose, which would you rather have, aptitude or attitude? (Watch out, this is a trick question!) Did you say aptitude? If you did, you gave both the right and the wrong answer. It is the right answer because aptitude is very important to success. At the same time, however, it is the wrong answer, because neither you nor anyone else has the ability to exercise any control over it. You either have it or you don't. And if you don't have it, then you have to blame your parents, your grandparents, your great-grandparents, and anyone else who has contributed to your genetic makeup. If you have accepted the concepts espoused in this book, then you recognize that this is really a moot point, because no matter how long you blame your ancestors, nothing will change. In fact, it is something that winners ignore.

Now for another trick question: Which is a better predictor of success, aptitude or attitude? Again, you are probably tempted to answer aptitude. But this time you are wrong. History books are full of people who lacked aptitude, but because of their attitude, their burning desire, and their relentless persistence they made it to the top. They include such well-known figures as Abraham Lincoln, Booker T. Washington, Golda Meir, Ronald Reagan, Martin Luther King, Jr., Franklin D. Roosevelt, Thomas Edison, Ty Cobb, Adolf Hitler, Joseph Stalin (had to throw in a couple of bad guys), Margaret Thatcher, Anwar Sadat, Indira Ghandi, Armand Hammer, and Lee Iacocca, to name a few.

Insight Break

Things may come to those who wait, but only the things left by those who hustle.

—Abraham Lincoln

My favorite is Wilma Rudolph. Born in 1940, three months prematurely, in a miserable shack in the woods of Tennessee, the little Black girl seemed destined to failure. Although she was able to overcome those terrible odds and live, lady luck did not look out for her. At age 4, Wilma contracted pneumonia and scarlet fever, a deadly combination that resulted in paralysis of both of her legs. She was told that she would have to wear an iron brace for the rest of her life, which meant that she would never again be able to walk normally. Wilma, however, with the help of her mother and an incredibly positive attitude, had a different idea.

She decided to prove the doctors wrong. Doing so meant learning to walk all over again. And, even though it was incredibly painful, she did not quit. She kept on practicing until one day, at the age of 9, she was able to do away with that ugly brace. That meant, though, that the learning process had to start all over again. Again, she persisted. About four years later Wilma Rudolph made medical history. She was once again able to walk normally. Something most of us take for granted cost Wilma over five years of relentless and painful practice.

But Wilma couldn't leave well enough alone. She decided that she was not just going to prove the doctors wrong, she was going to embarrass them. She decided to become (are your ready for this?) the world's greatest female runner! She entered her first race in high school at age 13. How well did she do? That depends on your perception. People full of PEP[2] would say that she did extremely well. After all, she finished the race. The skeptics, of course, noting that she came in last, would say that she did terribly.

They said her running was futile and self-destructive. Some even said that she wasn't "wired right." I would have to agree with them because she was not "wired" right; she was "wired" for success, and nothing was going to stop her. And nothing did. She continued racing, getting a little better each time she raced. Until finally, while still in high school, she began winning races. From that point on, nothing could slow her down.

After entering Tennessee State University, Wilma was fortunate to meet Ed Temple, a coach who recognized her determination and talent. The two began a journey, a journey of uncountable hours of intensive and painful training that culminated in Wilma Rudolph entering the 1960 Olympics. But the "miracle" did not end there. Wilma, after all her trials and tribulations, now faced her greatest challenge. To win in the Olympics she had to beat Jutta Heine, the young German woman known as the fastest woman of all time. And beat her Wilma did, but not just once. She beat Heine in the 100-meter race, in the 200-meter race, and, for good measure, again in the 400-meter relay, even after dropping the baton. That astonishing feat earned Wilma Rudolph, the crippled girl who was to never walk normally again, not just one, but three, gold medals.[1]

Now which would you rather have: aptitude or attitude?

Insight Break

It's not whether you get knocked down, it's whether you get up.
—Vince Lombardi

ATTITUDE: NATURE VERSUS NURTURE

But, you say, Wilma Rudolph had something I don't have: an incredibly positive attitude. She must have been one of those people who was born with it. For some reason, nature has endowed these people with that positive spirit. No matter how bad things get, they always have the ability to find something good in every tragedy. You may also be saying very quietly to yourself, Don't these people just make you sick?

I am not sure that I should answer that question. You can do that yourself. But what about the other question: Are people born with a positive attitude or is it something that one can learn?

Instead of getting into that scientific quagmire, which scientists have been debating since the dawn of civilization, I would like to share my story with you to see if that will help answer the nature versus nurture question. Generally speaking, I grew up in a fairly tough world. Experience and my parents had taught me that people could not be trusted. (I was able to internalize that primarily because I did not trust myself.) And because I did not like myself, most people, certainly the people who were different from me, were not very likable. I possessed an uncanny ability to focus on all the things that could go wrong. Most endeavors that I undertook were analyzed using the multiple-cost analysis method (instead of the cost/benefit analysis method). What I mean by that is that I would focus most of my mental energies on the costs and negatives of any new endeavor, decision, or event. After going through such an exercise, I generally found it impossible to see the good attributes or opportunities that were staring me right in the eyes. Because my mental shade had been closed, I succeeded in NIPing many a potentially great idea in the bud. (The PIN technique, which you have been applying since you read about it in Chapter 4, has helped me overcome this.) As a result, I tended to be generally negative, pessimistic, extremely conservative, mistrusting, and only moderately successful.

My parents were powerful role models for me, especially because I was an only child. Although always with my best interests at heart, they tended to be (and still are) very pessimistic. A specific example of their influence and the results of negativism dates back to the time when I was dating Marcela, the woman I have been happily married to for the past 23 years. When we were dating, my parents focused their mental energies on finding chinks in Marcela's armor. They pointed out that she was only of moderate means, that she did not have a college education, that her father barely spoke English, that she appeared to have little potential, etc. Even though I cannot remember all the things that they said were wrong with Marcela, I do remember being very critical and mistrusting of her. As a result, we argued frequently. Although you may think that is pretty normal, once we were married, I began reorienting my way of thinking. Instead of looking for the things that were wrong, I began to use my mental energies to focus on Marcela's strengths and to accept her for who she is instead of who I think she should be. The result? We have been happily married for 23 years. We trust each other implicitly, which is not an easy proposition because I am away from home quite a bit, and we seldom fight. In fact, we fought more during the 4 years that we were dating than we have during the 23 years that we have been married.

Humor Break

Friend talking to his buddy who is thinking about getting married: "Have you seen her mother?"

"Yep," answers the buddy, "but I'd rather marry the daughter!"

What is our secret? There are obviously many, but one strategy that I pursue vigorously is to accept my spouse *unconditionally for who she is, not who she should be.* The power of this was brought home to me recently when a friend confided that the reason she loved her puppy so much was that her puppy always loved and adored her. Her words: "It doesn't matter whether I'm made up, combed, or have my teeth brushed. Barney is always glad to see me."

Despite my efforts to persuade them otherwise, my parents continue to be saddled with negative thinking. In a short 5- to 10-minute telephone conversation, they are able to describe just about all of the ills of the world to me. The budget deficit is growing, politicians are crooked, AIDS is running rampant, Germany is spending too much money on rebuilding East Germany, one of their friends is again trying to take advantage of them, taxes are going through the roof, oil prices are out of control, the young people are dumb, Americans (or any ethnic group) are lazy, and so on—zappers ad nauscam. And that is during a short telephone conversation. You can imagine how much ground they cover during a visit. At times, all of the negativity overwhelms me and I have to take a walk just to rePEP[2] myself.

Why am I sharing these painful revelations with you? Because I have been able to overcome this legacy, which means that you can too! Just like that? you ask. Well, no, there is an *if,* which I think you know already. *If you want to badly enough.* But how did I accomplish it? That is what participants in my success workshops always want to know. The typical assumption is that some tragic event happened that forced a change upon me. Actually, that is not how it happened. It was a long, tedious process of about nine years, during which I relentlessly practiced what I now call the PEP[2] principles. My change process was initiated as a result of reading Denis Waitley's *The Psychology of Winning.*[2] It made me aware that being positive or negative is a conscious choice. I also became aware that life somehow seemed easier and more rewarding to the positive people I knew. Once I gained that recognition and accepted that attitude is a choice, I began to try out a wide variety of new behaviors. I began to build my positive thinking and language skills. I also reinforced my newly learned behaviors by repeatedly listening to a wide variety of motivational audiotape programs on my way to and from work.

Insight Break

The three great requirements for a happy life are something to do, something to love, and something to hope for.

—Joseph Addison

The other profound influence on my life is my wife, Marcela, who is one of the most upbeat and positive persons I have ever known. (I only began to really appreciate that after I started working on my own behavior change and became more positive myself.) Marcela supported and positively reinforced my new behaviors with her words and actions. Her support was critical because my colleagues and bosses, who for the most part were also stricken with "negativitis," were less charitable. I am sure that at times, when they were in an intense negative mode and I instead found something positive to say, they considered having me admitted for psychiatric care. (You see, anyone who behaves differently than everyone else must have a problem.) Fortunately, even though I was working in a medical center, that never happened.

My transformation, however, was not completed until I was able to move to an entirely different department, a department in which people were not nearly so afflicted by negativitis and therefore were able to more readily accept my behavior. Also, they did not have their minds made up regarding what they considered normal behavior for me. The concept of selective perception tells us that people only see, hear, or otherwise experience those things that they are ready to see, hear, or otherwise experience.

Now, you might say, what's the big deal? Well, when I completed my last military assignment, during the last four of my nine years of transformation, both senior officers (the commander and the executive officer of the huge medical center where I was assigned), commented on the positive impact that I had had on the medical center. To quote them, a positive impact because of "your numerous accomplishments and your ever-present positive attitude." Keep in mind that what they were talking about was the positive impact of 1 person in a hospital with 1,200 beds and some 3,000 employees. Alexander the Great was absolutely right when he said, "One can be a great many." In short, regardless of what you were born with (nature), regardless of how you were brought up, and regardless of how old you are, you too can develop a consistently positive attitude (nurture), *if you want to do it badly enough!*

Mental Stretch Break

In the next section, I want us to get serious and consider whether this positive mental attitude stuff is just a bunch of fluff or if it indeed has a scientific basis. Since I am going to ask you to stretch your assumptions, perhaps we should take a short break and exercise the right side of the brain. Just as before, translate each of the figures in Exhibit 7-3 into a meaningful word or phrase. (See end of chapter for answers.)

Exhibit 7-3 Brain Teasers

1 **HURRY** ↑	**2** *TIM ING*	**3** **H**A**I**R __
4 **THUMB**	**5** **s** **t** **one**	**6** **ankoolger**
7 STUD	**8** **HISTORY** **HISTORY** **HISTORY**	**9** **THIRIGHTNGS**

POSITIVE MENTAL ATTITUDE: FACT OR FICTION?

Let's put all this touchy-feely stuff aside and see if there is a bit more to this positive attitude idea. The mind–body connection has been explored by scientists and physicians since the days of Hippocrates, the father of medicine. There are numerous diseases, called psychosomatic illnesses, that acknowledge this relationship. The term *psychosomatic* is from the Greek words *psyche,* which means mind, and *soma,* which means body. Included in this category are such common ailments as tension headaches, body pains, upset stomachs, and more serious diseases such as depression, asthma, peptic (stomach) ulcers, rheumatoid arthritis (inflammation and stiffness of the joints), hypertension (high blood pressure), and neuroder-matitis (chronic skin disorders). Some physicians even include cancers. These ailments and diseases are so common that it has been estimated that about one-half of all visits to physicians in the United States are the result of psychosomatic illnesses.[3] Our collective consciousness about the importance of attitude on the healing process was raised by Norman Cousins in his best-selling book, *Anatomy of an Illness.*[4] Cousins, former editor of the *Saturday Review,* described how he "cured" himself from what doctors told him was an "incurable" disease (ankylosing spondylitis) by invoking a positive attitude and by laughter. Similarly, in *Head First: The Biology of Hope,*[5] Cousins made a very strong case that hope, faith, determination, and a positive attitude can strengthen the immune system and fight disease and even cancers. Since then, numerous scientific studies have demonstrated the importance of a positive attitude on one's perception of well-being, wellness, and health.

One example of the impact of a positive attitude on healing is a double-blind (meaning neither the patient nor the health care personnel knew what was going on), randomized study of surgical patients undergoing hysterectomies. This study, which was reported in the prestigious British medical journal *Lancet,* found that patients who received positive messages during general anesthesia "spent significantly less time in [the] hospital after surgery, suffered from significantly shorter period[s] of pyrexia [fever] and . . . made a better than expected recovery" in comparison with the group that received no such messages.[6]

Another longitudinal study of 57 breast cancer patients who had undergone mastectomies reported that 7 of the 10 women with "a fighting spirit" were alive 10 years later. On the other hand, 4 of the 5 women who, upon hearing their diagnosis, "felt hopeless" had died during the same time period. The remaining 32 women were classified as "stoics," meaning that they had simply accepted their diagnosis. Of the 32 stoics, 24 had also died.[7] Similarly, a two-year study of 200 burn victims at Harborview Medical Center in Seattle, Washington, found that burn patients with a positive attitude recovered more quickly.[8]

These results are similar to those found in a landmark study of women conducted by Stanford University psychiatrists George Solomon and Rudolf Moos, who were able to demonstrate a connection between emotional health and rheumatoid arthritis. Despite a genetic disposition to the disease, women who were emotionally healthy (not depressed, not alienated, and happily married) were "protected from" rheumatoid arthritis.[9]

These studies represent only the tip of the iceberg. Studies are increasingly linking attitude to the body's propensity to ward off disease and illness. An entire new branch of medicine—referred to as psychoneuroimmunology—

has been established. One of these scientists, Dr. Issac Djerrassi, director of oncology at Philadelphia's Mercy Catholic Medical Center, has concluded that "we now have convincing evidence that the right mental attitude can help your immune system function more effectively."[10]

Similarly, Bernard S. Siegel, M.D., noted cancer specialist and surgeon at Yale-New Haven Hospital and assistant clinical professor at Yale Medical School, firmly believes, based on numerous personal experiences with his own cancer patients, "that the best medical treatment is only as effective as the patient's unconscious mind allows and that a combination of stress reduction, conflict resolution, and positive reinforcement (in the form of visualizations and positive emotions such as hope and love) can stimulate the immune system and allow healing to take place."[11]

Insight Break

The care of tuberculosis depends more on what the patient has in his head than what he has in his chest.

—Sir William Osler, M.D., known as the father of modern medicine

---

These powerful statements pale in comparison with the teachings of Deepak Chopra, M.D. Dr. Chopra, a fellow of the American College of Physicians, former chief of staff of the New England Memorial Hospital, and author of *Quantum Healing*[12] and *Perfect Health,*[13] maintains that thinking of the mind and body as separate entities is based on obsolete knowledge. He, as well as many other scientists,[14] believes that the mind and body are not just forever evolving, but that they are inextricably linked, affecting one another on a ongoing basis. He believes that the body/mind is actually one, because both have the ability to think.

One image scientists have used is the mind as a "soup kitchen," in which brain chemicals called neuropeptides (*neuro,* in the brain, *peptides,* protein-like substances), of which there may be several thousand, although only about 12 are known today, exert their influence on the brain by bathing whole systems of neurons. The billions of possible combinations produce the infinite nuances of thought, emotions, and mood.[15]

Chopra maintains that neuropeptides are produced in the brain whenever we have a thought, a feeling, or an emotion. These neuropeptides speak to each other by latching onto chemical receptors found in the brain. Although fascinating, that is only half the story, because, according to Chopra, there are receptors to these same chemical messengers in other parts of the body. For example, monocytes, T cells, and B cells, cells of the immune system, which protect us from cancer and infectious and degenerative diseases, have receptors to chemical messengers that are the "material equivalent of thought."[16] This means that your immune system is eavesdropping on your self-talk, that it *knows* what is going on inside of your head whether you do or not. Now that is awesome.

But there is more. According to Chopra, this direct linkage is not confined to the mind and the immune system. He maintains that the same receptors and chemicals that exist in the mind and the immune system are also present in the stomach, the intestines, the colon, the kidneys, and other parts of the body. That means that the body and the mind are in fact one. Both are not only connected, the human body, according to Chopra, is actually a body/mind at the same time. This connectedness is what provides us with the ability to keep ourselves healthy or, conversely, to make ourselves sick.

Insight Break

[Research] has established that there are the molecular equivalent of telephone lines between the brain and the immune system.

—Stephen S. Hall

This idea may not be as far-fetched as it seems, considering that the body is in fact a marvelous walking pharmacy.[17] For example, stress, or because *stress* means different things to different people, an anxious feeling, causes your body to produce such chemicals as cortisol and adrenaline, which in turn cause certain negative physiological responses such as an increase in your blood pressure and your pulse. Conversely, if you feel calm and collected your body produces a Valium-like substance. That's right, the same stuff that the doctor prescribed for you the last time you were totally stressed out. The difference, however, is that the body knows exactly how much to make, when to release it, and when to quit. Similarly, when you get a natural high from a race you won, an important project you completed, or being involved in any other activity that gives you a euphoric feeling, your body responds by making interlukens and interferons, the same substances that scientists are currently using for anticancer therapies. (If you have been keeping up with this latest cancer research you know that this stuff is superexpensive—a tiny amount costs several thousand dollars. Your body makes it absolutely free. It costs you nothing. Who says there is no such a thing as a free lunch?)

I am sure that you are impressed, but the point is that your thoughts, your attitude, what goes on in your mind, whether you are aware of it or not, does not just influence your mind; it may influence whether you live or die. A dramatic example is the observation that more people in our society die on Monday morning than at any other time during the week.[18] Because Monday is a thought, not a physical event, it becomes evident that the effect of our attitudes on our well-being is unequivocal fact, not fiction.

Before I leave this topic, however, I would like to express a word of caution. What I have said in this section is that your attitudes, your thoughts, your feelings, and your emotions influence your well-being, your health, and probably even your longevity. I am convinced that what goes on inside of your head will control your future. It is, however, much less likely to affect what has happened in the past or what is happening in the present. In other words, if you have cancer or some other serious disease you cannot just think positive thoughts and make the disease go away! What you need to do is get expert medical treatment. Once you have received that treatment, you can use your incredible positive attitude as an adjunct therapy to help you get better. You can also continue that type of positive programming after you have licked the illness or disease and very likely decrease the probability of recurrence.

Insight Break

Dear Doctor:
Please do not tell me how long I have to live.
I alone can decide how long I will live.
It is my desires, my goals, my strengths, and my will to live that will make the decision.

—Excerpted from *The Cancer Patient's Bill of Rights*
by Bernard Siegel, M.D.

MIRROR, MIRROR ON THE WALL . . .

Attitude has a much greater impact than just on your own personal health and level of success. Your attitude also affects others, especially the people who are important in your life—your spouse, your children, your employees, etc. How important is a positive attitude? you ask. According to one estimate, a positive attitude accounts for 85 percent of why people succeed in life.[19] Your own experience will tell you that it is much easier to work with or for people who have a positive attitude. Somehow they tend to exude energy and make work much more fun. I have, and I am sure you have, worked for people with this unique human capacity.

Conversely, I am sure that you have had the misfortune to work for another type of boss, the boss spelled backward—the double SOB. No matter how hard you tried, he or she could be counted on to find something wrong. Remember when you burned the midnight oil to get that important report done—the one that was going to make or break the company and probably you as well? After giving it your all, wallowing in pools of perspiration, and feeling it was never going to get finished, you persevered and got it done. With considerable pride and elation, you brought it to your boss and placed it before him on his desk. He distractedly looked up from his current project, grabbed your report, flipped through it, wrinkled his forehead, said, "There's a typo in the last line on page 9," and handed it back to you.

I have worked for both types of boss. Working for the latter boss, the negative one, resulted in my feeling tired, stressed, and generally "wrung out." On the other hand, working for a positive boss, the one that was engaged in catching me doing things *right,* resulted in much less fatigue, stress, and emotional drain. In fact, I found myself working even longer hours in an attempt to go the extra mile, to make the boss look good. Still, I felt much better at the end of each day. It was a case of the body feeling tired but the mind being energized. Negative people are energy robbers; they drain your battery. Positive people are energizers; they charge your battery. So be careful when you pick your spouse, friends, and bosses.

What I am basically saying boils down to this: Life is like a mirror—you get from it what you put in. Your attitude toward other people will determine their attitude toward you. Treat people positively or negatively, it is your choice. Whatever choice you make, though, be assured that, in the long run, you will get back whatever you give, plus interest.

Humor Break

Think you're having a tough day? Just think how you would feel if . . .

—Your income tax check bounced.
—You put your bra on backward and it fit better.
—Your birthday cake collapsed from the weight of the candles.

Having reengaged your funny bone, let's take a look at what you can do to develop and maintain that positive attitude.

DEVELOPING AND MAINTAINING A POSITIVE ATTITUDE

Now that we have established that a positive attitude is essential to your success and well-being, let's shift gears and provide you with specific strategies that you can use, not only to develop such an attitude, but also to maintain it, even during tough times.

Start Your Day on a Positive Note

What is the first thing that happens to you every day? Is it a loud, clanking, old-fashioned alarm clock that literally makes you jump out of your bed? Or is it a modern clock radio that rings pleasing chimes or plays soft music? Do you rise at the last minute after repeated snoozes or do you give yourself extra time so that your day can evolve at an unhurried, gentle pace? Do you listen to the news while getting dressed, bathing your conscious and subconscious mind with extra heavy doses of stinking thinking, or do you instead listen to pleasant music? Do you sit on the "throne" thinking of all the problems you have to wrestle with during the day or focus your mental energies on the positive things you expect to accomplish? Do you eat breakfast (the most important meal of the day) or smoke a cigarette (shortening your life by about 16 minutes) and drink a cup of coffee? (I've been told that when you smoke you won't necessarily go to hell, you just smell like you've been there.) While eating breakfast, do you memorize the newspaper or do you pay attention to your spouse or significant other, focusing your mental energies on catching him doing something right? Do you go for a brief walk or jog or engage in some other exercise before going to work, or do you rush out of the house, late as usual? While driving to work, do you let other drivers control your behavior, sometimes for the rest of the day, or do you drive gently and use that unproductive time to invest in yourself by listening to motivational or educational audiotapes?

Just as with anything else in life, different things work for different people. Here is how Marcela and I start a typical day (when I am not on the road). I am a very fortunate man because I enjoy the luxury of being awakened gently by my better half; usually there is a kiss, a smile, and a friendly word. While Marcela gets ready for work, I make breakfast. We eat a leisurely breakfast for about 20 to 30 minutes. During that time, we discuss our plans for the day and scan the newspaper, focusing on the headlines to ensure that we don't get out of touch. (Note I said scan, not study or memorize. Why? Because to me the newspaper is a compilation of all the bad information that is fit [probably more correctly unfit] to print. To help you with this concept, remember Robert Fulghum's admonition that the news represents the *exception*, not the rule. If it were the rule it would *not* be news.[20] And I always finish with the comics, my antidote for all that stinking thinking the media elects to call news.)

Humor Break

Talking about getting up reminds me of a neat story.

Mom was trying to get John out of bed. After her third attempt, she got angry and shouted, "John, get up right now, or you'll be late for school."

Pulling the covers over his head, John protested, "I don't want to go to school. The kids pick on me, they give me a hard time, and they laugh at me. Why should I go to school?"

"Two good reasons," answered Mom. "First, you are 47 years old; and second, you are the principal."

Before Marcela leaves for work, I make it a point to find something positive to share with her. It might be her exceptional beauty, her outfit, her determination, or any other attribute that I can find. After she leaves, I take my three-mile jog (I do that every other day). During that time, I do some creative thinking and positive planning. I also use this time to program my biocomputer with positive thoughts. Using the PIN technique, I can always find something to be pleased about. It can be that it is a gorgeous day. Or, if it is very cold, it is a brisk, refreshing day that makes me look forward to a warm shower. If it is dreary, damp, and wet, it is a calming, melancholy day that reminds me of my younger days in Germany. If I can't quite get it together, I listen to motivational audiotapes. If absolutely nothing seems to work, which is rare, I remind myself that it is truly fantastic to be alive. (If you ever have any doubt about that, just skip a day *one time* in your life, and see how you like that alternative.) After I return from my run, I shower, and am ready for another exciting, positive, and highly productive day. Seven in a row represent a wonderful week, and 52 of those in a row make for a another positive year. I know that may sound simplistic, but that is how I have *made* it a great year every year since I became aware that great days are made, not had.

Use Positive Greetings

In these trying and rapidly changing times, maintaining that positive attitude throughout the day is tough to do. Most of us need reminders to help us stay on a positive course. What helped me immensely during the time that I was making this transition was taking advantage of the fact that many people want to know how you are doing when they meet you. They do, don't they? Why else would they say, "How are you?" (Are you chuckling, or are you taking me too seriously?) Of course, you're right, that's merely a rhetorical question that people use as a greeting. How you respond to that greeting is more important. Are you like many of the people I meet, who answer with an autopilot response such as "Fine"? Or worse, do you answer with a positive response that is negatively expressed, such as "Not too bad" or "It could be worse." Or do you describe how well you are surviving by saying such things as "I'll make it," "I'm OK, after all it is TGIF day," or "I am alright because today is hump day." Or do you forget that it is a rhetorical question, and proceed to tell the other party everything he *didn't* really want to know?

Instead of answering with an automatic or negative response, make it a habit to answer in a purposeful and positive fashion. Say that you are feeling "Great," "Fantastic," "Excellent," or, on the days when you don't feel quite as positive, "Great, and I'm getting better!" This strategy will provide you with several super positive results. First, people will notice you. (The negative thinkers will mutter under their breath something like "Wonder what's preventing his elevator from going all the way to the top?") That is OK. They are not the important people in your life anyway. The winners will recognize what you are doing, admire you for it, return the positive energy with an equally positive message, or respond with an empowering smile. More importantly, you have taken the opportunity to send a positive affirmation to your subconscious. This will continually reinforce the positive programming you started in the morning. Because your subconscious is unable to tell right from wrong, fact from fiction, and dreams from reality, it will accept everything you send it as if it were true. Therefore, you are creating your own positive reality. As Picasso said, "Everything you can imagine is real." I have found that this strategy turns most of my days into super days, and even my worst days into good days.

Also make it a point to depart on a similar positive note. Instead of saying "Have a good day," remind yourself and others that they are in charge of their lives, by saying "*Make* it a great day!"

Humor Break

Talking about defining your own reality reminds me of the following story.

A gentleman of considerable wealth was afflicted with an unusual problem that caused him to seek psychiatric care. When the psychiatrist asked him what his problem was, the gentleman answered, "I'm dead." The psychiatrist asked the patient, "How do you know that you are dead?" The patient answered, "I just know." After realizing that she was unable to convince the patient that he was not dead, the psychiatrist instructed him to say to himself three times a day for the next 21 days: "Dead men don't bleed." When the patient returned for his follow-up appointment, the psychiatrist asked him whether he had followed her instructions. Very proudly he assured her that he had done just as she had asked. The psychiatrist then advised the patient that she was going to conduct a brief experiment that would convince him that he is very much alive. Having said that, the psychiatrist pricked the patient's finger with a small needle. Upon noticing several drops of blood, the patient exclaimed in a bewildered voice, "Oh my God, dead men *do* bleed!"

Expect the Best

Just because things are tough today does not mean that they will continue to be that way tomorrow. Always expect the best. It is a crazy phenomenon, but we generally get what we expect from life. Tell yourself or someone else that you always get a cold in the winter, and indeed you will. Conversely, if you expect that your mind/body is an extremely well-integrated system that possesses the ability to stay in excellent health, then you likely will stay healthy and not suffer the myriad illnesses that others are always complaining about. This assertion is supported by six major studies that concluded that "those who rate their health 'poor' are four to five times more likely to die in the next four years than those who rate their health 'excellent.' "[21] It is the self-fulfilling prophecy at work, and how well it works. The most absurd example that comes to mind is Elvis Presley, who worried extensively about dying a premature death like his mother. We all know how well it worked, because he died almost to the day and from the same illness as his mother. Another example, which I heard on a radio news report, was a study of randomly chosen U.S. college graduates, both males and females. They were asked what they expected to earn annually in about ten years. The range given by females was $25,000 to $45,000, whereas their male counterparts stated that they expected to earn $45,000 to $75,000. I bet that both groups, on average, will earn close to what they expect.

Here is another example that vividly demonstrates that in the long run you get what you expect. My wife will tell you that I *always* get a parking spot right up front, no matter where we are going or how busy the event is.

I don't *always* get a spot right up front, just most of the time. Why, because I drive a tow truck? No, because I expect it! Let me explain. Because I expect it, I look for a spot up front. If, on the other hand, I expected not to find one, I would not bother wasting my time. I would instead take the first parking spot that I could find. Although that is an oversimplified example, that is how life is. If you don't expect it, you don't bother looking for it. If you don't look for it, whether it be a raise, good health, a wonderful spouse, a promotion, or anything else, you are not going to get it, even if it is right there waiting for you!

The field of medicine is full of examples of the self-fulfilling prophecy at work. There is even a name, placebo, given to medicine that is no medicine at all. In many controlled clinical trials, placebos have been found to be as effective as the real thing. (One study found that a placebo provided patients with the equivalent relief of a typical dose [6 to 8 milligrams] of morphine.)[22] So do yourself a favor—always expect the best. Over the long term, you will get what you expect.

Insight Break

The people who get on in this world are the people who get up and look for the circumstances they want, and, if they can't find them, make them.
—George Bernard Shaw

Get off Your Case

Another way to maintain a positive attitude is to learn to forgive yourself, or in today's lingo, to get off your case. Cognitive therapy, founded by Aaron Beck, M.D., in the early 1960s, identified the impact that our own self-talk has on our moods, behavior, interactions, and performance.[23] The effects of cognitive therapy are extremely positive. In a study conducted at the Washington University School of Medicine in St. Louis, Missouri, cognitive therapy was found to be "at least as effective as drugs for patients with moderate to severe depression."[24]

Cognitive therapists have found that thinking negative thoughts is only part of the problem. The major problem is that negative thoughts are almost always accompanied by major distortions. These cognitive distortions fall into six major categories:

1. *Exaggerating.* You overestimate problems and underestimate your ability to deal with them.

2. *Overgeneralizing.* You take an isolated event and generalize to an entire universe.
3. *Personalizing.* You think everything revolves around you.
4. *Either/or thinking.* You see things as mutually exclusive, even when they are not.
5. *Jumping to conclusions.* You take limited information and predict the future or make assumptions.
6. *Ignoring the positive.* You lock in on something negative to negate all the other positive things.

See Exhibit 7-4 for examples of these cognitive distortions and how to change your self-talk and get off your case.

Insight Break

Change your thoughts, and you change your world.
—Norman Vincent Peale

Experience has taught me that we are often our own worst enemy. It is not what others are saying or doing to us, it is what we are saying and doing to ourselves. What has worked well for me is to become future oriented. (Remember the "spilled milk" story in Chapter 5?) Again, I have not always been that way. I still remember several months after I had gotten my new Mercedes, my dream machine, my lifetime goal, I made what I considered an awfully stupid mistake. I was working in the yard, with the Mercedes in the garage. I needed to wheelbarrow something out of the garage. Instead of pulling the car out, I decided that there was enough room to get through. Of course there wasn't, and so I put a long scratch in the car. Talk about getting on your case and self-flagellation. You should have heard my internal conversations. You would have been surprised, amused, startled, horrified, and aghast. I carried on for quite some time. Isn't that crazy? No matter how long I berated myself, the scratch simply did not disappear.

The next time you get on your case, ask yourself two very basic questions:

1. If I do this long enough, will things get better?
2. If someone else were doing this, would I admire them?

Exhibit 7-4 Correcting Cognitive Distortions, or How to Get off Your Case in Six Easy Steps

Distortion	Wrong Thinking	Right Thinking
Exaggerating	I'm always late for meetings.	I usually make it to most meetings on time.
Overgeneralizing	I'm stupid.	This time I got a D, but I normally get As and Bs.
Personalizing	Everyone noticed that I wore the same suit two times in a row.	I am appropriately dressed for the occasion.
Either/or thinking	Either I get the promotion or I'm a failure.	My performance has been exceptional. I have a good chance to make my next promotion. If not, there will be other opportunities.
Jumping to conclusions Assumption	I didn't get the contract because I mispronounced the CEO's name.	I will call to find out why the contract was not awarded to me.
Predicting the future	She is not home yet. She must have been in an accident.	I will call to find out if she has left the party.
Ignoring the positive	I have a big nose.	I have a gorgeous body and great-looking legs.

If the answer to both questions is no, quit doing it! Acknowledge that you are a fallible human being and that all fallible human beings make mistakes. Even the most competent people make mistakes about 5 percent of the time. Make a written or mental note of what you learned from the mistake so that you can avoid doing it in the future. Then fix it, correct it, solve it, and, most importantly, make peace with yourself and get on with your life.

Humor Break

This is an appropriate place to share a supposedly true story with you, because it is directly related to taking a future perspective. It is said that a young vice president of IBM had made a serious mistake in the stock market. In fact, it was no ordinary mistake, because it cost IBM about $10 million. Shortly thereafter, the young vice president was summoned to the chairman of IBM, Tom Watson. Expecting to be fired—or because IBM tends not to fire people, to be sent to IBM's Siberia—the young man was not very happy when he arrived in Mr. Watson's office.

Bracing himself for the worst, he had his head hung low and listened somewhat defensively. However, as the conversation went on, it became apparent that Mr. Watson was talking about new opportunities, perhaps even a promotion. So the young vice president tentatively asked for clarification. When his initial perceptions were confirmed, he asked incredulously, "You mean you are not going to fire me?" Mr. Watson, equally startled, responded, "Fire you? After we just spent $10 million training you?"

Set Yourself up for Success

Nothing helps people succeed or enhances our positive attitude as much as success. It is odd, but for some reason we utilize this concept with little people (my preferred term for children), but either forget it or think it is inappropriate when we grow up or when we are engaged in managing adults. If you are a parent (if not, use your imagination), think back to the time when you were trying to teach your daughter to ride a bike. Did you get *your* bike out, get on it to show her how it is done, then put her on it, give her a shove and tell her to go for it? When she fell, did you call her a dummy? I am sure that your answer is no. I am certain that you got her a small bike and put on a pair of training wheels. Also, once she was barely propelling the bike forward, your spouse came outside and exclaimed over her accomplishment. Continued repetition, positive reinforcement, and near-tries finally gave your daughter enough confidence for you to take off the training wheels. At that point the whole process started over again, with you holding onto the saddle. And, after much more practice and encouragement, your daughter finally rode that bike all on her own.

If you use this simple, elegant, and extremely basic approach to set yourself and others up for success, you will succeed more often, feel better about your abilities, and find it easier to maintain a positive attitude. When you have to learn a new and seemingly overwhelming task, start with what you currently know, build on that in small increments, reward yourself for near-tries as if they were giant accomplishments, forgive yourself for misses because they are a natural part of learning, supply some type of internal or external reward, and you will be on the way to success. All human beings, regardless of age, are much more effective learners if they can start with "training wheels" and if they receive positive instead of negative reinforcement. If you are a manager, these strategies work equally well for teaching and empowering the people on your team.

Quit Being a Perfectionist

Directly related to setting yourself up for success and expecting the best is giving up perfectionism. For me that was easier said than done. Being brought up with the belief that anything worth doing is worth doing right made me into a "crippled" perfectionist. Crippled, because doing everything perfectly results in perfectionism, and people who are afflicted with this dreaded disease accomplish relatively little. I still remember the first few articles I ever wrote. It took forever because they had to be perfect. After the first dozen, I began to catch on. What I noticed was that the editor or the reviewers made my *perfect* articles even more perfect. Then I began to experiment. Instead of sending in perfect articles, I submitted articles that were well written but had not been fine-tuned. What I found was that there was absolutely no correlation between how perfect I felt the original article was and the number of changes suggested by the reviewer. That taught me that it is more important to *do the right things right* than to do all things right.

I am now convinced that being a perfectionist is extremely counterproductive and sets you up for perpetual failure and disappointment and the consequent negative feelings. Life, people, and nature are extremely imperfect; you could even call them messy. If you can accept that premise (which took me only about 40 years to do) then being a perfectionist is unrealistic, even unnatural. "Murphy" was on to something when he conceived his pessimistic "laws." Everything does seem to go wrong when you least expect it (otherwise it would not bother us and we would not notice it), people do let you down and disappoint you, and the weather does not cooperate when you want it to. We live in an imperfect world. Conducting yourself as if you live in a perfect world will certainly set you up for some major disappointments, stress, and maybe even illness. The solution is to accept imperfection as the normal order of things; continue to expect the best, because most of the time, especially with a long-term perspective, you will get what you expect; and most importantly *go with the flow.*

Mental Stretch Break

In front of you is a set of matches arranged to form six squares (see Exhibit 7-5). Your task is to remove no more than two matches so that four equal squares remain. (See end of chapter for solution.)

Exhibit 7-5 Match Exercise

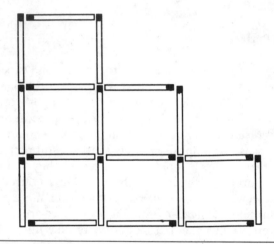

HOW TO GIVE YOURSELF A PEP² TALK

As mentioned earlier, you program your internal computer (your subconscious) every waking moment of the day and even in your sleep. To ensure that you maintain that powerful positive attitude, you must get in the habit of using positive language. Communication expert George Walther calls it "power talk."[25] I call it "PEP² Talk."

Treat Successes as the Rule and Failures as the Exception

Psychologist Martin Seligman maintains that people have consistent explanatory styles.[26] Optimists express successes in global, internal, and stable terms, and failures in local, external, and unstable terms. Pessimists reverse that process. *Global* means that you generally see yourself succeeding, that success is something you expect to happen. *Local,* on the other hand, means that a specific occurrence is viewed as an exception. If a winner makes a very difficult sale she says, "I knew I could do it. I am a great salesperson and I make most of my sales." A loser making the same sale will be surprised and wonder what happened. When things go bad, however, and sooner or later they will, the winner will perceive the situation as an exception. The loser might say to herself, "I'm not making my sales quota. I'm in debt. I'm not getting along with my husband. Everything in my life is just going wrong for me all of the time."

Internal means that you assume full responsibility for everything that happens to you in your life, both good and bad. *External* means that you attribute all events to something over which you have no control. If an internal accomplishes a particular difficult project, he will be proud of his accomplishments. He will respond to a compliment with a simple "thank you." By the same token, he will also confess to any failures and take complete ownership without making excuses or providing lengthy explanations. Externals tend to externalize successes, attributing them to astrology, karma, or luck. Externals are embarrassed by compliments and try to minimize them. When they fail, however, they tend to either externalize the failure by blaming others or internalize it by blaming it wholly on themselves.

Stable means that a specific successful event is just a part of an overall pattern, a part of the grand scheme. *Unstable* means that it is an exception, a random event. Winners see success as a continuing event and failure as an unstable event. They are not surprised when they experience success; after all, they expected it. When they run into a roadblock, they are quick to pick themselves up, dust themselves off, and go on with their lives. Losers reverse the process, considering success as an unstable event, something that happens occasionally. Failure is the rule, not the exception.

Insight Break

Words are magical in the way they affect the minds of those who use them.

—Aldous Huxley

Use Positive Language

When we speak, we can express things in negative or positive language. For example, you can say, "Don't walk on the grass" or "Please help keep our lawn green by walking on the walkways." "Don't litter" or "Please put your trash in trash cans." "I can't get this project completed until two weeks from now" or "I'll have this project completed in two weeks." In each case, both statements say the same thing. Which do you think is easier to understand and more effective? According to Walther, research has demonstrated that positively worded statements are one-third easier to comprehend than their negative counterparts.[27] The reason is that human beings are unable to move away from the reverse of an idea. Instead, we move toward that which we visualize in our minds. Take advantage of this phenomenon by taking the extra minute to figure out how you can express yourself in positive terms. Avoid identifying what it is that you do not want. Instead, identify what you want to have happen.

Substitute the Word Can *for* Can't

Most of us have the potential to do just about anything we want to do. I will go so far as to say that the word *can* applies to about 90 percent of the opportunities that you face in life. In other words, it is not a question of whether you can or can't; the real question is how badly you want it. (My daughter Nicole wrote a poem that I think provides a vivid example of what I am talking about. See Exhibit 7-6.)

Exhibit 7-6 "I Can" Poem

> I can dance,
> I can chant,
> I can even go to France.
> I can love,
> I can hug,
> I can even catch a bug.
> I can write,
> I can draw,
> I can even fly a kite.
> I can cry,
> I can be shy,
> I can do anything . . .
>   as long as I try.
>
> —Nicole Rinke, age 11

Substitute the Word Will *for* Try

The word *try* provides for built-in failure before you even start. Even a lack of success will meet the requirements you have set for yourself. After all, you did try. *Will,* on the other hand, demonstrates commitment, action, and a high probability of success.

Let's look at an example of how this works. You have a serious medical complication and your dietitian wants you to lose 10 pounds in 2 months. You assure the dietitian that you will try to do your best. Two months later you are back in the dietitian's office, having lost only 2 pounds. You protest to the dietitian that you did your best to lose 10 pounds, which is exactly what you did. You complied with what you had promised to do. You did not agree to lose 10 pounds; you only promised to *try.* On the other hand, what type of commitment is expressed when you say, "Well, it is going to be tough, but I am making a commitment to lose 10 pounds in 2 months." When you come back after 2 months and have lost only 2 pounds, which can still happen, you will have broken your commitment, both to yourself and to your dietitian. Most people, however, live up to their commitments. Be careful to avoid the use of the word *try* unless you want to fail by design.

Substitute the Words Challenge/Opportunity *for* Problem/Failure

The Chinese vocabulary is very sensitive to the minute differences in the words we choose to express ourselves. For example, the Chinese symbol for *crisis* consists of two words: danger and opportunity. This illustrates that words create powerful perceptions that invoke either fear or desire. Fear causes negative responses in our mind/body, whereas desire generates powerful forces that will energize us. Words such as *problem* and *failure* immediately paint a negative picture in the mind. They connote something to be avoided, something that means trouble, headaches, heartburn, and no way out. *Challenge* and *opportunity,* on the other hand, express a sense of competition, excitement, and adventure. Ultimately, if we use our creative potential and productive energies, we know that we have the potential to succeed. So be mindful of the words you choose and select only those that create desire and set you up for success.

Insight Break

Whenever I make a bum decision, I just go out and make another one.
—Harry Truman

Take Ownership of Your Communication

Many years ago I read a powerful little book titled *Declare Yourself— Discovering the ME in Relationships,* by John Narcisco and David Burkett.[28] From it, I learned that most of us behave in one of three ways in interpersonal transactions: deferring, demanding, and defecting. All of these are intended to help us get what we want in the short term. In the long run, however, they are ineffectual, manipulative, and self-defeating. The only way to get out of these self-destructive behavior patterns is to learn how to take ownership of your behavior by declaring in the first person singular what you want to have happen in operational terms. Instead of saying to your spouse, "You make me so mad when you ignore me," you substitute, "Please look at me when I speak, because when you ignore me I feel angry."

Another technique that I have used to take ownership of my communication is to recognize that when I point a finger at anyone there are three fingers pointing back at me. What I have learned over the years, sometimes with very painful results, is that I cannot control other people's feelings—*I can only control my own.*

As icing on the cake for this chapter, I would like to share my favorite poem with you. Enjoy!

Exhibit 7-7 You Can Fly, If You Try

You can fly, if you try!
You can soar with the eagles, if you dare
Or you can run with the turkeys who don't care
You can watch life on the TV tube
Or invent some great, new Rubick's Cube
You can fly, if you try!

Getting high on yourself!
You can run with your earphones—full of hope
Or you can fall in the shadows full of dope
You can get depressed and try to fake it
Or get up, get dressed, and try to make it
Getting high on yourself!

Set your course and keep on trying
And you'll find that soon you're flying
Doesn't matter who you are
Spread your wings and be a star!
You can fly, if you try!

—Unknown

PEP² IN ACTION—POSITIVE ATTITUDE: DANIELLE KENNEDY

Danielle Kennedy embarked on a real estate sales career at the age of 27 while six months pregnant with her fifth child. With little formal sales training, but driven by her personal motivation to provide for her family, she became one of history's most successful real estate agents. In one year alone, she sold more than 100 resale homes, worth $6 million, earning the title of the Six Million Dollar Woman.

Today, Kennedy is a best-selling author, a popular motivational speaker, a certified aerobics instructor, wife, and the mother of eight children. She has hosted her own television talk show, made numerous television commercials, and appeared as a spokesperson for PBS. She has been widely recognized for her accomplishments, has received the prestigious Council of Peers Award of Excellence from the National Speakers Association, and has been profiled in a variety of publications, including The Republic, The Los Angeles Times, Vogue, *and* Cosmopolitan.

WR: Why did you go into real estate?

DK: Well, I had four children, I was pregnant with my fifth, and we had trouble making ends meet. Real estate seemed to be one thing that at the time I could do. I can remember how fearful I was when I began my first career in sales in the early 1970s. There were very few women in the field at that time—only 1 out of 16 members of our board was female—and none of them was pregnant. So when I tried to get a job, no one would hire me. Finally, someone said, "OK, you can hang your license here. But you can't work in the office. You'll have to do this out of your house and get your own prospects." But more than anything else I was motivated by a freezer.

WR: Did I hear right, you were motivated by a freezer?

DK: Yes, I was motivated by a freezer. I used to go to the grocery store with three or four children on my hip. When I'd get to the checkout counter, I'd be praying that the amount of money I'd see when the total was hit on the register was the same amount that I had in my pocket. Three or four people would be in line behind me. I'd be holding up things for the checker to subtract from the total—I'd have to return items to the shelves. People would look at me with all these children and say to each other, "How can she do this? How can she stand in line with all that food and not be able to afford to buy it all? Look at all those kids. What's the matter with this woman?" I hated that feeling. So, when I first began my career, I would picture a truck delivering a freezer to my garage. After seven months in real estate, that freezer finally came and I filled it with food. Every night when I came home, the children and I would go out to the garage and open the freezer door. I'd say, "Look at all that food! This is amazing! I'm so excited!" And we'd just stare at the stuff. Then I'd slam the freezer door shut and say, "Boy, am I exhausted. Does anybody want to take me to dinner?"

WR: That's a great story. But there must have been more to your success than a freezer.

DK: Right you are. I think the question was, how did I succeed in real estate? I did what I thought I needed to do, the sowing and reaping. I really didn't know any better, so I didn't do all the things that many of my colleagues did. I didn't spend time in the office. Instead, I put a 20-foot cord on my kitchen phone and started cold calling. And I simply would not quit.

I sold my first house after three months. After that, I quadrupled my sales every year from 1972 to 1977. I was selling 100 houses per year. The industry was calling me the Six Million Dollar Woman. I was breaking records and winning awards. In 1981, together with my husband, I formed Danielle Kennedy Productions, my speaking company.

WR: I imagine that during that time things were not all milk and honey all the time?

DK: You can say that again. In 1978, my dad passed away. He was very young, about 62, and had had health problems for about 10 years. Three weeks after that, my grandfather passed away. Six months later, my best friend, who was in sales and under a lot of stress, more than we realized, took her life. And so, here I was 33 years old. Even though this was a very traumatic time of my life, I was working full time. I think in some cases my career and my work was therapy for me. I was so passionate about my work that it gave me a sense of keeping on. But I also think that after the initial shock and the bitterness of it, you think nobody has problems as big as yours when you're in the first stages of grief. After about six months, I got a call from a former client, the wife of a very successful doctor in the community and someone I had always admired. She had never gone to work. She had raised her children for 30 years, and they were all gone now. She seemingly had the perfect marriage. This was a woman who I thought had really been fortunate. She had something I had dreamed about having but didn't. But when I got to her house, I found that she was devastated. She said, "I need your help. I have to sell my home." I asked why. And she said, "Well, my husband came home out of the blue and said that he wants a divorce." She said, "I have no job skills. I've never balanced a checkbook. I have to sell this gorgeous 5000 square foot home and move into a condominium." It was weird, because how can somebody else's bad news be my good news? But that's exactly what happened.

I went home and began to look around. I said, "My career made all this possible." I always wanted to have a big family, and there they were, children everywhere. I began to reflect that life wasn't so bad for me after all. When I looked around, I realized there was a lot to be grateful for. I got back that attitude of gratitude that we lose sometimes in the middle of our own desperation. Little by little, because I think we heal in little spurts, we got stronger and stronger as a family. In 1980, I fell in love and remarried. My husband and I have been partners in this business for the last 11 years, and we had a child together when I was 40. That brought me up to six pregnancies, and he had two children, so as a combined family we have eight children. It's almost been like I've been living a completely different life since the age of 36. It's like I lived two lives. But I say to a lot of people that I'm awfully happy that if I had to go through what sooner or later everybody goes through, some shocking event, some tragedy, I'm glad it happened to me early. I have a tremendous appreciation for the simpler things now, whether it's the smell of cut grass or a sunset. You learn from the negative as well as the positives. Each life event brings a new lesson. Of course, there are some people who'll go through something like this and never recover. They're chained to the past and wish things were like they used to be. That's the real tragedy.

WR: Let me back up a bit. Positive attitude is one of the key success principles that I talk about in my book. What I have found out is that you, unlike many people, appear to have a seemingly unending positive attitude. You just alluded to the fact that things have not always been all milk and honey in your life, so the question I would like you to address is, when you are facing troubles, when you are facing tragedies, how do you keep yourself up? How do you maintain your positive attitude?

DK: There are several things I do. First of all, a certain amount of pain has to be confronted. I think just being able to face your emotions, whether anger or grief, is very important. Believe me, I like a good cry every now and then. Besides, I was brought up in a very positive environment. But don't misunderstand me. We had our problems. My father was an alcoholic, and I'm sure that my mother would have had a very different perspective. In any event, I was an only child, and I remember that my parents were always very encouraging and very positive with me.

WR: That's interesting, Danielle. What I am hearing you say is that you feel that all those positive strokes have helped you to weather the trials and tribulations when you encountered them. In my book, I use the analogy of "money in the bank." That is, if we put positive affirmations in the "bank" when things are good, then when things go bad we can draw on the interest to maintain that positive attitude.

DK: That's a great analogy.

WR: You said that there are several strategies that you use to maintain your positive attitude even when things are tough. What are the others?

DK: I also use physical fitness. Originally, I got involved in running and dancing and exercise because I wanted to look good physically. I gained and lost 50 pounds with each pregnancy. I'm a small person, and I've always had a fast metabolism, but when you have one baby after another it can sure change the look of your body if you don't do something about it. And so, originally I got into exercise because of the physical benefits. But at this point in my life I am involved in physical fitness because of how it affects me mentally. It releases endorphins and other chemicals in my brain and keeps me on a natural high. It also controls depression and helps keep negative thoughts out of my mind. I tell people when things come up, such as anger that you think you can't control, go for a brisk walk, go ride a bike, go run, or go dance, because physically you need some kind of an outlet. By the way, being an athlete also helped me succeed in business. In fact, succeeding in business and in sports have a lot in common.

WR: That is an interesting observation. What I am hearing you say is that the discipline that you developed as an athlete is the same discipline that you need to succeed in the business world. The reason I find that so interesting is that discipline, I call it perseverance, is one of the six success principles I discuss in my book.

DK: Another way that I keep myself positive is through meditation. I certainly enjoy meditation tapes. I enjoy just being quiet, sitting alone, breathing deeply, and spiritually taking retreats. My own special relationship with God through silent prayer and my own background in the Catholic faith have been very important to me. You'll notice that I said faith, not religion. I think there's a tremendous difference between being a religious fanatic and a faith fanatic. Faith is something that happens inside of your heart, and it's a private thing. You respect other people's religions, but it's a relationship you have between yourself and your higher power or God. A lot of times I've turned to my faith to see me through.

Also, I have my work that I love. I love to write and I love to speak and I have a wonderful, wonderful family surrounding me that acts as a buffer against anything that could possibly get me down. I have too much to be thankful for to let it last too long. As soon as I get down, I begin to think about people who are much more underprivileged than I am. The other day I had a tour of the Children's Hospital ward in Orange County, the oncology center. Over 80 percent of these kids are being cured, as opposed to the late 1960s, when they hadn't developed bone marrow transplants and all that other stuff that they are able to do today. I went to the neonatal center and saw the small babies who were born with bad valves in their hearts and needed open-heart surgery at the age of 2 weeks. I looked around and realized how grateful I am for all the healthy family members I have. Imagine what it must be like for these parents who have a baby 15 weeks early or have a child with a heart problem or a child with leukemia. These kind of experiences immediately get me away from myself, my ego, and my own petty thoughts.

WR: What I hear you talk about is choosing your attitude. A lot of us give that choice to somebody else, our spouses, our boss, or even the weather. How often do we hear people say, "My wife makes me so mad" or "My boss ruined my day" or "This weather depresses me." What I'm hearing you say is that you slow yourself down, you reformulate your thoughts, and refocus on what you should be grateful for. In short, you *choose to have a positive attitude* instead of a negative attitude. That is an exciting observation, Danielle, because the theme of my book is that most people choose to lose, but we can instead *choose to win!*

You have a huge and happy family, you are happily married, and you have a very lucrative business. Some people would say why not just sit back and relax. You are not doing that. You are even going back to school. Tell me about that.

DK: I'm halfway through the master's in writing program at the University of Southern California. It's a 30-unit program, and I just completed my 17th unit, so I'm planning on finishing by the fall of 1992. I'm doing it for lots of reasons. I love writing, and I'm very passionate about it. I'm finding that writing is one of my strengths. What all of us should do is figure out what our strengths are and build on that. The fact is that some people take an awful lot of time to figure that out. Some never figure it out.

WR: I am really getting excited now, because you are reinforcing a critical principle that I would like my readers to internalize. If you want to succeed in life, you have to build on your strengths. But let's get back to the other reason why you are going to school.

DK: Well, I mentioned that I want to get better at writing. I want to learn different types of writing, not just nonfiction. I want to try my hand at play writing, fiction, short stories, and screenplays, maybe. I know a lot of stories about people, and my life has been very interesting. That should be the first qualification of any speaker or writer. If you've spent your whole life in a closet and confined yourself to non-risky activities, you're not going to have much to offer an audience. At this point in my life, looking back, there's a wealth of information that I'd like to share. I'd like to become a better writer. I want to associate with people who are better than I am. That's why I'm going back to school, and I find it extremely inspiring. It gives you a sense of balance again to realize how little you know. I constantly put myself in new situations so that I'm green and growing, as opposed to ripe and rotting.

WR: That is a very interesting observation; it reinforces one of the six principles I talk about, education, namely, being a voracious lifelong learner. I think you just put a different twist on it. The twist is that all of us need to recognize that there is always something new to learn. Even though you are good at what you do, you are also at the same time very ignorant. The only way you can come to that realization is to put yourself in a learning environment. Once you become a lifelong learner, life stays exciting because it is a perpetual growth experience. Or as you put it, it keeps you green and growing instead of ripe and rotting.

DK: I think the older you get, the more you realize just how little you know. I like that concept because it takes that awful pressure off, that you have to know everything about everything. Once you realize that it is a lifelong process, it's a relief.

WR: I think that it also gives you a connectedness to the people you work with. In my interview with Dr. Ben Carson, the physician who separated the German Siamese twins, he said, "That was a 70-member team. Yes, I was important, but I was no more important than anyone else on the team." That is indeed a unique skill, to value every human being for their certain special abilities instead of pigeonholing them because of title, rank, religion, color, or sex. I have found that the minute you begin to see yourself as smarter or so important that you're better than anyone else, you have lost.

You speak to a lot of female audiences. Women in our society have always been, and continue to be, discriminated against. They are the ones who have to do it all. They go to work, sometimes more than one job, but almost always still maintain the responsibilities of running the household. Yet they are often held back, whether it be the "glass ceiling" in corporate America or in other ways. What do you say to women, you, who appear to have been able to do it all?

DK: Well, you're not going to do it all, at least not all at the same time. The advice I have for women is that you can't be a perfectionist. You can't have a kitchen counter polished at all times, the bed won't always be made. There will be times in your life and passages during certain stages of kids' lives when it's more difficult than others. For example, when you have two kids in diapers at one time or when they're in school and one has to be at ballet and one has to be at Little League and you have to be at an appointment or whatever. There are going to be times when it's going to be very confusing and you're going to have to be able to keep your head above water. You're going to have to delegate, have good help to take care of the house, whether it's cooking, cleaning, or whatever. Sometimes women don't want to give up. They want to do everything, and then they have a nervous breakdown. I've been in situations where I've said I can't do any more, this is what I can do. You have to teach your kids and encourage independence from the time they are little. Encourage them to do things for themselves as opposed to saying, "Only I can do it, you can't do it well enough." Even if it's not done to your specs, they're doing their best to make their beds, to rinse off their plates. Let them do it when they want to. There is a natural willingness in children that is often squelched by parents because they are perfectionists. Become their friends. Talk to them like they are human beings instead of little dolls. They're not stupid. We talk down to children in our society, and it's ridiculous. Explain your work to them. Let them know what your work is all about. Let them know how money affects the family. Let them know how the ballet lessons get paid for—not that you want them to feel indebted to you, but it's a team effort. And being part of the team means that they cooperate and take good phone messages and understand that today you have to work late and there will be a baby-sitter but there will be a payoff for that because you're not always going to say yes to the working world and no to the family. Some people have more respect for their customers or clients than they do for their family. They'd never break a commitment with a client but think nothing of breaking commitments with their child or spouse. I've always tried to keep that balance.

WR: Balance is certainly critical, and often tough to accomplish. What about the issue of fairness in the workplace?

DK: I think there is no such a thing. Perhaps, I was lucky to get my start in real estate. In real estate it does not matter what sex you are. Results are the only thing that counts. In fact, I outperformed all my male counterparts, so much so that someone in the office suggested that I should be handicapped. They felt it wasn't fair that I should keep winning all the sales awards. They wanted a chance too. Here were these young single males suggesting that I should be handicapped. I said, "Handicap me, muzzle me, tie one arm behind my back. I don't care. I'll still outsell all of you." And I did. Why? Because I was willing to work harder than they did! And that is the secret, if there is a secret. Women basically have to work three times as hard as their male counterparts to make it in the business world. Some women maintain that that is not fair. And I agree. But what are you going to do about it? Complain or get on with your life? My experience has taught me that if you consistently deliver excellence, if you are consistently more productive than others, may they be male or female, sooner or later your competence will be recognized and you will succeed accordingly.

WR: I'm glad to hear you say that. I maintain that, in general, life is not fair. What I find is that most people want to succeed, but they do not want to pay the price. Unfortunately, at the counter of success there are no discounts. One always has to pay full price up front.

DK: I totally agree.

WR: It's been my distinct pleasure to chat with you today. My readers and I thank you for your time and your wonderful insights. I hope you continue to *MAKE it a WINNING life.*

SUMMARY: A TRIP BACK TO THE FUTURE

- Attitudes are created.
- A positive attitude is the one characteristic that all successful people have in common.
- Other things being equal, attitude is a better predictor of success than aptitude.
- Individuals can learn to change their attitude response patterns.
- Attitudes are infectious.
- Research provides evidence that the mind and body are connected and that both have the ability to think.
- Research has demonstrated that a positive attitude can strengthen the immune system, ward off illness, help fight disease, and influence healing and recovery from long-term illness.
- Positive people are energizers. Negative people are energy robbers.
- A positive attitude is developed and maintained by
  —starting your day on a positive note;
  —using positive greetings;
  —expecting the best;
  —getting off your case;
  —setting yourself up for success;
  —avoiding perfectionism; and
  —giving yourself a PEP[2] talk.
- You can give yourself a PEP[2] talk by doing the following:
  —Treat successes as the rule and failures as the exception.
  —Use positive language:
    Substitute the word *can* for *can't*.
    Substitute the word *will* for *try*.
    Substitute the words *challenge/opportunity* for *problem/failure*.
    Take ownership of your communication.

SUCCESS ACTION STEPS

- ❏ Ask three people you know and consider to be positive role models what strategies they use to maintain their positive attitudes.
- ❏ Reformulate your language, both internal and external, by substituting positive words for negative words.
- ❏ Build a network of positive friends, colleagues, and acquaintances.

❏ Commit to being your own best cheering squad.
❏ Whenever anyone asks, "How are you doing?" answer, with enough enthusiasm to convince yourself and the other person that you really mean it, "GREAT!"
❏ Appreciate yourself for who you are instead of who you ought to be.
❏ Conduct an experiment. For just 1 day, treat every human being as if he or she were the most important person in the world. At the end of the day, ask yourself what kind of a day you had. If you liked the day, repeat the same process tomorrow, and the next 21 days, until you have developed a new habit.
❏ Stop fretting about anything that has already happened. Look for a lesson, if there is one to be found, then forget about the mistake.
❏ Accept that mistakes are part of life and that without them there is no progress.
❏ Conduct another experiment. For 1 full day, starting in the morning, tell yourself that you are going to focus all of your mental energies on positive things in your life, your language, and the people you associate with. If you like the way the day turned out, repeat the process for 21 days.
❏ The next time you are involved in an important project, do more than is expected of you, then expect to be "compensated" accordingly.
❏ When you make a mistake, treat it as an exception. Never call yourself a dummy or a similar negative affirmation again.
❏ Accept that how you feel about anything or anyone is your choice.
❏ Invest in yourself by spending just 10 percent less time in front of the television for the next month. Spend that newly found time doing something that will enrich you, such as reading, exploring a hobby, going to school, or listening to educational or motivational audiotapes. The next month after that, reduce your television watching time by another 10 percent, and so on, until you are down to "purposeful and positive" television watching, meaning that you watch only programs that will enrich your life.
❏ Pick one day a week to remind yourself that you are the only one who can maximize your ability.
❏ Let your language reflect that you are in charge of your feelings by getting in the habit of using "I" statements. For example, instead of saying, "You make me so mad!" say instead, "I am upset, and this is the reason why."
❏ Make it a habit to give yourself credit for what you have accomplished and to forgive yourself for anything that has happened in the past.
❏ Listen to yourself talk. Notice when you eliminate the words *try* and *can't,* and give yourself credit for it.

❑ Catch yourself taking charge of your life, and give yourself positive feedback when you do.

NOTES

1. S. L. Stetler, *Almanac of Famous People* (Detroit, MI: Gale Research, 1989).

2. D. Waitley, *The Psychology of Winning* (Chicago: Nightingale-Conant, 1979).

3. *Encyclopedia Americana* (Danbury, CT: Grolier, 1989).

4. N. Cousins, *Anatomy of an Illness as Perceived by the Patient* (New York: Norton, 1979).

5. N. Cousins, *Head First: The Biology of Hope* (New York: E. P. Dutton, 1989).

6. C. Evans and P. H. Richardson, "Improved Recovery and Reduced Postoperative Stay after Therapeutic Suggestions during General Anaesthesia," *Lancet* 8609 (August 27, 1988): 491–493.

7. D. Robinson, "Mind over Disease I: Your Attitude Can Make You Well," *Readers' Digest* 130 (April 1987): 73–76.

8. Ibid., p. 75.

9. S. Hall, "A Molecular Code Links Emotions, Mind and Health," *Smithsonian* 20 (June 1989): 62–71.

10. Robinson, "Mind over Disease I," p. 75.

11. B. Siegel, quoted in E. Padus, *The Complete Guide to Your Emotions and Your Health* (Emmasus, PA: Rodale Press, 1986), p. 529.

12. D. Chopra, *Quantum Healing: Exploring the Frontiers of Body, Mind, Medicine* (New York: Bantam Books, 1989).

13. D. Chopra, *Perfect Health: Maharishi Ayurveda, the Mind-Body Program for Total Well-Being* (New York, Crown, 1990).

14. S. Hall, "A Molecular Code Links Emotions, Mind and Health."

15. G. Bylinsky, "The Inside Story on the Brain," *Fortune* 122 (December 3, 1990): 87–100.

16. D. Chopra, "Magic Mind, Magic Body," *Insight* 96 (1991): 26–35. Audiotape program with accompanying written materials. Nightingale-Conant Corp., 7300 North Lehigh Avenue, Chicago, IL 60648.

17. J. L. Hopson, "A Pleasurable Chemistry," *Psychology Today* 22 (July–August 1988): 29–33.

18. D. Chopra, "Magic Mind, Magic Body," p. 34.

19. Z. Ziglar, *See You at the Top* (Gretna, LA: Pelican, 1985).

20. R. Fulghum, *All I Really Need to Know I Learned in Kindergarten: Uncommon Thoughts on Common Things* (New York: Ivy Books, 1988).

21. D. Goleman, "Patients Know Best," *New York Times,* summarized by *Reader's Digest* 139 (August 1991): 31.

22. J. Hopson, "A Pleasurable Chemistry," p. 30.

23. H. B. Braiker, "The Power of Self-Talk," *Psychology Today* 23 (December 1989): 23–27.

24. E. Padus, *The Complete Guide to Your Emotions and Your Health*, p. 105.

25. G. R. Walther, *Power Talking: 50 Ways to Say What You Mean and Get What You Want* (New York: Putnam's Sons, 1991).

26. M. E. Seligman and P. Schulman, "Explanatory Styles as a Predictor of Productivity and

Quitting among Life Insurance Sales Agents," *Journal of Personality and Social Psychology* 50 (August 1986): 832–838.

27. G. Walther, *Power Talking*.
28. J. Narciso and D. Burkett, *Declare Yourself: Discovering the ME in Relationships* (Englewood Cliffs, NJ, Prentice-Hall, 1975).

ANSWER TO MENTAL STRETCHING EXERCISE
Page 210

Exhibit 7-8 Solution: Match Exercise

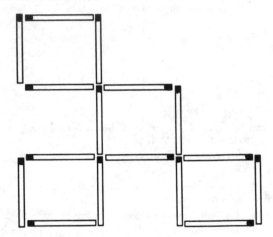

ANSWERS TO BRAIN TEASERS
page 195

1. Hurry up
2. Split-second timing
3. Receding hairline
4. Thumbscrews
5. Cornerstone
6. Looking back in anger
7. Strip tease
8. History repeats itself
9. Right in the middle of things

8

Perseverance

Nothing in the world can take the place of persistence.
Talent will not;
nothing is more common than unsuccessful men with talent.
Genius will not;
unrewarded genius is almost a proverb.
Education will not;
the world is full of educated derelicts.
Persistence and determination alone are omnipotent.
—Calvin Coolidge

Now we've got it made. We are at the top! Your PEP^2 rocket is in orbit. Why don't we take a break, and just hang out and do nothing? That is a great idea; in fact, you deserve a break today. But make sure that it is only a temporary break. If it is not, you will stagnate and become like a burnt-out rocket circling the earth in the same orbit until it falls from the sky. To sustain your journey, you must continually strive toward new horizons, toward new challenges and goals. To do that, we must install a set of very powerful engines and keep those engines properly tuned so that they can work relentlessly and at peak efficiency for you. Only then will you be able to propel yourself into new and even higher orbits. In other words, you must be willing to persevere; success is not achieved by traveling a straight line between points A and B. It is not even achieved by reaching *one* goal. Success consists of traveling the journey; reaching one worthwhile goal after another; enduring the persistent disappointments, the obstacles, and the setbacks; and enjoying the ultimate victory.

Let's crank up and fine-tune the engines of your PEP^2 success rocket so that you can find out what it takes to persevere and make it to the very top (see Exhibit 8-1).

PREVIEW OF COMING ATTRACTIONS

In this chapter, we will begin by determining how much you are willing to PAI by having you complete the Perseverance Assessment Inventory (Ex-

Exhibit 8-1 Your PEP² Rocket—Part 6: Engines at Full Blast (Perseverance)

hibit 8-2). Then we will find out why positive thinking is not enough. From there, we will take a brief look at people who have succeeded to find out what sets them apart from the "also-rans." Next we will consider three types of optimists and discuss the three universal laws that govern our lives. That discussion will be followed by a description of the six stages most of us go through when we are confronted with failure or a traumatic event. The chapter will conclude by providing you with seven powerful steps to help you turn future failures into opportunities and help you succeed.

Insight Break

Great works are performed not by strength, but by perseverance.

—Samuel Johnson

POSITIVE THINKING DOES NOT WORK

Did I catch your attention with that heading? I hope so, because I need to have you fully aware, turned on, and tuned in for the tough part. So far, we have talked about positive self-esteem, purpose, energy, education, and positive attitude. All of these are absolutely essential if you want to succeed in the game of life, love, and business, but they are worth absolutely nothing unless I can get you to buy into the last success principle: *perseverance*. Many of the people I have studied have been exposed to the importance of feeling good about themselves, having dreams and goals, keeping themselves motivated, and maintaining a positive mental attitude. Many have done it all, and many have done it well. But they soon become discouraged because nothing magical seems to happen. They have not committed to the long term, and they have not accepted that you have to pay the price. They have not made a long-term commitment to persevere.

I am not sure, but I think that looking for "easy street" is a key attribute of the American psychology. We all want it now, and we want it without effort. For example, some people spend 30 years of their lives being inactive and overeating until they have gained enough weight to be classified as obese. But once they make a decision that they want to lose weight, they expect to go on a magical diet that requires no effort and no behavior modification. In addition, they also want to be able to maintain their sedentary life style. If the diet doesn't help them take off the 30 extra pounds in 30 days or less, the diet obviously is not any good. That type of expectation is as American as apple pie. Perhaps it is because we live in a

Exhibit 8-2 Perseverance Assessment Inventory (PAI)

Instructions

Circle true (T) if you agree with the statement, false (F) if you disagree.

T F   1. Success is primarily a function of luck.

T F   2. Most self-made millionaires work more hours than people with average incomes.

T F   3. People who have succeeded have failed more often than people who have not succeeded.

T F   4. All you need to succeed in life is to have a positive mental attitude.

T F   5. Visualizing your goals will increase your rate of success.

T F   6. Succeeding in life, love, and business requires a lot of hard work.

T F   7. Life is fair.

T F   8. Most people who lose their job find a better one.

T F   9. Life is in balance.

T F   10. Success is primarily a function of being in the right place at the right time.

T F   11. Life is a game of probabilities.

T F   12. Sending positive affirmations to yourself will help you succeed.

T F   13. The more often you fail, the more likely you will succeed.

T F   14. You should not accept no until you hear it from the "horse's mouth" seven times.

T F   15. Human beings are predictable.

T F   16. Most people work through specific and predictable stages when tragedy strikes.

T F   17. Every tragedy has a hidden opportunity.

T F   18. Obstacles in life can be overcome by assuming a problem-solving attitude.

T F   19. When things go wrong, all you have to do is think positive thoughts and everything will be all right.

T F   20. Networking will contribute to your success.

__ __   Total

_____   Total Correct

Exhibit 8-2 continued

Scoring Key

(See end of chapter for answers.)

Interpretation of Your Score

   20 *Exceptional.* You are an expert and should have written this chapter.

18–19 *Excellent.* You've got it together and know all about hanging tough.

15–17 *Very Good.* You are doing well, but you can do even better. (I don't know anyone who can't.)

14–16 *Good.* Study this chapter carefully.

  <13 Retake this quiz after you have read the chapter. It is important. You need to master these principles so that you will succeed in the game of life, love, and business.

country that has always been a land of incredible abundance. Unfortunately, that kind of expectation is not very realistic, because succeeding at anything, regardless of how you define success, takes work, an awful lot of hard work, and an incredible degree of perseverance.

Consider the simple process of boiling water. If you put it on the stove and are impatient and take if off when you think you have waited long enough, you may simply have warm water. That is sufficient if you want to wash your face. But if you are a bit more persistent and wait until it just starts to bubble, let's say at 211 degrees Fahrenheit, you will have some real hot water that you can use to make soup. But let's say you are persistent and wait just a bit longer than seems bearable, until the water reaches 212 degrees. What do you have now? You have steam! And with steam you can move mountains. In fact, with steam you can move just about anything. If you want to experience true success you must internalize this last principle, the principle of perseverance.

Humor Break

The only difference between a big shot and a little shot is that the big shot simply keeps on shooting.

Study after study has demonstrated that there simply is no shortcut to success. In his study of self-made millionaires, Brian Tracy found that all were hard workers. Most worked from 10 to 14 hours per day.[1] He further quoted a newspaper interview with a self-made millionaire who was asked why he worked 12 to 14 hours a day. The millionaire responded, "It took me 15 years . . . to realize that in our society you work 8 hours a day for survival. . . . Everything over 8 hours is an investment in your future. Everything over 8 hours is an investment in your success."[2]

In other words, there are no discounts at the counter of success. You always have to pay full price, and you have to pay in advance. OK smarty, you're right, there are exceptions. For example, you could win the lottery, inherit a fortune, or find a pot of gold. These exceptions, however, are so rare and so random that you have a greater chance of being struck by lightning. Further, I suggest that you do not count on them, because you can wait for a long time. In fact, hell may freeze over long before you get lucky. (You're right again— I don't play the lottery. That makes me a winner every week. Think about it!) When I gamble (which happens very rarely) I do it for entertainment, not to win. True success, success that you can be proud of when it is featured on the front page of your local newspaper, is almost always proportionate to the amount of time and effort you expended to achieve it. Think of any field of endeavor. Those people you admire and perhaps even envy have usually dedicated their life to their avocation or profession.

Insight Break

The heights by great men reached and kept
Were not attained by sudden flight,
But they, while their companion slept,
Were toiling upward in the night.

—Henry Wadsworth Longfellow

HOW ABOUT THEM FAILURES

Let me introduce you to a failure. This person failed in business at age 22; he was defeated in the legislature at age 23; he failed once more in business at age 24; he was elected to the legislature at age 25; his sweetheart died at age 26; he had a nervous breakdown at age 27; he was defeated for public office again at age 29, at age 31, and at age 34. He was elected to Congress at age 37; he was defeated for public office again at age 39, at age 46, at age 47, and again at age 49. This man who failed in public office eight times was finally elected to the presidency of the United States at age 51. His name was Abraham Lincoln.

But he is not the only famous "failure" I can name. How about Thomas Edison? He tried to build an incandescent light bulb and couldn't get it right even after 10,000 tries. Not only that, he was also a workaholic, working up to 115 hours per week. How about Helen Keller? After all, she couldn't hear or see. Babe Ruth, now there was a failure if I ever saw one. He struck out 1,330 times. How about Lee Iacocca? He was fired from the Ford Motor Company. How about Winston Churchill, another failure? He was deathly afraid to speak in front of people, and was repeatedly defeated for various public offices for over 50 years. But, you protest, these people aren't failures. They were incredibly successful. You are right. But they also failed more than their unsuccessful counterparts. What distinguished them from their less fortunate colleagues was their ability to persevere even under the worst of circumstances. Truly successful people hang tough when things seem to be going the worst, when obstacles seem insurmountable; they are able to go just one more mile, make just one more call, lift just one more shovel, or type just one more page, until finally they get what they want. In short, having a dream, translating it into specific goals and objectives, and then sticking with it, over the long term, are the most basic ingredients for success.

Insight Break

The late Armand Hammer, at age 92, when asked by Barbara Walters to what he attributed his success, responded, "When you work 14 hours a day seven days a week, you get lucky."

That is why I know that you are going to succeed! How do I know that? Well, you made it through most of this book, didn't you? Behavior characteristics and traits are stable for most sane human beings. That means that most of us are fairly predictable. If you want to predict how someone will behave, observe and note her behavior in a specific situation. You will know, with a fair degree of accuracy, how she will behave in a future comparable situation. What does that have to do with reading this book? you ask. Well, the people who are full of PEP[2] will make it to the end of the book. The others, the also-rans, will not even come close (unless they got here by skimming). To them, success, or in this case wisdom, is supposed to come easily. They will try some of the principles in this book. They might even practice the positive attitude principle for a while (after all, that seems easy). But over the long run, they will become disillusioned, throw in the towel, and say that the principles in this book just don't work. But you, you will implement *each one* of the PEP[2] principles for 21 days or until they become your autopilot. You will persevere and, as a result, you will succeed!

Humor Break

A story that has been told many times bears repeating to emphasize this important point. Thomas Edison, while toiling to build an incandescent light bulb, was being interviewed. The young reporter said, "Mr. Edison, how does it feel to have failed 10,000 times?" Astonished and perplexed, Edison looked up and replied, "Failed 10,000 times? I have not failed 10,000 times. I have successfully found 10,000 ways that will *not* work."

The concept of seeing failures as steppingstones instead of as insurmountable obstacles was verified by Warren Bennis and Burt Nanus in their study of what makes people leaders.[3] One of the key leadership attributes they discovered was that leaders never saw themselves failing. In fact, they religiously avoided the word *failure*. It was as if that word was simply not in their vocabulary. They substituted such synonyms as "mistake," "glitch," "hash," "setback," "error," or "bungle." Never failure. To them, there simply was no such a thing. One of the individuals interviewed for this study said, "A mistake is just another way of doing things."[4] Another said, "If I have an art form of leadership, it is to make as many mistakes as quickly as I can in order to learn."[5] Similar sentiments were expressed by Thomas J. Watson, the founder and CEO of IBM, who said, "To be successful you have to double your failure rate."

Insight Break

Ships in a harbor are safe, but that's not what ships are built for.
—John Shedd

THREE TYPES OF OPTIMISTS

Perhaps one of the reasons that the positive mental attitude (PMA) movement has gotten such a bad rap is that too many people focus only on establishing a positive attitude. The advocates of this movement make it appear that all you need to do to succeed is to think positive thoughts, and if you are good at it and do it long enough, you will be successful. (There is that quick and easy stuff again.) Although I agree that with a positive attitude you can do anything—*anything better than with a negative attitude*—establishing such an attitude is simply not enough. In this respect, Stephen Covey, author of *The Seven Habits of Highly Effective People,*[6] was absolutely right. You have to superimpose on top of a PMA the realities of life. Understanding these realities, which I refer to as the basic laws of the universe, will transform you from an unrealistic optimist into a pragmatic optimist. Although that sounds like another oxymoron, I believe that it is absolutely essential to superimpose pragmatism on optimism to ensure that you will have the emotional resilience to stick with it when the going gets tough.

Humor Break

If you don't know where you're going, the last thing you want to do is get there any faster.

Type 1: The Unrealistic Optimist

My study of people has suggested that there are essentially three types of optimists. Type 1 is the *unrealistic optimist.* These are the people who have learned that it is important to think positive. They unfortunately have learned only half the lesson. They did not make it to the end of this book or many other books they have read. (Studies have shown that of the 55,000 new books published every year in the United States, only about 5 percent of all nonfiction books purchased are read from cover to cover.[7]) They *talk* about all the things they plan to accomplish in their lives, but they have no fire in the belly, no clearly defined action plan. When things do not go the way they expect them to go, they are stranded (after all, they believe that as long as they maintain their PMA everything will work out). Ultimately, however, they become upset and discouraged, and give up. They continue to smile, maintain a superficial positive attitude, and pretend that everything will turn out for the better. Often it will not, and as a result, they end up becoming disillusioned and cynical.

Type 2: The Eternal Optimist

Type 2 optimists, the *eternal optimists,* are like the people I recently met in Jamaica. Regardless of what happens to them, no matter how bad things get in their lives, they are governed by the axiom "Don't worry, be happy." Some of the people I have met in the Middle East live with a similar belief system. When things do not work out they shrug and say, "That's Allah's will." In the face of adversity, calamity, tragedy, and failure, they invoke a higher order, shrug it off, and just go on with their lives. They are almost on the right track. Some even have dreams, but most lack passion, that fire in the belly, the action plan, the energy, and the will to persevere when the going gets rough. In short, they talk a good game, but they don't persist. They just do not have all of the PEP^2 needed to succeed.

Type 3: The Pragmatic Optimist

Type 3 optimists, the *pragmatic optimists,* adhere to all six of the PEP^2 principles. They recognize that they live in an imperfect world, a world in which success is not a straight line. (I know your geometry teacher taught you that the shortest distance between any two points is a straight line, but she did not say that that is the distance to success.) The road to success is fraught with obstacles, pain, hard work, sweat, blood, and tears. (Sorry, I didn't mean to get that dramatic.) Pragmatic optimists accept setbacks, tragedies, losses, and disasters as the *normal* order of things, as lessons from which to learn, and as challenges to be mastered. Because they do not perceive obstacles as the exception, they are able to deal with negative events constructively. They have the capacity to persevere.

Mental Stretch Break

Before we discuss the three universal laws of life, let's take a brief break to ensure that you have both sides of your brain engaged. Translate each of the figures in Exhibit 8-3 into a meaningful word or brief phrase. (See end of chapter for answers.)

TIME TO FACE THE MUSIC

Let's take a look at several of the universal laws that govern all of us so that you can become a pragmatic optimist.

Universal Law Number 1: Life Is a Bitch

One of my workshop attendees once said to me, "Life is a bitch, and then you die." I bet you didn't expect to hear that kind of language from

Exhibit 8-3 Brain Teasers

1 ma✓il	2 MOMANON	3 _AR ^{Y L I} B A R R R A B _{I L Y} R
4 Clams She	5 GEORGE	6 age a g e age
7 WRITERS	8 FALL ALOHA SUMMER HI WINTER HELLO SPRING SHALOM	9 C C GARAGE R R

me. You didn't. Remember, it was one of my workshop attendees. Be that as it may, my personal life experience has certainly taught me that life is tough. It consists of never-ending problems, disasters, hardships, rejections, and frustrations. Ignoring these problems in yourself, your family members, or your employees by telling them that they just have to think positive thoughts and all will work out is simply counterproductive. In fact, just the opposite will likely happen. If serious problems are ignored, they usually get worse, not better. Pragmatic optimists accept these occurrences as normal events. They know that the only time that all of their problems will cease to exist is when they are looking at the radishes from the other side. Because they accept traumatic events as normal occurrences, they are empowered to act and do something about them. Unrealistic optimists, on the other hand, are devastated and paralyzed by difficulty. You might hear them say that life isn't fair. (They are right. It is *not*.) Or they might ask, Why me? (See the humor break that follows.) These people perceive themselves as victims. They therefore assume a defensive and helpless behavior pattern. Of course, when we perceive ourselves as helpless, we are unable to act. Because we cannot act, all that is left to do is to complain, bitch, and whine.

Humor Break

A well-to-do gentleman, let's call him Bill, was going through a very serious midlife crisis. To fix things, he decided to have himself made over. First, he had a complete medical checkup. Then he had a facelift, a tummy tuck, and a hair transplant. This gentleman was really serious. He also stopped smoking, cut down on fats and junk food in his diet, and initiated an aerobic exercise program three times a week. To complete the makeover, Bill bought a new Porsche and found a mistress 20 years his junior. Did it work? Well, let's just say Bill felt like a million dollars. In fact, he was reflecting on just how good he felt while crossing the street. Unfortunately, at that very moment, Bill was hit by a truck, with devastating, or should I say deadly, results. When he arrived at the pearly gates, Bill cried out in anguish, "Why me, God?" God took one look at Bill, clasped his hand over his mouth, and said, "Oops. I didn't recognize you!"

Universal law number 1 was demonstrated to me while I was dating Marcela, my superwoman. At the time, she was a beautiful 16-year old, with a sharp mind, wonderful disposition, gorgeous body, and beautiful face. (I'm not sure why I'm using the past tense—all still apply, except, of course, her age.) She was everything a young man could want in a sweetheart. Unfortunately, a small lump in her neck, which seemed to be getting bigger all the time, was diagnosed as a malignant thyroid tumor. She was admitted to the hospital, and skilled surgeons spent just about a full day cutting my beautiful girlfriend's neck into shreds, removing all of her thyroid and much else that used to be the left side of her neck. With medication and her wonderful positive disposition, Marcela overcame what many a young woman would consider devastating. After all, she would have a disfigured neck for the rest of her life, which meant that she could never again wear her hair short, wear a dress with a low neckline, or feel comfortable in a bathing suit. But with chemotherapy, a lot of support and love, and an incredible, vivacious, and positive attitude, Marcela did overcome this handicap. Because of that vivacious attitude, most people do not even notice her scarred and uneven neck.

Unfortunately, the story does not end there, as anyone who has battled with cancer knows. Uncertainty and stress were reawakened every year during her follow-up studies. Unanswered questions kept being repeated like a broken record: Will the tumor recur? Will it recur in another part of the body? But lady luck was kind. In spite of several minor "hot spots," all was well for 26 years. But then lady luck took a day off, and the next checkup revealed another growth in her neck. Even though it was growing on the same side of her neck, this tumor, also diagnosed as malignant, was totally unrelated to the first tumor. This one was in the salivary gland. And so, while the surgeons had Marcela in the operating room, especially after she had been in there for more than six hours for a surgery that was to take only three hours, I kept asking, Why Marcela? Why twice? The same trauma? The same anguish? Why couldn't misfortune have picked on someone else? Why does this always happen to the "good" people? (You know all the irrational thoughts that go through our mind when we are stricken with grief.) In spite of an extremely lengthy and complicated surgery, my superwoman pulled through again. She got better, and her powerful positive personality again took over. Today she is as beautiful as she ever was. In fact, to me, she is even more beautiful than she was when I first met her, because I have come to respect her incomparable strength, her vibrancy, her energy, and her incredible positive attitude. And even though we do not want to push our luck, we both expect to live until we are 100 and 102, respectively.

Universal Law Number 2: Life Is in Balance

All things in life are in balance. For every positive action, there is a negative reaction. The ancient Chinese philosophers, especially Lao Tzu and those who practiced Taoism about 300 B.C., called these forces Yin and Yang (female and male). And so it is with all things in the universe. Day is followed by night, life by death, victory by defeat, summer by winter, good by bad, warm by cold, health by disease, fire by ice, and success by failure. Without positives there can be no negatives, and without negatives there can be no positives. Nothing in the universe is, over the long run, just one way. To expect it to be otherwise sets you up for perpetual disappointment, stress, and failure. The next time things seem to be going badly for you, remind yourself of universal law number 2, and recognize that if you hang in there long enough, things will take a turn for the better.

Insight Break

The road to success requires constant course corrections.
—Wolf J. Rinke

Universal Law Number 3: Life Is a Game of Probabilities

Statisticians tell us that life is predictable. For example, any human trait, whether hair color, intelligence, or height, is distributed in accordance with the standard curve. If you have enough people, a statistician will be able to predict with a defined level of accuracy how many people will be blond, how many brunette, and so on. The laws of probability provide statisticians with an indication of how often a certain event will occur. That is how casinos structure their payout schedules and insurance companies develop their actuarial tables, which help them decide how much to charge you so that over the long term they can remain profitable and stay in business.

Of course, all of this is based on the long term and repeated tries. For example, if you toss a coin, would you expect the coin to show heads about 50 percent of the time and tails the other 50 percent of the time? Yes and no. Let's say you throw the coin 6 times. Would you expect it to come up heads 3 times and tails 3 times? Of course not! That would be rare indeed. But what if you tossed it 60 times, 600 times, or even 6,000 times? The chances for success are much better with each zero you add. Statisticians call this the law of large numbers.[8] Similarly, if you want to succeed at anything you can increase your chances proportionately with the number of tries you make. If you want to hit a home run, you can double your chances by stepping up to the plate 4 times instead of 2 times; you can triple your chance of making a sale by calling on a client 15 times instead of 5 times; and you can quadruple your chance of meeting the right spouse by going out with 40 prospective spouses instead of 10.

Although it is extremely basic, the law of probabilities is almost universally ignored. The sales literature tells us that most salespeople make about two sales calls before they give up. They quit after two calls even though many know that most sales are made only after the sixth sales call. The reason for this seemingly counterproductive behavior is that most of us do not like to face failure and rejection. Once you internalize the law of probabilities, however, you recognize that a no has absolutely nothing to do with you. In fact a no just brings you one closer to a yes. Because of the phenomenon of the law of probabilities I have made it one of my golden rules to never accept a no until I hear it from the horse's mouth at least seven times. (I should not have used the absolute term *never*, because if it is a really important goal, I might still be asking after the 12th try.) If you adhere to this rule you will obviously not always end up with a yes, but you will be confident that you have given it your best shot. (See Exhibit 8-4.)

Exhibit 8-4 Don't Quit

When things go wrong as they sometimes will;
When the road you're trudging seems uphill;
When the funds are low, and the debts are high;
And you want to smile, but you sigh;
When care is pressing you down a bit—
Rest if you must, but don't quit.
Success is failure turned inside out;
The silver tint of the clouds of doubt;
And you never can tell how close you are;
It may be near when it seems afar.
So stick to the fight when you're hardest hit—
It's when things go wrong that you mustn't quit.

—Unknown

Let me share a basic application of universal law number 3. My previous book, *The Winning Foodservice Manager: Strategies for Doing More with Less,* has a foreword by Bill Marriott, the CEO of the Marriott Corporation, and was positively endorsed by such notables as Ken Blanchard, coauthor of *The One-Minute Manager;* Tom Monaghan, CEO and founder of Domino's Pizza; the late Earl Nightingale, the dean of self-development; and Denis Waitley, author of *The Psychology of Winning.* My workshop participants frequently want to know how I was able to get so many famous people to endorse my book. They often assume that I personally know them all or that I paid them for their endorsements. When I tell them that all I did was to ask, I get numerous startled and doubting looks. But that is the truth. All I did was ask, but I asked more than once, and I did not just ask those who ended up endorsing my book. Isn't it funny how somehow we never find out about all the failures people experience? All we notice are their successes. If you want to succeed in life, pay attention to the law of probabilities. Make them come out in your favor by always going for more than you actually need. Then, with a bit of luck (see the definition of *luck* that follows), things may just work in your favor, and you too may be one of the "lucky" ones.

Insight Break

Luck: Preparedness meets opportunity.

—Napoleon Hill

HOW TO BEAT YOURSELF UP BY THE BOOK (NOT MINE)

The previous discussion should have made you sensitive to the fact that life can be very cruel at times. (Like you really needed to be reminded of that.) At times, we must deal with tragedies and even that dreaded *f* word (*failure*). After all, even if you persist beyond the call of duty, not every one of your efforts will lead to success. Not only that, being very ambitious increases your probability of failure. Working through the aftermath of such an event can be improved if we become aware that most of us go through specific stages when we are traumatized.

According to Linda Gottlieb and Carole Hyatt, authors of *When Smart People Fail*,[9] there are five stages—shock, anger and blame, fear, shame, and despair—that people go through any time we are traumatized. I have added a sixth: repair. Let's consider each of these stages in the context of a traumatic event, such as getting fired, and more importantly, identify what you can do to minimize the effect and get on with succeeding:

- *Stage 1: Shock.* This is like being hit by the proverbial five-ton truck. You cannot quite believe that they fired you. You of all people.

  Antidote: Remind yourself that losing is part of winning. Also review the preceding three laws of the universe.

- *Stage 2: Anger and Blame.* This is when you get mad at yourself, someone else, the system, the organization, anyone or anything as long as you can find a scapegoat. You might be saying such things as Why did they fire me? I've tried so hard. I'm so much better than Harry, John, Jane, and all the others in my department. Why me? I'm the most loyal, most trustworthy, and most dependable. That double

SOB (boss), he just never liked me, even after all I've done for him. Life is not fair.

Antidote: Analyze your actions. Listen to yourself speak. Ask yourself whether you are being rational or whether it is part of the process (stage 2) that you are going through.

* *Stage 3: Fear.* This is when you get that funny feeling in the pit of your stomach, which is especially pronounced when you are having to confront the unknown. You might be saying to yourself, Where am I going to find a new job in this recession? How am I going to feed my children? Who would want me at this age?

  Antidote: Identify specifically what you are fearful of. Make a list. Get it on paper. Dissect it. Figure out which are rational fears so you can deal with them, and which are irrational fears so you can throw them out.

* *Stage 4: Shame.* This is the sense that something is not right. You feel anxious to tell your spouse, your children, and other family members about getting fired. After all, someone with your experience should never have been fired. There must be something else going on.

  Antidote: Isolate what you feel ashamed about. Find out where your feelings originated. Is it something that someone else said? Do they have the facts? Get rid of those feelings that you determine to be irrational. Get answers to rational feelings from the "horse's mouth."

* *Stage 5: Despair.* This is the feeling of having lost all your momentum. You feel alone, depressed, defeated, and all washed up. You just don't know how you are going to deal with this tragedy.

  Antidote: Confide in your closest friend, your spouse, your parents or anyone else who can help you rebuild your positive self-esteem and confidence.

* *Stage 6: Repair.* This is when you pull yourself up by your bootstraps, sort it all out, put things in perspective, establish an action plan to fix the problem, and reengage the PEP² principles.

  Antidote: See the discussion that follows on turning failures into opportunities.

Mental Stretch Break

In the next section comes the important part: how to turn failures into opportunities. So let's take a brief mental stretch break so that you will be refreshed. Your task is to divide the square in Exhibit 8-5 with no more than three straight lines so that each dot is in a separate section. (See end of chapter for solution.)

Exhibit 8-5 Separate the Dots Exercise

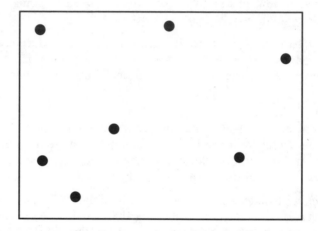

HOW TO TURN FAILURES INTO OPPORTUNITIES

Someone once said that when the going gets tough, the tough get going. (Of course, my wife changed that to When the going gets tough, the tough go shopping.) So what do you do when you hit a deep slump, when you are seemingly being overwhelmed by a tragedy of monumental proportions? For example, you lose your job, you have a tragedy in the family, your car gets broken into, your daughter tests positive for drugs, or any one of the many negative things that happen to all of us throughout our lives. Although there are no quick fixes for these situations, here are seven steps you can take to help you out of the slump.

Insight Break

I shut the door on yesterday
and threw the key away.
Tomorrow has no fears for me
Since I have found today.

—Anonymous

Believe in Yourself and Your Skills, Products, and/or Services

When things get tough, reaffirm for yourself the value of what you stand for and the benefits that your products and/or services are providing for your clients. Do this over and over again. Literally psych yourself up. If you have been fired, pull out all the awards you have received, your past positive evaluations, your "atta-boy (girl)" file containing your letters of appreciation, and your ledger in which you have detailed your strengths and weaknesses. Find anything that documents how good you are and how valuable your skills, products, and services are. Immerse yourself in those positive affirmations. Let this "objective data" reaffirm for you that you are an extremely valuable human being. Then tell yourself over and over again: I'm great. I have an incredible number of very positive strengths that are highly valued by others. Look at all the awards I have received. Why is psyching yourself up important? Because if you don't believe in yourself, how can others believe in you? Any excellent salesperson can reaffirm this for you because they have learned from experience that you will never be excellent at selling something you do not believe in.

We recently had to go through this process with our oldest daughter, Jeselle. She had just started her first semester in college and was struggling in several of her classes. She was not just struggling, she was finding great enjoyment in self-flagellation: "I'm not smart. I can't learn like the others. It takes me much longer to study than all my classmates." To overcome this self-defeating behavior, we pointed out to Jeselle that she had been an excellent student in high school, graduating in the top 10 percent of her class with a 3.2 average. We provided her with objective information that would help dispel her irrational fears. Although it was by no means easy, she survived her first semester, which did not surprise us at all. Not only did she pass all of her classes, but she got all As and Bs, with a 3.46 average.

Insight Break

Imagination rules the world.

—Napoleon Bonaparte

Visualize Success Instead of Failure

Cognitive psychologists tell us that the human mind has the capability to focus only on one major thought at a time. We also have the unique ability to make those thoughts come alive as if they were reality. That process is called visualization.

The advertising industry takes advantage of this phenomenon. For example, Marcela and I decided to take a cruise last year. Reviewing the sales literature that the travel agent had sent us helped us visualize just how wonderful that cruise was going to be. There were people just like us having fun, eating wonderful food, marveling at wonderful sights, snorkeling in crystal-clear waters, sunning themselves on sun-drenched beaches, and enjoying all of the exciting shows and activities aboard a fantastic-looking cruise ship. (Could you see it, feel it, touch it, smell it, and hear it while I was describing it? If so, you were visualizing even without the benefit of beautiful pictures.) They did not show all the negative things that are part of even that experience. Here is just a small sample of what actually also happened: having to take a very early and grueling morning flight to Miami, waiting "forever" on luggage, getting stuffed on an over-crowded bus, waiting "forever" to get off the bus, waiting in incredibly long lines to board the ship, waiting in more incredibly long lines to be assigned to a dining table to be with people who we didn't particularly care to be with three times a day for the next seven days, sleeping in a bed that isn't particularly comfortable or spacious, and living on something that absolutely refuses to hold still. And that is only the first several days. (I'd better shut up. I think you get the picture. If I go on, you may never take a cruise, and that would be a shame, because it is really a wonderful experience.) The point of all that is this: When you make your vacation plans, may it be for a cruise, a camping trip, or any other vacation, you choose to focus most of your mental energies on all the wonderful things that you expect to have happen. You might briefly think of potential problems, but that is not typically what you think about when you make these plans. On the other hand, when confronted with a new lifetime opportunity, most of us focus our energies on all the things that might go wrong. In either case, *we bring to pass what we visualize.* What I am suggesting is that you use the same positive visualization techniques that you use in planning a vacation to plan your life and to take advantage of any new projects and challenging opportunities (or what some would refer to as problems).

What about the possible problems? Should I ignore them? you ask. I am glad that you asked. No, I don't want you to ignore them. What I would like you to do is analyze the situation objectively. One way to do so is to make up another ledger. Take a blank piece of paper and a pen or pencil. On the top, write down what opportunity you are evaluating. Underneath it, divide the paper into two columns. Head one column "Benefits," the other "Disadvantages." (Some people call this the Ben Franklin decision-making method.) Now put on your optimist hat and write down all the possible things that can go *right* if you chose to take this course of action. Then take that hat off, put on the pessimist hat, and write down all the things that can possibly go *wrong*. This is the time to get it all out of your system. Then analyze the two columns to determine which is longer. If you are making a major life decision, you may want to get more sophisticated and assign a weight to each benefit and disadvantage. Now make a decision. (There is that action stuff again. Sorry. Just do it!)

Humor Break

This decision-making stuff reminds me of a story that I know you will enjoy.

A young man was being interviewed for a position as a railroad "switcher." (That is the person who shunts the trains onto the right tracks.) The job would be very convenient because the switching tower where he would be employed was just a few minutes from home. The engineer conducting the interview said to the young man, "When you become a switcher you have to be able to think on your feet. So what I like to do is set up a hypothetical situation and have you tell me what you would do." After the young man agreed to answer the questions, the engineer described the following scenario: "Imagine that you are in the control tower and you note on the monitor that there are two trains, one northbound, the other southbound, headed directly for each other on the same track. What would you do?" The young man answered, "I would telephone one of the trains and order it to stop immediately." The engineer complimented the applicant, and said, "Suppose neither train can be reached by telephone. What would you do then?" "I would throw the emergency switch and shunt one train out of harm's way onto the emergency track." "Suppose that track was inoperable, what would you do then?" the engineer asked. "I would get my kid brother," the applicant responded. "Why would you do that?" the puzzled engineer asked. The young man answered, "Because my kid brother has never seen a train wreck before!"

So much for levity. Let's get back to our decision-making process. If you should decide not to take advantage of this opportunity, challenge, or problem, be sure to forget it. Do not fret about it, or engage in what Arthur Freeman, a cognitive therapist from the University of Pennsylvania, calls woulda, coulda, shoulda thinking.[10] You have decided not to act on this option. You have done your homework, thought it through, decided on the basis of the best currently available evidence not to do it, so now it is time to forget that option. (It is in the past and you cannot make the past come back, can you?) So get on with your life and forget it once and for all. To help you do that, immediately focus on another goal, objective, or task so you can push those nonproductive thoughts out of your mind.

On the other hand, let's assume that the benefits appear to outweigh the disadvantages and you decide to go for it. (Note that I said *appear*. Certainty is such a rarity, why look for it?) What you want to do now is to analyze the disadvantages one more time and see which ones you can control or avoid. Develop an action plan for these to ensure that they are minimized. Then (I know you have heard it before) work your plan. Next, you want to shift your visualization gears and engage your positive visualization process. Visualize yourself succeeding. Picture yourself in the new situation in living color, with all the accompanying sounds, sights, and smells. To add realism to this process, you may want to find an actual role model who exemplifies what it is you want to have happen. Forming such a holistic mental success picture in your mind will facilitate what has been called a "force field" of energy in you. That field of energy will seemingly magically attract all the right resources, people, ideas, and situations that are consistent with your holistic success image. Once that has happened, you will find that you will dramatically increase your probability of success. You will magically begin to "act as if you are," which will lead to the second step of the visualization process, which is that you will "act as you become." Finally, you will sustain and reinforce that new success behavior because you will "act because you are."

Visualizing success in this manner has been practiced by the greats throughout history. For example, Michelangelo saw the completed statue in his mind before he ever began. Once he started, it was simply a matter of chipping away at the block of marble until the image he had visualized became a reality. Martin Luther King, Jr., talked about having a dream, and President John F. Kennedy helped our nation buy into his vision of putting a man on the moon. Successful authors visualize the entire story in advance. Effective house executives (that's what I think homemakers should be called) visualize the successful party long before the guests arrive. Olympic athletes run their races in their imagination before going to the track. Successful speakers deliver their presentations, and hear the applause, in their imagination in advance. And so it goes with all successful people, both in their personal and professional lives.

Send Yourself Positive Affirmations

In Chapter 3, we talked about the fact that you and I talk to ourselves all day and all night. It has been estimated that the average person thinks 60,000 thoughts every day.[11] Unfortunately, 95 percent of the thoughts that we have today are the same as the ones we had yesterday. That startling statistic leads to the following insight.

Insight Break

If you always think what you have always thought, you will always get what you have always gotten. If you are not happy with what you have gotten in the past, start thinking new and different thoughts.

—Unknown

Basically, to change and succeed, we must supplement our visualization with positive internal affirmations. (*Affirmation* just means that you talk to yourself (affirm yourself) in positive ways.) To make this process work for you, I recommend that you get all of your affirmations A P P P R O V E D (see Exhibit 8-6). (Sorry about that spelling, but perhaps you will remember the acronym whenever you talk to yourself.)

To help you put this into action, let's pretend that you have hit a major roadblock. Say you are in sales and have hit a slump. No matter what you do, you just can't seem to make that next sale. You try all the magic success strategies that have worked for you in the past and nothing happens. To overcome this "downer," the successful salesperson continues to feed herself positive affirmations, such as "I am the best salesperson in the company." "For the last three years in a row I was voted salesperson of the year." "I'm number one." "I'm the best." Each one is repeated over and over again. She might even review her enviable sales record from the same

Exhibit 8-6 How to Have All Your Affirmations A P P P R O V E D

- **Accurate**
  Your affirmations are correct and not exaggerated. They can be verified.
  Good example: I run a mile in seven minutes.
  Poor example: I outrun everyone.
- **Personal**
  Using personal pronouns such as I, my, mine, and me will make your affirmations more powerful and help you internalize them.
  Good example: I know that I will have a high probability of succeeding.
  Poor example: People are never given a chance to succeed in this organization.
- **Positive**
  State what you want to happen, not what you do not want to happen.
  Good example: I will get to work on time every day.
  Poor example: I won't be late for work anymore.
- **Present**
  State your affirmations in the present tense, as if they are happening. You have no control over the past and very little control over the future.
  Good example: I am very organized.
  Poor example: As soon as I have the time, I'll get organized.
- **Realistic**
  Your affirmations are attainable.
  Good example: I will join Greenpeace and devote four hours each week to the cause of preserving the environment.
  Poor example: I'm going to save the planet.
- **Observable**
  Make your affirmations observable, which means that they are specific.
  Good example: At the end of 1992, I will have earned $50,000.
  Poor example: Someday I'll make lots of money.
- **Valued**
  Your affirmations should be consistent with your values and lifetime goals.
- **Energizing**
  When you mess up, your affirmations should reenergize you instead of sapping your positive attitude. This refers to how you talk to yourself when you have messed up. Since you cannot make things go backward, refocus on the future.
  Good example: Make a note of what you have learned, and then say to yourself, I really messed that one up. The next time . . .
  Poor example: I always mess up. I can never get anything right.
- **Dominant**
  Make your positive affirmations your dominant thoughts. This acknowledges that you will occasionally forget and get back into that negative self-talk. If you do, make a note that you did, forgive yourself, shift mental gears, and get on with it.

time the previous year. If all else fails, the experienced salesperson will set herself up for success by selling the easiest product to the easiest client she can find. Then, after succeeding, she will return to increasingly more difficult products and clients. Successful salespeople, probably more than many others, know that life is governed by the law of probabilities. That is, if you make enough calls, sooner or later you will get another sale. They also have learned another law of human nature, which is that nothing begets success as much as success. So they set themselves up for success. You can use the same strategies with equally positive results.

Insight Break

There will never be another now—
I'll make the most of today.
There never will be another me—
I'll make the most of myself.

—Robert H. Schuller

Become a Problem Solver

Whenever you are confronted with a problem, a crisis, or a failure, think of it as a problem that needs to be solved. Look on it as an opportunity. Instead of being intimidated by the obstacle, let it energize you. Perceive it as a challenge, a puzzle that needs solving, or a code that needs to be cracked. Step back, avoid personalizing the problem, and pretend that you are on the outside looking in. Play Sherlock Holmes, make a game out of it, and solve the puzzle. To assist in this process, I suggest that you use the PIN technique and the creative thinking process described in earlier chapters of this book.

Mental Stretch Mini-Break

Talking about becoming a problem solver, here is a riddle that will stretch your assumptions. According to international law, if an airplane should crash on the exact border between two countries, would unidentified survivors be buried in the country they were traveling to or the country they were traveling from? (See end of chapter for answer.)

Look for the Good Stuff

In the previous example, we talked about the depressing event of losing a job. Please do not think that I am minimizing that, especially in these difficult times. But let me ask you this: How many people have you known who were fired or laid off, or for some other reason lost their job, who subsequently ended up with a better job or vocation as a result of it? That is exactly what happens many times.[12] Remember the symbol for crisis? It consists of two words: danger and opportunity. It reminds us that virtually every failure is accompanied by an opportunity. To find it, we must make a conscious mental effort to look for it. For most of us, that is easier said than done. The reason is that most of us have been conditioned to wallow in our own misery. That is what often got us the results we wanted when we were children. Since we are not little anymore, we must learn to PEP[2] ourselves up and shift into a positive gear. (The PIN technique discussed in Chapter 4 will help you accomplish this.)

Insight Break

I am reminded of Thomas Edison, who, while surveying the damage after his laboratory was completely burned down in 1914, exclaimed, "There is great value in disaster. All our mistakes are burned up. Thank God we can start anew."

Let me share a specific example with you to make this point. After my previous book, *The Winning Foodservice Manager: Strategies for Doing More with Less,* had been in print for a little more than a year and a half, I received a letter from my publisher advising me that they had decided to not reprint it. I had to read the letter numerous times to make sure that I had read correctly. After all, the publisher had just recently declared it a best seller, it had received numerous powerful endorsements, and I had received many unsolicited letters from readers and educators who told me how great the book was. I was so flabbergasted that I had to call the publisher just to make sure that they had not made a mistake. After I found out that no mistake had been made, I went through the five stages, shock, anger and blame, fear, shame, and despair, that I discussed earlier in this chapter. I even went so far as to consult with my lawyer to find out how I could "make" them print my book. Given that I am pretty stubborn, this took a couple of months. But after lots of study and introspection, I finally figured out that what was happening with my book had nothing to do with the quality of the book or even me. It had to do with the book publishing business and the fact that most book publishers are really much better at book *printing* than they are at book *promoting and selling*. I guess that is really not that surprising once you realize that there about 55,000 new book titles published *every* year.[13] What I also learned is that publishers, just like most people, like to take the path of least resistance. What they do is publish as many new books as possible every year because they have learned that any book, regardless of quality, will sell a certain minimum number of copies. However, after that initial easy sell, books really have to be promoted to continue to sell. Only about 40 percent of all books make any money for the publisher.[14] Getting books to actually make big money obviously takes a lot of effort and financial investment. Instead of doing that, publishers just print another new one, betting on the law of probabilities. Meanwhile, the authors are left holding the bag (I guess I should have said the book), since it takes much longer to write a book than to print one.

After I worked myself through all five stages, I began to move into stage 6, repair. That is when I began to look for the good stuff. And it was really not very hard to find, once I committed to finding it. The solution was to start my own publishing company, Achievement Publishers. Now, instead of making a measly royalty, I am rewarded handsomely for my significant initial investment and considerable effort. (Yes, as always, I have to pay the price in advance, because there is a lot more to self-publishing than originally meets the eye.) The additional benefit that resulted from this "tragedy" is that for the first time I had complete control over the jacket design, insertions, layout, and many other things that the publisher and I could previously not agree on.

The moral of this story is obvious. *The good stuff is there, but you have got to look for it.* So go ahead, work yourself through those five stages (after all, you are human). But don't quit there. Go on to stage 6, repair, and you too will find in every failure at least one new opportunity.

Humor Break

Here is a brief story directly related to what we have been talking about.

There were twin brothers—one was an eternal optimist, the other a superpessimist. Both were told by their mother that there was a surprise in the barn for them. The pessimist went first. He opened the barn, and found it to be full of horse manure. He immediately ran out, complaining loudly,

"Darn it, there is nothing but horse s—t in the barn." The other brother went to look for his surprise. After he had been gone for about an hour, the mother got worried, and went to the barn to see what her son was doing. As she approached the barn, she heard him singing at the top of his lungs. She opened the door and there was her son, bathed in perspiration, shoveling horse manure. She asked him what he was doing. He answered, "With all the horse manure in here, there's got to be a pony in here somewhere."

Take an Inventory

It helps to take either a verbal or written inventory of all the good things still left in your life. If you set this up as a ledger with the credits (positive things) and debits (negatives) on one sheet of paper, you will usually find that no matter how bad things appear to be, the positives in your life still outweigh the negatives.

Recently, a colleague confided in me that he was finished, through, kaput. He had just declared bankruptcy after having invested his life savings and over ten years in his business. He was extremely depressed and was virtually ready to check out of life. I said to him, "I'm sorry that your wife has left you." He said indignantly, "Who said that my wife has left me?" I said, "You mean to tell me that you still have the most important person in your life?" I continued, "I'm sorry that your son has become a drug addict." Again he objected, telling me that he was very proud of his son's and daughter's accomplishments. After I continued this a bit longer, his face suddenly lit up, and he said, "I guess things are not nearly as bad as I thought they were."

It also helps to put things in perspective. Even though grief is personal, it is also relative. When you see what other people who are less fortunate than you go through, especially if you can take a worldwide perspective, you begin to realize that your tragedy is not really as calamitous as it initially appeared. You might also find it useful to confide in a close friend, seek counsel, read a motivational book, or listen to a motivational audiotape program.

Insight Break

I had no shoes and I complained until I met a man who had no feet.
—Anonymous

Establish a Strong Bond with a Significant Other, a Support Group, or a Network

Some wise person once said that no man (or woman) is an island. All of us need someone we can confide in when things are particularly bad. This applies even when things are particularly good. Have you ever noticed how much less stunning a gorgeous sunset is when you are viewing it by yourself? Of course, in times of trouble that important other, group, or network becomes even more critical. It provides you with a mechanism to talk things through, to tease apart the rational from the irrational, to generate those innovative solutions, and to come up with all the opportunities. I believe that if more of us had such a network, many mental health professionals would be out of a job.

Humor Break

Our discussion of the value of a strong support system and letting others help you reminds me of a story. As a result of Hurricane Bob, Mr. Smith's house flooded. Police advised people to evacuate. As the flood rose, Smith prayed, asking God for help. When a neighbor came by offering him a lift, Smith answered, "Thanks very much, but I'm going to stay here because I have faith in God and know that he will help me." Smith continued his prayers, but the flood waters continued rising, forcing Smith to the second story. Just then, a boater came by and offered Smith a ride. Again Smith rejected the offer, telling the boater, "I have faith in the Lord, and I know he will save me." Despite his prayers, the flood waters continued rising, and Smith had to escape to the roof. While on the roof, a police helicopter came by and attempted to rescue him, but again Smith resisted help, restating his belief in the Lord. The flood, however, had no mercy, and Smith was swept away by the waters. Following his entry to the pearly gates, he expressed his frustration by asking God, "Why did you let me down?" God answered, "Let you down? I didn't let you down. I sent your neighbor, a boat, and even a helicopter after you."

Now that I have gotten you to laugh, I would like to introduce you to a man who has had little reason to laugh. A man who has faced more adversity in his life than most would expect to experience in ten lifetimes. A man who, despite all the adversity in his life, has accomplished all that we have talked about in this book and more. A man who persevered more than anyone I know. A man who is a living legend, who knows what it takes to *MAKE it a WINNING life.*

PEP² IN ACTION—PERSEVERANCE:
W MITCHELL

Probably more than anyone else in these pages, W Mitchell is living proof that all of us, regardless of obstacles, handicaps, or even tragedies, can choose to MAKE it a WINNING life. His unfortunate but true story will no doubt bring tears to your eyes.

W Mitchell, born William John Schiff (he changed his name to honor his late stepfather, Luke Mitchell), dropped out of high school in the tenth grade and joined the Marines. While he was in the service, he got his high school equivalency diploma. Following his four-year hitch, he bounced between various jobs, including radio announcer, bartender, cab driver, and part-time college student. In 1969, he became a San Francisco cable car gripman and piloted the city's famous trolleys. On July 19, 1971, he bought a beautiful new motorcycle and, for the first time, soloed an airplane. He was 28 years old, healthy, and popular. In short, he was on top of the world.

All that came to an abrupt end when, while riding his motorcycle to work, he collided with a laundry truck. The motorcycle went down, crushing his elbow and fracturing his pelvis. The gas cap popped open on the bike, gas poured out, and the heat of the engine ignited it. Someone nearby doused Mitchell with a fire extinguisher and saved his life. But his face had been burned off; his fingers were black, charred, and twisted; and his legs were nothing but raw, red flesh. Mitchell was burned over 65 percent of his body. He remained unconscious for two weeks. During four months in the hospital, Mitchell underwent 13 transfusions, 16 skin-graft operations, and a variety of other surgeries.

When he finally awoke, he had time, lots of time, to reflect on his life. To say the least, things did not look bright. Mitchell was so badly disfigured that first-time visitors had trouble looking at him. And when they did, they often fainted. At this point, he could have decided to feel sorry for himself. He had a choice, though: He could focus on what he had lost or focus on what he had left. Mitchell decided to do the latter. This is best expressed in one of his most memorable quotations: "Before the accidents there were 10,000 things I could do. Now there are 9,000. I could dwell on what I lost, but I prefer to focus on the 9,000 things I have left." Instead of feeling sorry for himself,

Mitchell asked for his flying manuals. (No, this is not a typo.) He was determined to get better and practice his favorite hobby, regardless of the obstacles before him.

With that spirit, and $500,000 awarded him in a lawsuit, Mitchell moved to the picturesque ski town of Crested Butte, Colorado, 230 miles southwest of Denver. He bought a lovely Victorian house, an airplane, some real estate, and a bar. Early in 1975, Mitchell teamed with two friends, invested $25,000, and cofounded Vermont Castings, Inc. As chairman of the board, he helped make the tiny wood-stove company into Vermont's second-largest private employer. Eventually, his net worth climbed to nearly $3 million.

Then, on the morning of November 11, 1975, when once again he seemed to be on top of the world, lady luck took another day off. Unfortunately, it was on a day when Mitchell and four passengers took off in his turbocharged Cessna. At 75 feet, the plane stalled and dropped like a rock, straight back onto the runway.

Upon impact, Mitchell told the others to get out of the plane, but he was unable to. Excruciating pain shot from his lower back, impeding his ability to move his legs. When they finally "dug" him out of the wrecked plane, Mitchell was once again taken to the hospital. This time, his 12th thoracic vertebra was crushed and his spinal cord was bruised beyond repair. He was a paraplegic.

At that point in his life, even the relentlessly optimistic Mitchell began to have dark moments. As he described it, "I wondered what the hell was happening to me. What did I do to deserve this?" But he still had his friends and a profound sense that he could create his own reality by focusing on the "can" rather than the "can't." He decided to follow the advice of the German philosopher Goethe, who said, "Whatever you can do, or dream you can, begin it. Boldness has genius, power and magic in it."

While in the hospital recuperating, he began to articulate his philosophy and reassess his values. He began to think about the Rocky Mountains he had come to love. In particular, he thought about Mount Emmons, called the Red Lady because of the rouge tint it takes at sunrise. It forms the backdrop of Crested Butte, and is regarded by many as unspeakably beautiful.

One of the world's largest mining companies was staking claims on the mountain to extract molybdenum. Many residents regarded the mine—and the more than 1,500 workers who would descend on their quiet town—as inevitable, but not Mitchell. Utilizing the determination that had reawakened during his lengthy hospital stay, Mitchell decided to do something about it. He ran for mayor, won, and, as he puts it, "hit the ground rolling." From 1977 to 1981, he spent an estimated $120,000 of his own money in a pitched battle to preserve the mountain and the town. He buttonholed politicians, *captured media attention, and prodded lawyers. In August 1981, after four years of fighting one battle after the other, the mining company withdrew.*

The next summer yielded an even happier moment. On June 19, 1982, Mitchell married Annie Baker at the base of Oh Be Joyful, a mountainous wilderness that Mitchell's lobbying had helped to protect.

In February 1984, Mitchell decided to run for Congress. He turned his odd appearance into an asset, with slogans such as "I'm not just another pretty face." Mitchell won the primary, but the Reagan coattail effect made 1984 a bad year for Democrats in Colorado, and he lost the election. He has no regrets, and says, "I would not trade that experience for anything in the world."

Today he is a millionaire, a respected environmentalist, a sought-after speaker, a former mayor and Congressional candidate, a happy husband, and even a river rafter and skydiver. And, he became all of these things after *his accidents.*

WR: Mitchell, you have had an incredibly tough time, yet you have been able to overcome, persevere, and succeed. What are some of the important principles that have allowed you to succeed?

WM: After the accident, when I was lying in the hospital, I started to think about some lessons I had learned about taking responsibility for my own life. I realized that if I did not take responsibility, nobody else was going to. Responsibility doesn't mean finding someone to blame, or feeling guilty or even finding fault. Responsibility just means the ability to respond. Fortunately, I had the belief that I was able to respond to any situation, even while I was in the hospital. I believe that was one of the great benefits that I had. I was able to recognize that it was my life, that it was my decision as to what I was going to do. The problem with not taking responsibility is that if you will not take responsibility for what has happened in the past, then you cannot be responsible for what is going to happen in the future. Fortunately for me, I also understood another principle. I think it is one of the key principles to a successful life. That is, there is no absolute relationship between any two variables. There is no absolute relationship between being odd-looking, unusual, and different and being unsuccessful, any more than there is a relationship between having a million dollars in the bank and being happy. When you say, "When I have this, then this will be the result, this will happen," you make a big mistake.

WR: That is right. That belief is similar to a metaphor I use throughout this book: Life and success are a journey. The idea is to experience the joy while you live it instead of always looking to the end of the journey.

WM: Exactly. When you are waiting for some of that to happen or because some of that does not exist in your life, no other good things can happen. You miss an awful lot. Fortunately, I had those two philosophies. Again, it did not make being burned the greatest thing that ever happened to me, but it allowed me to recognize and understand that *it is not what happens to you, it is what you do about it.* Now, I did not actually use those words until later. In fact, I started using them once I started to speak. But even though I did not have those precise words in my mind, that was the feeling I had.

WR: One of the things I talk about in this book is that there are three types of optimists: an unrealistic optimist, an eternal optimist, and a pragmatic optimist. Unrealistic optimists are the people who basically operate under the premise that all they need in life is a positive mental attitude, and everything else will be fine. I am trying to convey to my readers that that is a heck of a good start, but it is not enough in and of itself. How do you feel about that?

WM: I agree absolutely. I think you need much more than just optimism. You need tools. You need a sense of purpose. You need a mission. You need goals. You need focus. You can be wonderfully optimistic and sit under a tree, but the chances of a million dollars fluttering down into your lap is slight to nonexistent. You can start a business and have the most positive attitude in the world, but if you do not get a good bookkeeper to do the necessary ABCs of business, that business is likely going to fail. It takes a lot more than just a positive mental attitude to make things work. I think things work a lot better with a positive outlook, and I think when you are looking for positive solutions, when you are going out and seeking them, having the right mental attitude helps a lot. But without the other essentials, the rest is not going to happen.

WR: The other principle I talk about in the book is three universal laws: Life is a bitch, life is in balance, and life is a game of probabilities. I think when I was writing this section I was thinking about you. Many people, when something happens to them, belabor the fact that something bad happened to them. They feel sorry for themselves and keep digging themselves a proverbial hole that keeps getting deeper and deeper. The more they feel sorry for themselves the less they are able to get themselves out of this rut. If anything has happened to anybody, it has happened to you. Yet, you have been able to pull yourself up by the bootstraps and turn yourself around. What advice do you have for my readers? How can they overcome the obstacles that they face?

WM: I talk about the children in the schoolyard calling me a monster, and I talk about the fact that for a long time I avoided people's gazes. I did not want to answer the questions they were asking with their eyes. But after about two years I had forgotten how "funny looking" I was. I was thinking about other things. And when I began to concentrate on the positive, and quit concentrating on the negatives, my life changed; other people were concentrating on what I was concentrating on. When I was focusing on what was *wrong* so were they. When I began focusing on what was *right,* so did they. And that gets back to the question of focus. It doesn't work just to be positive. You have to have a focus, a purpose, a direction. When you are headed in a direction, people will, more often than not, head in that direction with you.

WR: The first P in the PEP^2 principles stands for positive self-esteem, which is the ability to feel good about yourself. I believe that that is what you were just describing. The next P stands for *purpose,* which you have been referring to as that important sense of direction. *Energy* is the ability to constantly remotivate yourself. *Education* is about being a lifelong voracious learner. *Positive attitude* is that attitude that you demonstrated when you were lying in the hospital bed, virtually a cripple, but asking for your flying manuals. The last P in the PEP^2 formula refers to *perseverance,* the ability to not give up, even when it seems the whole world is out to get you. To me, all six are of equal importance. If you take one away, the probability of your ability to succeed becomes slimmer. It is not impossible, but your chances become slimmer. How do the PEP^2 principles fit with your personal experiences?

WM: I think your formula is right on. For example, you cannot say that something can't be done. But what one does can make things harder or easier. There are people who overcome impossible odds. There are people who do things that seem quite easy and everything is handed to them. Again, that is what it is all about—increasing the odds in your favor. Practicing what you call the PEP^2 principles will certainly increase the odds in your favor.

WR: This idea of increasing the odds is illustrated by the following, for lack of a better analogy: If you want to catch fish, the more lines you have in the water, the greater the probability of catching fish. You talk about failures. If anyone has personally experienced failure, you have certainly had more than your share. To help people overcome their failures, I impress upon them that life is a bitch. I don't say that to be ugly. But the bottom line is this: People who expect things to be rosy all the time are just setting themselves up for stress, anger, and myriad other health problems. Instead of just saying, "Everything is supposed to be rosy," what I am trying to get my readers to think is, "Hey, I am going to have problems in life because failures and problems are part of life. But, because life is in balance, sooner or later things will turn around, and I will succeed again." How does that fit with your experiences?

WM: Again, my greatest successes have come from my greatest failures. That is not a new phrase on my part. We have all heard other people use that term. It certainly has been true for me. I wouldn't trade for anything what I have learned, what I have received from these experiences. Now, I wouldn't recommend that people go get burned or go get paralyzed, and I do not think that you need to do that to experience these realizations. But, the fact is, those experiences taught me an enormous amount. I don't know how many mistakes I have made as the mayor of my community. I have made bunches of them. I could have put my head down and said, "Well, life's just impossible, and I'll never be able to do it." Instead I was fortunate enough to find lessons in my failures, which enabled me to win the next time around. These lessons perhaps even enabled me to win in a better way, to win more dramatically than if I had not stumbled the first time.

WR: Let me give you an example. My father has glaucoma and has been diagnosed as being legally blind. Certainly that is not something one would wish on anyone. Relatively speaking, though, comparing his inability to see well with what has happened to you makes one aware that it is really not a *major* tragedy. But, for my father, glaucoma has literally debilitated him. It is his crutch, the excuse he uses to avoid doing all kinds of things. He will not go along to the grocery store with my mother, he will not come visit us. Instead, you have said, "Before the accidents there were 10,000 things I could do. Now there are 9,000. I could dwell on what I lost, but I prefer to focus on the 9,000 things I have left." How can you help my father and my readers, who have not gone through those horrible experiences, to focus on the things they have *left,* instead of on the things they no longer have?

WM: It is not easy. There is the old saying that you can lead a horse to water but you can't make it drink. Some people can't even be led to water. They don't want to do it, they don't want to think about it, they feel that they are fine the way they are, they don't want to be bothered. There are a lot of folks out there who don't want to hear it. People have to be looking first. If they are not looking for it, then you have a real challenge. With a book it is a little easier. Usually you are reaching people who are already looking. They have bought the book, so they are at least interested. At least they are moving in the right direction.

WR: After having gone through some of the challenges you have faced, do you feel there are specific steps one must take when one experiences a personal or a business loss? Do you think there are specific steps one can take to pull oneself out of the "hole"?

WM: I think that you have to focus on what is *right*. You have to stop from time to time and think about what is working. We frequently think about what is not working when we are in a tough situation. We can get ourselves spiraling downward. We think about how bad it is. We think about all the consequences of how bad it is. Then we think about all the things that are going to happen to us if we don't fix it. And then we think about how bad that will be. We just spiral downward. We have to catch ourselves and have time to just think about what is going *right* in our lives. Tony Robbins uses a series of questions that he encourages people to ask themselves every morning: What is right in my life? What am I proud of in my life? What do I feel good about? Who do I love? Who loves me? Even when things are as bad as they could ever be, even when things are a horrendous disaster, there are still things going right in your life. There is something out there— a memory, the magnificence of your brain, your resourcefulness, whatever allows you to live on the planet—that enables you to survive against all the odds. There is something there. I think it is important to catch yourself and get a positive perspective, regardless of the situation.

WR: In other words, you want to avoid digging yourself a hole that gets ever deeper. It is almost like a black hole. You cannot see it, but it has a force so powerful that it sucks everything in its path into it and devours it.

WM: Exactly! At least you can think, "Here is one speck of light." Look at that speck of light for a second. There's another old saying, "What you focus on is what you become." When you think about what is going right in your life, then you can get perspective on what is going wrong. Once you are operating from a position of positive perspective, or balance, other bright lights can start shining and illuminate or solve your problem.

WR: In the book I talk about eight different steps to take to turn failure into opportunity. The fifth step is looking for the good stuff. That is basically what you have been telling us, isn't it?

WM: When I was lying in the hospital, I didn't have any fingers anymore and I was a pretty unusual sight. I asked someone to bring my flying manuals, my instructional materials. It seemed pretty improbable to most people that I was going to fly an airplane again, but it wasn't improbable to me.

WR: You asked for your manuals for your flying lessons while lying in your hospital bed?

WM: It was during a time when I had the opportunity to reflect on all the things that were wrong. Fortunately, I was able to marshal my thoughts and start to think about a few things that were right. Thinking about flying was a very pleasant thing. I soloed in an airplane the day I was burned. I was able to think about that. It's a fascinating thing, the great fortune cookie proverb that says, "The longest journey begins with a single step." Here we are in a world of plenty in which so many people refuse to take that first step. I don't know what would have happened if I had not asked for the flying materials in the hospital. People thought I was a little crazy thinking about trying to fly an airplane when I didn't have the hands to do it. It was a very interesting experience. After I got out of the hospital I started flying lessons again, with the same instructor I had before the accident. We flew for a long time, day after day after day. When I asked him when I could solo again, he kept saying, "I don't know. We'll talk about it." Finally, one day when I confronted him, he said, "How can you fly without any hands?" I had been flying him around for months! All he could do was look at my hands and say it was impossible even though I had been flying him around for months.

WR: In other words, he had his mind made up. What he saw caused him to disregard what he had actually experienced.

WM: That is exactly right. He had decided something was so, and he couldn't change; he was unable to change.

WR: That is a beautiful example of how all of us are ready to see and hear what we are ready to see and hear and that all improvement in life has to begin with self-improvement. That is the ability, as the oracle of Delphi proclaimed, to know thyself. Thanks for giving so generously of yourself. You have been an extremely powerful role model to me and my readers. I hope that my readers can gain your powerful insights without experiencing multiple tragedies. Thanks for helping all of us to *MAKE it a WINNING life!*

SUMMARY: A TRIP BACK TO THE FUTURE

- Positive thinking by itself will not ensure that you make it to the top.
- There is no shortcut to success.
- There are three types of optimists:
  —the unrealistic optimist;
  —the eternal optimist; and
  —the pragmatic optimist.
- Pragmatic optimists are the ones who generally succeed in the game of life, love, and business.
- All human endeavors are governed by three universal laws:
  1. Life is a bitch.
  2. Life is in balance.
  3. Life is a game of probabilities.
- Pragmatic optimists have the ability to take advantage of the three universal laws and succeed even in tough times.
- When tragedy strikes, most people go through five stages:
  1. shock;
  2. anger and blame;
  3. fear;
  4. shame; and
  5. despair.
- To transform despair into positive action, you must add stage 6: repair.
- You can turn failures into opportunities by
  —believing in yourself and your skills, products, and/or services;
  —visualizing success instead of failure;
  —sending yourself positive affirmations that are A P P P R O V E D (accurate, personal, positive, present, realistic, observable, valued, energizing, and dominant);
  —becoming a problem solver;
  —looking for the good stuff;
  —taking an inventory; and
  —establishing a strong bond with a significant other, a support group, or a network.

SUCCESS ACTION STEPS

❑ Identify one lifetime goal that you are currently pursuing with all your energy. If you cannot identify at least one, go back to Chapter 4, and get busy. Remember that success is a journey, not a destination and that satisfaction and happiness come from traveling the journey.

❏ Set up an appointment or create an opportunity to talk for at least 15 minutes with someone who has made it to the top. Find out how long they have been practicing their craft, how much time they typically dedicate to their "work" and how much time, effort, and money they dedicate to their own self-development.

❏ Evaluate your past to determine what has had the greatest impact on getting you where you are today. Once you have isolated what it was that made a significant difference in your career, consistently do more of it for the next 21 days or until it becomes a new habit.

❏ Starting tomorrow, treat yourself as if you are the most important asset you will ever own. Why? Because you are!

❏ The next time you experience a tragedy, analyze what stages you go through to deal with your grief. Recognize that these stages are normal. Also recognize that no one ever guaranteed you that life was going to be fair. Then proceed to stage 6, repair, and get on with your life.

❏ If you have not already done so, establish a PEP² file. Use it to file all positive actions, accomplishments, and anything else you are proud of. Refer to this file any time you are beginning to doubt your own abilities or if you are down for any other reasons.

❏ The next time you start on an important project, visualize yourself succeeding in advance. Make that picture as dramatic, vivid, colorful, and realistic as possible. When you find that you are doubting yourself, pull that positive picture back up, recharge that image, and go on with your plan.

❏ Any time you need to make a major decision about an action, use the Ben Franklin method to analyze your options.

❏ The next time a close friend is in despair because of a serious personal tragedy, do not just feel sorry for him. Help your friend put things in perspective by taking an inventory of his life. Then help him focus on the positive things that are left.

❏ Grade your self-talk. If your language is generally positive, you pass. If it is not, use the acronym A P P P R O V E D to help you make your affirmations accurate, personal, positive, present, realistic, observable, valued, energizing, and dominant.

❏ The next time you face a "problem," make a bet with yourself that you can find something positive in it. If you win the bet, treat yourself and your significant other to something special.

❏ Do you have a support person or persons in your life with whom you can share both pain and joy? If you don't have at least one, make finding one a priority on your lifetime goal list, and pursue it as if your life depends on it. It does!

❑ There are enough suggestions in this book, in fact, just in this chapter, to help you succeed in the game of life, love, and business, even during tough times.

NOTES

1. B. Tracy, "Seven Secrets of Self-Made Millionaires," *Insight* 64 (1987): 25–42. Audiotape program with accompanying written materials. Nightingale-Conant Corp., 7300 North Lehigh Avenue, Chicago, IL 60648.

2. Ibid., p. 36.

3. W. Bennis and B. Nanus, *Leaders: The Strategies for Taking Charge* (New York: Harper & Row, 1985).

4. Ibid., p. 69.

5. Ibid., p. 69.

6. S. Covey, *The Seven Habits of Highly Effective People: Powerful Lessons in Personal Change* (New York: Simon & Schuster, 1989).

7. J. Kremer, *1001 Ways to Market Your Books* (Fairfield, IA: Ad-Lib Publications, 1990).

8. T. Gilovich, *How We Know What Isn't So* (New York: Free Press, 1991).

9. L. Gottlieb and H. Hyatt, *When Smart People Fail: Rebuilding Yourself for Success* (New York: Penguin, 1988).

10. A. Freedman, *Woulda, Coulda, Shoulda: Overcoming Regrets, Mistakes, and Missed Opportunities* (New York: Harper & Row, 1989).

11. D. Chopra, "Magic Mind, Magic Body," *Insight* 96 (1991) 26–35. Audiotape program with accompanying written materials. Nightingale-Conant Corp., 7300 North Lehigh Avenue, Chicago, IL 60648.

12. C. Kleinman, "Dismissals Can Bring Brighter Days," *Washington Post,* Nov. 25, 1990, H3.

13. J. Kremer, *1001 Ways to Market Your Books.*

14. Ibid.

SCORING KEY TO THE PERSEVERANCE ASSESSMENT INVENTORY (PAI)
Page 230

All questions are true (T) except 1, 4, 7, 10, and 19.

ANSWERS TO MENTAL STRETCHING EXERCISE
Page 251

It is not nice to bury survivors, especially if they still have enough strength to object. In fact, it is against the law in *any* country.

Page 244

Exhibit 8-7 Solution: Separate the Dots Exercise

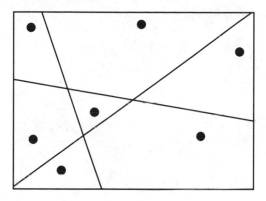

ANSWERS TO BRAIN TEASERS*
Page 237

1. The check is in the mail
2. The man in the moon
3. Circulating library
4. Clams on the half shell
5. George Burns
6. Middle-age spread
7. Writer's block
8. Season's greetings
9. Two-car garage

*I hope that you have enjoyed the brain teasers and mental stretching exercises in this book. If you come up with others, I would appreciate receiving them in the mail—with the answers, of course, just in case you stump me. If I use them in a future book I will give you credit *and* send you a free autographed copy of the book.

Mail your brainteasers to:
Wolf J. Rinke
c/o Achievement Publishers
P.O. Box 1289
Olney, MD 20830-1289

Thanks in advance.

9

The Commencement

*Knowledge plus action will change your life. So what are you waiting
for? Do something NOW!!!*
                                                                —*Wolf J. Rinke*

Weird book, right? Here you thought that you had finally finished it and
it says "The Commencement." It really is your commencement, though. If
you look up *commencement* in your trusty *Webster's New Collegiate Dictionary* you will find that it is defined as "an act, instance, or time of
commencing." Sounds just like Webster, doesn't it? If we pursue it just a
bit further we find that *commencing* means "to enter upon; begin" and "to
initiate formally by performing the first act of . . ." In other words, this is
the beginning for *you*! This is where I leave you and you take the controls
and become the commander of your own PEP² rocket. Only if you consistently apply the PEP² principles advanced in this book and unfailingly put
the winning action steps I've provided you to work will you thrive in the
tough times ahead and succeed in life, love, and business. I would like to
encourage you—no, implore you—to *act now*. Because Will Rogers was
absolutely right when he said, *"Even if you're on the right track, you'll get
run over if you just sit there."* In other words, no matter how much you
enjoyed reading this book, no matter how much knowledge you gained,
nothing will come of it unless you *do something*. It is just like reading the
best diet book money can buy. No matter how good the book, and no
matter how well you know the principles, you just are not going to lose any
weight until you do something! So what are you waiting for? Don't just sit
there. *Do it NOW! And you too will become a most uncommon man or
woman.*

Exhibit 9-1 The Uncommon Man

Crystal Ball, Oh Crystal Ball, Will my empire rise and fall
Like the Roman Legions must, Ash to Ash and
        Dust to Dust?
Is there something more to life,
        than to build it for my wife
And to give our children more,
        than their parents had before?

I go to work, I earn the bread, I watch TV and go to bed
Sunrise, Sunset—year to year,
        before I know it winter's here.

But it's no scrimmage or practice game, and there's no Martyr's Hall of Fame.

Time, the speedster, takes it toll, and every day's the
        Superbowl!!
Losers live in classic style—The never world of
        "Someday I'll,"
They blame bad luck each time they lose, then hide with sickness, drugs and booze.

But losing's a habit and so is winning,
and the way to change is by beginning . . .
to live each day as if my last—
Not in the future—Not in the past.

To dream it now, to plan it now, to want it now,
        to do it now!
To close my eyes and clearly see
        that person I'd like most to be.

I think I can, I know I can
                become my greatest coach and fan,
And love myself and give away all the love I can today.
I think I can, I know I can
                become a most uncommon man.

—Denis Waitley

Source: Reprinted from *The Psychology of Winning Workbook* by D. Waitley, with permission of Denis Waitley, Inc., © 1983.

As you travel down the road of life, be sure to remember that *success is a journey, not a destination.* Keep your life in balance, have fun at whatever you do, nurture a positive attitude in yourself and others, and always keep your eye on your long-term goals. Most of all, be supremely confident in your own abilities and you will become

positive
appreciated

accomplished
energetic
valuable
unique
purposeful
remarkable
poised
articulate
dedicated
resolute
treasured
enthusiastic
prominent
vigorous
admired
recognized
renowned
coveted
acclaimed
bright
esteemed
honored
respected
praised
sharp
brilliant
tenacious
dynamic
charismatic

In other words, you will be full of PEP^2, and most importantly, successful in life, love, and business.

Remember *there is no time to lose, but so much time to WIN, so begin right NOW to*

MAKE it a WINNING life!

For Your Continuing Learning . . .

Here is a list of related books and articles that I have found to be particularly useful. They will help you *MAKE it a WINNING life* and succeed in life, love, and business.

Adams, J. L. *Conceptual Blockbusting: A Guide to Better Ideas.* 3d. ed. Reading, MA: Addison-Wesley, 1990.

Albrecht, K. *At America's Service.* Homewood, IL: Dow Jones Irwin, 1988.

Albrecht, K. *Brain Power: Learn to Improve Your Thinking Skills.* Englewood Cliffs, NJ: Prentice-Hall, 1980.

Bennis, W., and Nanus, B. *Leaders: The Strategies for Taking Charge.* New York: Harper & Row, 1985.

Blanchard, K., and Johnson, S. *The One-Minute Manager.* New York: Morrow, 1982.

Bloomfield, H. *The Achilles Syndrome: Transforming Your Weaknesses into Strengths.* New York: Random House, 1985.

Blotnick, S. *Ambitious Men.* New York: Viking Press, 1987.

Braiker, H. B. *Getting Up When You're Feeling Down.* New York: Pocket Books, 1990.

Brockner, J. *Self-Esteem at Work: Research, Theory, and Practice.* Lexington, MA: Lexington Books, 1988.

Burns, D. *The Feeling Good Handbook.* New York: Morrow, 1989.

Chopra, D. *Quantum Healing: Exploring the Frontiers of Body, Mind, Medicine.* New York: Bantam Books, 1989.

Cohen, H. *You Can Negotiate Anything.* New York: Bantam Books, 1980.

Cousins, N. *Head First: The Biology of Hope.* New York: E.P. Dutton, 1989.

Covey, S. *The Seven Habits of Highly Effective People: Powerful Lessons in Personal Change.* New York: Simon & Schuster, 1989.

Druckman, D., and Swets, J. A. *Enhancing Human Performance: Issues, Theories and Techniques.* Washington, D.C.: National Academy Press, 1988.

Dyer, W. W. *You'll See It When You Believe It.* New York: Morrow, 1989.

Fisher, R., and Ury, W. *Getting to Yes: Negotiating Agreement without Giving in.* New York: Penguin Books, 1981.

Freedman, A. *Woulda, Coulda, Shoulda: Overcoming Regrets, Mistakes, and Missed Opportunities.* New York: Harper & Row, 1989.

Fritz, R. *Creating.* New York: Ballantine, 1990.

Garfield, C. *Peak Performers: The New Heroes of American Business.* New York: Morrow, 1986.

Gottlieb, L., and Hyatt, H. *When Smart People Fail: Rebuilding Yourself for Success.* New York: Penguin Books, 1988.

Hill, N. *Think and Grow Rich.* New York: Fawcett Crest, 1987.

Karp, H. B. *Personal Power: An Unorthodox Guide to Success.* New York: AMACOM, 1985.

Kimbro, D. *Think and Grow Rich: A Black Choice.* New York: Ballantine, 1991.

Knowles, M. *Self-Directed Learning: A Guide for Learners and Teachers.* Englewood Cliffs, NJ: Cambridge Books, 1988.

Kotter, J. P. *A Force for Change: How Leadership Differs from Management.* New York: Free Press, 1990.

Linkletter, A. *Yes, You Can! How to Succeed in Business and Life.* Boston: G.K. Hall & Co., 1980.

Livingston, J.S. "Pygmalion in Management." *Harvard Business Review.* 66 (September–October 1988): 121–130.

Mackay, H. *Beware the Naked Man Who Offers You His Shirt.* New York: Morrow, 1990.

Mackay, H. *Swim with the Sharks without Being Eaten Alive.* New York: Ivy Books, 1988.

Manz, C. C., and Sims, H. P. *Super-Leadership.* Englewood Cliffs, NJ: Prentice-Hall, 1989.

Molloy, J. T. *New Dress for Success.* New York: Warner Books, 1989.

Naisbitt, J., and Aburdene, P. *Megatrends 2000: Ten New Directions for the 1990's.* New York: Avon Books, 1990.

Padus, E. *Your Emotions and Your Health*: *New Dimensions in Mind/Body Healing.* Emmanaus, PA: Rodale Press, 1986.

Peale, N.V. *The Power of Positive Thinking.* Pawling, NY: Center for Positive Thinking, 1987.

Peters, T. J. *Thriving on Chaos: A Handbook for a Management Revolution.* New York: Knopf, 1988.

Peters, T. J., and Waterman, R. H. *In Search of Excellence.* New York: Harper & Row, 1982.

Pirsig, R. M. *Zen and the Art of Motorcycle Maintenance: An Inquiry into Values.* New York: Bantam Books, 1974.

Rinke, W. J. "Empowering Your Team Members," *Supervisory Management 34,* no. 4 (1989): 21–24.

Rinke, W. J. "Encouraging and Recognizing Employees Builds Winning Teams," *Provider* 16, no. 11 (1990): 35.

Rinke, W. J. "Maximizing Management Potential by Building Self-Esteem," *Management Solutions* 33, no. 3 (1988): 11–16.

Rinke, W. J. *The Winning Foodservice Manager: Strategies for Doing More with Less.* Rockville, MD: Achievement Publishers, Inc., 1990.

Rinke, W. J. *The Winning Manager: A "Tool Box" of Strategies to Help You Do More with Less.* Rockville, MD: Wolf Rinke Associates, Inc., 1989. (Six cassette audiotape program).

Rinke, W. J. "Winning Management: Doing More with Less." *Supervisory Management 36,* no. 6 (1991): 4.

Robbins, A. *Unlimited Power.* New York: Simon & Schuster, 1986.

Robbins, A. *Awaken the Giant Within.* New York: Simon & Schuster, 1991.

Ruggiero, V. R. *The Art of Creative Thinking.* 2d ed. New York: Harper & Row, 1988.

Seligman, M.E.P. *Learned Optimism.* New York: Knopf, 1991.

Senge, P. *The Fifth Discipline: The Art and Practice of the Learning Organization.* New York: Doubleday/Currency, 1990.

Schuller, R. H. *Tough Times Never Last, But Tough People Do.* New York: Bantam Books, 1984.

Stayer, R. "How I Learned to Let My Workers Lead," *Harvard Business Review.* 68 (November–December 1990): 66–83.

Stewart, T. A. "Brainpower: How Intellectual Capital Is Becoming America's Most Valuable Asset." *Fortune* 123 (June 3, 1991): 44–60.

Toffler, A. *Powershift: Knowledge, Wealth and Violence at the Edge of the 21st Century.* New York: Bantam Books, 1990.

Ury, W. *Getting Past No. Negotiating with Difficult People.* New York: Bantam Books, 1991.

Waitley, D. *The Psychology of Winning.* Chicago: Nightingale, 1979.

Walther, G. R. *Power Talking: 50 Ways to Say What You Mean and Get What You Want.* New York: Putnam, 1991.

Ziglar, Z. *See You at the Top.* Gretna, LA: Pelican, 1987.

Ziglar, Z. *Top Performance: How to Develop Excellence in Yourself and Others.* New York: Berkley, 1986.

Three excellent sources of audiotape programs to help you MAKE it a WINNING life:
Nightingale-Conant Corp., 7300 North Lehigh Avenue, Chicago, IL 60648
The Zig Ziglar Corp., 3300 Earhart, Suite 204, Carrolton, TX 75006
Achievement Publishers, P.O. Box 1289, Olney, MD 20830-1289

Index

About the Author

Wolf J. Rinke, R.D., Ph.D., is the president of Wolf Rinke Associates, Inc., a human resources development and management consulting company dedicated to helping organizations and individuals maximize their potential.

Dr. Rinke is

- A winner who started to work full time as an apprentice steward aboard a German ship at age 14 with an eighth-grade education and worked his way to the top.
- A seasoned professional with over 30 years of solid management and leadership experience.
- An expert in educating, training, motivating, and energizing people at all levels of the organization.
- A widely published author of numerous publications, audio- and video-tape programs.
- A highly effective consultant who helps his clients build winning teams, enhance quality, deliver superior service, and improve the bottom line.
- An associate professor with part-time faculty appointments at the University of Maryland and the Johns Hopkins University.
- A dynamic public speaker who is nationally recognized for his highly informative, down-to-earth, and entertaining keynote presentations, seminars, and workshops on motivation, personal effectiveness, management, leadership, creativity, and innovation.

Wolf holds a Ph.D. from the University of Wisconsin and has been honored for his many accomplishments by various professional associations and the military. He is a member of four honor societies and has been listed in *Who's Who in the World* and nine other international biographical references.

Wolf and his wife, Marcela, have two children and live in Rockville, Maryland.

What Do You Think About This Book?

This is your chance to let me know what you think of this book. You can even become an expert contributor. Please answer the following questions in enough detail so that I have a clear idea of what, why, when, where, and how something did, or did not, work for you. If I incorporate your input in the next edition or in another book, I will send you a personalized copy of the book absolutely free.

Wolf, the strategies you described in Chapter _____ on pages _____ worked for me.

This is how I applied them:

These are the results I got:

Wolf, the strategies you described in Chapter _____ on pages _____ did not work for me.

This is how I tried to use them:

These are the results I got:

This is how I fixed it:

Wolf, the following pages describe a personal experience related to the topic of your book. Please feel free to use it as you wish.

Your signature _____ Today's date _____

Your name, complete mailing address, and telephone number:

Mail to: Achievement Publishers
P.O. Box 1289
Olney, MD 20830-1289

Thanks in advance for taking the time to provide me with your feedback and/or expertise!

You and your group will be energized, entertained, motivated, and inspired!

Wolf J. Rinke, Ph.D custom designs and delivers stimulating and informative key-note presentations, interactive problem-solving workshops and highly effective training programs. They will meet your needs, solve your problems, and **improve your bottom line.**

MOTIVATION
- MAKE It a WINNING Life: Success Strategies for Life, Love and Business (based on this highly acclaimed book)
- Winning Sales Strategies: The Art of Making the Sale
- Winning Strategies to Maximize Potential
- Self-Motivation: The Key to Peak Performance

LEADERSHIP
- Leadership: Creating a Climate for Achievement
- The Art and Skill of Empowering Others
- Leadership Strategies to Maximize Employee Performance
- How to Negotiate Win-Win Outcomes

MANAGEMENT DEVELOPMENT
- Winning Management: Strategies for Doing MORE with Less (based on Dr. Rinke's best selling book)
- Winning Management: How to Build the Foundation for Effective TQM
- Service Management: How to Deliver Outstanding Service and Improve the Bottom Line
- The Art and Skill of Delegation
- Building and Managing Winning Teams
- How to Resolve Conflicts and Get Win-Win Results

CREATIVITY AND INNOVATION
- Think Creatively: Manage Effectively
- How to Promote Innovation in Your Organization
- How to Generate Creative Ideas that Make Money

PERSONAL EFFECTIVENESS
- How to Communicate Effectively with Individuals and Groups
- How to Maximize Your Creative Potential
- Time Management: How to Stretch the Time Rubber Band
- How to Make Winning Presentations

GUARANTEE: I deliver what I promise, or you don't pay my fee!

CONSULTING SERVICES

If you, your organization, or your company wants to build a winning team, enhance quality, deliver superior service, and **improve your bottom line,** contact us! We will help you maximize the only resource that has the potential to appreciate: **YOU** and your **PEOPLE!**

To find out how you can benefit, write to:

Wolf J. Rinke, Ph.D.
Achievement Publishers
P.O. Box 1289
Olney, MD 20830-1289

or call toll free **1-800-828-WOLF**

YOU will succeed when you put Wolf Rinke's strategies to work!

Order Now!!!

❏ YES, I want to MAKE it a WINNING life and SAVE! Please rush me the following:

NO.	DESCRIPTION	QTY.	PRICE	TOTAL
B101	MAKE It a WINNING Life: Success Strategies for Life, Love and Business (book)		24.95	
V101	MAKE It a WINNING Life: Success Strategies for Life, Love and Business (videotape & manual)		49.95	
A101	MAKE It a WINNING Life: Success Strategies for Life, Love and Business (audiotape)		12.45	
S101	SUPER BARGAIN: B101 (book), V101 (videotape) and A101 (audiotape) SAVE 20%		69.95	
B102	The Winning Foodservice Manager: Strategies for Doing More with Less (book) SAVE 8%		29.95	
A103	The Winning Manager: A "Tool Box" of Strategies (6 audiotape album)		49.95	
S102	SUPER BARGAIN: B102 (book) and A103 (audiotape album) SAVE 15%		69.95	
A105	The PEPP Principle: Success Strategies for a Rapidly Changing World (audiotape)		12.45	
A106	WINNING Management: How to Empower Your Team (audiotape)		14.95	
S105	SUPER BARGAIN: A105 and A106 (2 audiotapes) SAVE 20%		21.95	
			Subtotal	
	If your order is more than $200.00, deduct an additional 10%			
	Maryland residents, add 5% sales tax			
	Handling & shipping: $4.50 for the first $50.00, $2.50 for ea. additional $50.00 or fraction thereof (outside USA x 2)†			
	International orders: Payable in U.S. funds by credit card. Foreign checks add $10.00		TOTAL	

†Overnight available. Call for rates.

For faster service FAX your credit card charge order to (301)570-0303 or call (800)828-9653

Please UPS my order to: (Please print)

Name_____

Telephone # (_____)_____

Company_____

Address_____

City_____State_____Zip_____

Payment:

❏ Here is my check or money order for the TOTAL amount **payable to Achievement Publishers**

❏ Please charge $_____ to my MC/Visa card

No._____Exp.Date_____

Signature_____
(We need your credit card number, the expiration date, and your signature to ship your charge order.)

UNCONDITIONAL GUARANTEE: You will be totally satisfied with our products or you may return your order and get your money back!

Please send me information about:

❏ CE credit for reading this book
❏ Other educational products and home study courses
❏ On-site training and consulting services
❏ Details about Wolf Rinke speaking to my group

Need more than 6 of anything? Call us for generous bulk discounts!

Thanks for your order!
MAKE it a WINNING LIFE!

ACHIEVEMENT PUBLISHERS

P.O. Box 1289, Olney, MD 20830-1289

New Website
www.wolfrinke.com